Praise for

TOP *of the* ROCK

"Engrossing and lively. . . . [Littlefield] enlists the voices of many of the actors and creative forces behind such hits as *Seinfeld*, *Will & Grace*, *Cheers* and *ER* to help him chronicle the glory days of 'Must See TV.'" —*Chicago Sun-Times*

"An essential oral history." —*Detroit Free Press*

"A chronicle of the last golden age of network television, [*Top of the Rock*] is the literary equivalent of a former NBC Thursday night lineup. . . . Littlefield is the ultimate Must See insider. The mini-histories are a blast . . . full of fresh detail." —*The Hollywood Reporter*

"Warren Littlefield has reminded us of what was possible not so long ago. . . . [Recounting] his successful run at NBC and the inside stories of the shows that made it happen." —*TV Guide*

"A fascinating oral history of shows like *Seinfeld* that defined an era." —*Daily News*

TOP *of the* ROCK

WARREN LITTLEFIELD

Warren Littlefield is the former NBC President of Entertainment. Previous to that, he was the NBC comedy executive who developed such hit shows as *The Cosby Show* and *The Fresh Prince of Bel-Air*. He currently runs his own television production company.

T.R. PEARSON

T. R. Pearson is the author of fourteen novels, including *A Short History of a Small Place*, and a dozen screenplays.

TOP *of the* ROCK

WARREN LITTLEFIELD

with T. R. Pearson

ANCHOR BOOKS
A Division of Random House, Inc.
New York

TOP

of the

ROCK

Inside
the Rise and Fall
of Must See TV

Behind every successful television series
is a development executive who, at some point in the insanity
of the development process, put his ass on the line
so that the show might live.
This book is dedicated to those executives.

Contents

TOP *of the* ROCK

Introduction

One phone call changed everything.

After a decade as Brandon Tartikoff's lieutenant at NBC, I'd finally gotten the chance to run the entertainment division on my own. Brandon had taken a job at Paramount Pictures, leaving me as the guy to pick the shows and set the schedule. Credit for NBC's success would be mine, but so would blame for its failure. At that moment, the latter seemed far more likely than the former.

It was the early nineties, and we were flagging as a network. We were flagging a little as a nation as well. Economic malaise had returned with the beginning of the Gulf War and an accompanying spike in the price of oil. High unemployment and government deficits were putting downward pressure on the advertising marketplace. My timing sucked. We'd had a good run, but our shows were old. In the fall of 1991, *The Cosby Show* was entering its eighth season. *The Golden Girls* its seventh. *L.A. Law* its sixth. Viewership was off for each, and our general audience numbers across the schedule had plunged by double digits in a year's time. We'd managed to win the May sweeps, but it was the barest of victories. We were neck and neck with CBS and ABC after leading the pack throughout the eighties.

Brandon had timed his departure impeccably. I found myself holding both an exalted new title—NBC Entertainment president—and the bag.

I drew my chief strength and consolation from our top-rated comedy, *Cheers*. It may have been approaching its eleventh season, but *Cheers* wasn't showing its age. Its audience was larger than ever. *Cheers* had started life in the cellar—it was the seventy-seventh highest-rated show out of seventy-seven at the end of its opening season—but it had become a perennial top ten show and a revenue powerhouse for NBC.

For me, *Cheers* was a sentimental favorite as well since I'd been associated with it from its inception. I could well remember the pitch for *Cheers*, conducted over breakfast in the private dining room at NBC in Burbank. Director Jim Burrows with Les and Glen Charles, who would create and executive produce the show, had visited a Boston bar where customers (and their stories) entered through a revolving door. Over scrambled eggs and bacon, they spun out the nearly limitless comic possibilities such a setting would afford. The only sensible response was "Let's do it!"

We knew we had a gem from the beginning, even if viewers needed a year or so to catch on. With the premiere of *The Cosby Show* in 1984—*Cheers'* third season on the air—NBC could boast a Thursday night lineup consisting of *Cosby*, *Family Ties*, *Cheers*, *Night Court*, and *Hill Street Blues*. These five shows made for a remarkable evening of television, what we at the network thought of as our "Night of Bests."

NBC may have been floundering generally in the early nineties, but *Cheers* remained our rock. Its audience was huge and reliable (for both original episodes and repeats) and was divided almost evenly between men and women. That's rare enough in the TV business to approach unique. Better still, *Cheers* was a bull's-eye show for advertisers' dream demographic, the coveted eighteen- to forty-nine-year-old urban viewer with disposable income. It was also an Emmy magnet of unquestioned quality and pedigree.

Produced on stage 25 on the Paramount lot in Hollywood, *Cheers* was dependable and trouble-free. Two dozen high-caliber episodes each season. A great stable of series regulars with new ones thrown in for variety from year to year. The show was funny as hell and functioned as the spine of the network. It was a tent pole smack in the middle of Thursday night. Without it, we were sure to wallow and drift. I knew I'd need *Cheers* and its reliable success if I were to have any hope of turning NBC around, and there was no reason to think I wouldn't have *Cheers* to lean on.

Then the call came in.

I was in a meeting in my office at the NBC complex in Burbank when Patty, my assistant, stuck her head in the door.

"Ted Danson is on the phone," she said.

Professionally, I knew Ted well. Personally, only a little. I'd skied with him once in Colorado, but he rarely phoned me. I decided to step out and take the call at Patty's desk. I thought Ted might have a cause he wanted me to contribute to or an event he wanted me to attend.

Like most Americans who'd passed a newsstand or checked out at a grocery store in the previous six months, I had a fair idea of what Ted had been up to. During his last hiatus from *Cheers*, he'd starred opposite Whoopi Goldberg in *Made in America*, a limp comedy about artificial insemination. In the course of the ten-week shoot in Oakland, Ted and Whoopi had become an unlikely item.

I can't say I was terribly surprised. This sort of thing happens regularly in the entertainment business. Actors on a movie set often behave like counselors at summer camp, so liaisons and divorces are more the rule than the exception. I was only troubled by the fact that Ted starred in a wildly popular weekly comedy that Whoopi claimed to have never seen. The TV executive in me took wounded offense.

Ted and I exchanged pleasantries, and then he dropped the bomb.

"This is my last season on *Cheers*," Ted told me. "I'm not coming back."

I was staggered. I hoped it was a negotiating ploy, but I couldn't imagine why it would be. Ted was already the highest-paid actor on television at $400,000 an episode.

"I've thought about it a lot and discussed it with Whoopi," Ted told me, "and we think this is what I need to do."

By this point, panic had set in. I perched on the edge of Patty's desk and tried to figure out what to say. What to do. How to breathe.

"Whoopi thinks I need to find out who Ted is. If I don't, she says I'll never grow as a person."

"I know who Ted is," I wanted to tell him. "Ted's the guy who makes $10 million a year starring in one of the highest-rated shows on television. Ted can afford to find out who Ted is in the off-season."

I had the sharp, metallic taste of rank desperation in my mouth. My mind was racing. I began to wonder what my next career might bring. Back in New Jersey, I'd put myself through college as a teamster truck driver. Maybe they'd take me back?

"I just wanted you to hear it from me," Ted said. That was him all over. Classy as hell. I couldn't fault Ted, but I was devastated nonetheless.

Looking back, I can appreciate how pivotal that moment was. NBC's "Night of Bests" was well behind us, and the phenomenal success of Must See TV was just over the horizon. But I was too shaken and too close to the ground to see any of that at the time. *Cheers* was suddenly in my rearview mirror. Ahead lay barren road. What would happen next was anybody's guess.

Fortunately for me—fortunately for us all—what did happen next was television at its very best. From 1993 through 1998, NBC exploded every conventional notion of what a broadcast network could accomplish with a prime-time lineup. On Thursday nights in particular, everybody watched the peacock. We beat the three other networks combined by wide margins. *Mad About You. Frasier. Seinfeld. Friends. Will & Grace. ER.* At its height, NBC's Thursday prime-time schedule of Must See shows attracted a staggering seventy-five million viewers and generated more revenue for NBC than the other six nights of the week combined. In today's fractured entertainment market, NBC averages an anemic audience of less than six million for its Thursday night lineup.

At the time, we hardly understood the magnitude of what we were accomplishing in broadcast television. I'd like to say the remarkable success of Must See TV was the result of impeccable foresight and strategy from me and my team at NBC, but there was a lot of luck and no little alchemy involved as well. At the network, we developed and steered where we could, but our fundamental goal—and my guiding principle as president of entertainment—was to get into business with talented people and let them be talented. It sounds simple enough, but when I look at NBC's fortunes this past decade, I wonder if it's not a lesson that needs relearning.

To that end, here's the story of how *we* did it, the ultimate insider's guide to Must See TV. Because our success was a team effort, this is a team history, an intimate account of a golden era in broadcast television told by the people who helped make it happen—the writers, the directors, the producers, the actors, and, yes, the suits like me. Whatever you do, don't touch that dial.

Players Guide

Talent

JASON ALEXANDER—Actor, writer, producer, and singer. Best known for his role as the neurotic George Costanza on *Seinfeld*.

ANTHONY EDWARDS—Actor, producer, and director. With a big-screen blastoff in *Top Gun*, is best known for his soulful lead role as Dr. Mark Greene for eight seasons on *ER*.

KELSEY GRAMMER—Five-time Emmy Award–winning actor, director, and producer. Best known for his historic twenty-year portrayal of psychiatrist Dr. Frasier Crane in *Cheers* and *Frasier*. Currently executive producing and starring in *Boss* on Starz.

SEAN HAYES—Multiple Emmy Award–winning actor, comedian, and producer. Known for his role as Jack McFarland in *Will & Grace*. Currently cast as Larry in the upcoming *Three Stooges* feature film and executive producer on NBC's new drama *Grimm*.

HELEN HUNT—Academy Award–winning actress for *As Good as It*

Gets. Writer, director, and producer who starred in *Mad About You* with Paul Reiser.

Lisa Kudrow—Emmy Award–winning actress and producer. Best known for her role as the offbeat and unpredictable Phoebe Buffay in *Friends.*

Eriq La Salle—Actor, producer, director. Best known for playing the hardwired Dr. Peter Benton on *ER* for eight seasons.

Matt LeBlanc—Actor and producer who played the lovable Joey Tribbiani on *Friends.* Also starred in the spin-off *Joey.* Currently plays a fictional version of himself in *Episodes* on Showtime.

John Lithgow—Multiple Oscar-nominated actor, musician, and author. Known for his tremendous range in his feature film roles and playing Dick Solomon, the head of the alien household, in *3rd Rock from the Sun.*

Julianna Margulies—Emmy Award winner. Will always be remembered for her portrayal of nurse Carol Hathaway for six seasons on *ER* but is currently giving that legacy a challenge as the star of *The Good Wife* on CBS.

Eric McCormack—Emmy Award–winning actor, musician, writer, and producer best known for playing Will Truman on NBC's *Will & Grace.* Currently stars in the TNT drama series *Perception.*

Debra Messing—Emmy Award–winning actress best known for playing Grace Adler in *Will & Grace.* Currently starring in the NBC drama *Smash* from executive producer Steven Spielberg.

MEGAN MULLALLY—Multiple Emmy Award winner for playing the opinionated Karen Walker on *Will & Grace*.

DAVID HYDE PIERCE—Four-time Emmy Award–winning actor, director, and musician. Best known for playing psychiatrist Dr. Niles Crane on *Frasier*.

PAUL REISER—Comedian, actor, author, and musician. Best known for creating, co-writing, executive producing, and starring in *Mad About You*.

DAVID SCHWIMMER—Multiple award–winning actor, producer, and director. Best known for playing paleontologist Ross Geller on *Friends*.

JERRY SEINFELD—The King of Comedy. Emmy Award–winning writer, executive producer, actor, director, and comedian. Best known for starring as a semi-fictional version of himself on *Seinfeld*.

MARK SWEET—The king of multi-camera comedy audience warm-up. Over four thousand episodes from *Cheers* to *Mike & Molly*.

NOAH WYLE—One of *ER*'s brightest stars who began his eleven-year *ER* run playing medical student John Carter. George Clooney once proclaimed, "If I ever get to be young again, I want to be Noah Wyle." Currently starring in *Falling Skies* on TNT.

Writers, Producers, and **the** Director

JIMMY BURROWS—The most successful director in television comedy—ever. Multiple Emmy–winning executive producer of *Cheers* and *Will & Grace*. Directed the pilots of *Taxi*, *Cheers*, *Wings*, *Frasier*, *Friends*,

Will & Grace, NewsRadio, 3rd Rock from the Sun, Dharma & Greg, Mike & Molly, 2 Broke Girls, and many more.

MARCY CARSEY—Perhaps the most creative nonwriter in the TV business. Former ABC TV executive who together with Tom Werner formed Carsey-Werner Productions, television's most successful modern-era independent production company. Their hits include *The Cosby Show, Roseanne, That '70s Show, A Different World,* and *3rd Rock from the Sun.*

PETER CASEY—Multiple Emmy Award–winning writer and producer who went from *The Jeffersons* to *Cheers* and then created and executive produced *Wings* and *Frasier* with writing partners David Lee and David Angell. Sadly, David Angell died on September 11, 2001. He and his wife, Lynn, were aboard American Airlines Flight 11, which crashed into the North Tower of the World Trade Center.

DAVID CRANE—Multiple Emmy Award winner and brilliant comedic writer. The creator and executive producer of *Friends* along with his longtime friend and writing partner, Marta Kauffman, with whom he also created *Dream On.* Kevin Bright was also an executive producer of *Friends.* David is currently co-creator and executive producer of *Episodes* on Showtime.

MARTA KAUFFMAN—Multiple Emmy Award–winning writer, producer, co-creator, and executive producer of *Friends* and *Dream On.*

DAVID KOHAN—Emmy Award winner who co-created and executive produced *Will & Grace* with his longtime writing partner and best friend, Max Mutchnick.

DAVID LEE—Multiple Emmy Award winner, executive producer, writer, and director who went from writing on *The Jeffersons* to *Cheers* and then created and executive produced *Wings* and *Frasier* with Peter Casey and David Angell.

STEVE LEVITAN—Multiple Emmy Award–winning writer and producer whose credits include *Frasier* and *The Larry Sanders Show*. Created *Just Shoot Me!* and co-created and executive produces ABC's hit comedy *Modern Family*.

MAX MUTCHNICK—The comedically larger-than-life Emmy Award–winning co-creator, writer, and executive producer of *Will & Grace*.

GEORGE SHAPIRO—Jerry Seinfeld's loyal, trusted, and lifetime manager and an executive producer of *Seinfeld*.

JOHN WELLS—Multiple award–winning writer and executive producer who was the creative glue of *ER* for fifteen years. Currently executive producing *Southland* on TNT and *Shameless* for Showtime.

TOM WERNER—Like his partner, Marcy Carsey, a former ABC TV executive who created a comedy hit machine with Carsey-Werner Productions. In 2002 became a co-owner of the Boston Red Sox.

HOWARD WEST—With George Shapiro, also Jerry Seinfeld's longtime manager who was considered "the money man" in Jerry's deals.

DICK WOLF—Creator and executive producer of all of the *Law & Order* series brand (over 900 hours of television).

The Suits

JOHN AGOGLIA—The highly regarded head of NBC business affairs from the mid-eighties through the mid-nineties. A strong deal maker who was so comfortable wearing the "black hat" in a negotiation that he kept one hanging in his office.

PRESTON BECKMAN—The son of a New York City taxi driver and proud of it. Holds a Ph.D. in sociology and was NBC's iconic scheduler and strategic planner throughout the nineties. Currently executive vice president for strategic program planning at the highest-rated network, Fox Broadcasting.

BOB BRODER—A legend in the talent agency business and the only agent that director Jimmy Burrows has ever had. Transformed the boutique agency he created when International Creative Management acquired it in 2006. His handpicked management team became ICM's senior management, and Bob became ICM's vice-chairman.

HAROLD BROOK—Rose to executive vice president of business affairs at NBC and NBC Studios, replacing John Agoglia. In 2003, founded Point Media, a business-affairs-for-hire company.

KAREY BURKE—Began her career as an assistant at NBC and rose to executive vice president of prime-time series. Briefly partnered with Jamie Tarses and currently partnered with the director and producer Todd Holland at Universal Television.

DAN HARRISON—Handpicked by Preston Beckman as his protégé, strategic planner, and scheduler. Launched multiple cable networks for NBCUniversal and currently is senior vice president of strategic development at CBS Corporation. Loves baseball and is a resource for just about anything.

JOHN LANDGRAF—Vice president of series programs working under David Nevins at NBC during the Must See era. Currently president and general manager of FX Networks.

RICK LUDWIN—A thirty-plus-year (and counting) NBC executive vice president who oversaw late night and specials. He was also the steadfast development and current executive on *Seinfeld.*

MIKE MANDELKER—Charismatic vice president of sales at NBC in New York throughout the Must See era. Currently vice president of eastern sales at Fox News Network.

PATTY MANN—My trusted guardian and assistant since the early eighties at NBC who continues to watch my back under my deal at ABC Studios.

STEVE MCPHERSON—Vice president of prime-time drama at NBC in the Must See era. President of Touchstone Studios, where he developed the *CSI* franchise for CBS. President of ABC Network from 2004 to 2010. Currently a wine entrepreneur.

JOHN MILLER—Through good times and bad for more than thirty years the brilliant advertising and promotion czar of NBC. Currently the chief marketing officer of the NBCUniversal Television Group.

DAVID NEVINS—Senior vice president of prime-time series during the Must See era. Former executive vice president of programming at Fox and president of Imagine Television. Currently president of entertainment at Showtime Networks.

LORI OPENDEN—The industry's best eye for talent who began her casting career at MTM Enterprises. Head of casting at NBC throughout the nineties' Must See era. Post-NBC, ran casting for UPN and now the CW network.

GLENN PADNICK—The president of Castle Rock Television who also oversaw the development and episodic execution of *Seinfeld.*

BRIAN PIKE—A successful television packaging agent (and my agent) at CAA. Formerly a Movie of the Week development executive at NBC whom I moved into drama series development, where he flourished.

JOHN PIKE—Larger-than-life, shoot-from-the-hip head of Paramount Television during the *Cheers* era and a critical part of the development and launch of *Frasier*.

PERRY SIMON—Currently general manager of BBC America. A senior-level creative executive whose imprint is on NBC's historic success in both the eighties and the nineties.

JAMIE TARSES—Began her career in NBC's associate program, and as vice president of comedy development was instrumental in the development of *Friends* and *Frasier*. President of ABC Entertainment from 1996 to 1999 and currently a prolific executive producer of both comedy and drama on network and cable.

JACK WELCH—Former CEO of GE. In the nineties considered the most successful CEO on the planet. Best-selling author.

BOB WRIGHT—Jack Welch's replacement for Grant Tinker as CEO of NBC. Bob's vision for NBC yielded the modern-era multiple-cable-channel portfolio of the peacock, which also included the acquisition of Universal Studios.

1

*Where Everybody
Knows Your Name*

Warren: I arrived at NBC in December 1979, hired by Brandon Tartikoff to work in the comedy department. I was manager of comedy development, the junior member of the department. Brandon was a newly minted vice president of development at the network, which was mired in last place. I was twenty-seven years old, and though I had watched a lot of it, I knew next to nothing about network television. Brandon, my boss, was all of thirty.

In what was just a three-way race for audience (there'd be no Fox Broadcasting until 1987), NBC was jokingly derided as number four. CBS had ten comedies on its schedule, including *M*A*S*H*, *WKRP in Cincinnati*, *The Jeffersons*, *Alice*, and *One Day at a Time*. ABC could boast fourteen sitcoms, among them *Happy Days*, *Laverne & Shirley*, *Barney Miller*, *Soap*, *Taxi*, and *Three's Company*. At NBC, we had *Diff'rent Strokes* and *Hello, Larry*.

In terms of general viewership, CBS led the way with about sixteen million households. ABC was a close second with fifteen million. NBC lagged well behind at twelve million. For the 1980 season, *Little House on the Prairie* was our top-rated show at sixteenth. We placed only four shows in the top thirty. There was nowhere to go but up.

Worse still, NBC's head of programming at the time was a man named Paul Klein. He had a background in audience research and had come up with the strategy of LOP, which stood for Least Objectionable Programming (I'm not kidding). The object was to piss off as few viewers as possible. The network product line was largely geared toward big events, so we became the *Big Event* network.

A TV critic once asked Paul Klein, "How do you know when you've got a big event?"

Klein said, "We sit around a table, and people throw out ideas, and somebody says, '*That's* a big event,' and that's when we know."

It was an insane form of programming, expensive and not in the least bit habit-forming. NBC had essentially abandoned weekly series as the spine of the network. As a remedy, the legendary Fred Silverman had been brought over from ABC to turn things around. Fred didn't waste a lot of time in making Brandon the new head of the entertainment division. I hoped that would also be good for me.

By then, Fred had already enjoyed remarkable success at the other two networks. A *Time* magazine cover piece on Silverman had called him "The Man with the Golden Gut." NBC was in desperate need of a programming miracle, so maybe a golden gut would do.

My first encounter with Fred was pretty alarming for me. It took place in a conference room on the second floor at NBC in Burbank. We were meeting to review the current development slate. Fred wasn't very happy. In fact, he was screaming that it was impossible to turn NBC around if deals couldn't be made faster.

Fred shifted in his chair, looked at me, and shrieked, "Why haven't you closed any of those deals yet!?"

I experienced major shrinkage and couldn't get any words out.

Finally my boss jumped in and said, "Fred, this is Warren. He's the new guy in comedy development."

"Oh," Fred said. "Where the fuck is the business affairs guy?"

My only words to the legendary Fred Silverman that day were "Don't know. Not me."

We were so desperate for quality programming that we had to

wave a series commitment at Les and Glen Charles and Jimmy Burrows. The trio had never created a show, but they had worked on more than a few iconic programs: *The Mary Tyler Moore Show*, *Phyllis*, *The Bob Newhart Show*, and *Taxi*. We guaranteed them thirteen episodes on the air just to lure them to pitch us. Nobody wanted to be on NBC. To get Jimmy and the Charles brothers, we knew we'd have to overpromise and overpay, and, boy, did we.

That's a pitch meeting I'll never forget. Over breakfast, Brandon Tartikoff, Michael Zinberg, and I first got wind of what would become *Cheers*.

Jim Burrows: *Cheers* was pitched as a Miller Lite commercial. Those commercials with the jocks, Marv Throneberry and all that. We had an athletic leading man. Sam Malone, originally, was a wide receiver. That's how we pitched it. NBC made a deal for us—two for one. They had to put one on the air. We had to write two. The pitch wasn't too difficult. Since the three of us had run *Taxi* for about three years, we knew what we were doing, and NBC knew it. It's not like today, where they hire kids who've never run a show, based on one script.

Bob Broder: Grant Tinker had hired the Charles brothers at MTM, and they'd worked their way up to executive producers on the final year of the original *Newhart* show. Jimmy Burrows was a director who hadn't directed television but had been the stage manager in New York for a very unsuccessful musical, *Holly Golightly*, with Mary Tyler Moore and Richard Chamberlain. It had closed very quickly. Out of that, Jimmy developed a relationship with Mary and Grant, and he begged for an apprenticeship to come out and work with the MTM company.

At the time, I was representing Jay Sandrich, who was Jimmy Burrows before Jimmy Burrows became Jimmy Burrows. Jay Sandrich was the top multi-camera director at the time, in 1970. He did the pilot for *The Mary Tyler Moore Show*, and he went on to do *Cosby* and *The Golden Girls*.

Grant Tinker asked Jay Sandrich to mentor Jimmy. Jimmy asked me, "Would you represent me? I know Jay Sandrich can't do all the work he's being offered. Maybe you could get me a couple of gigs." I've been Jimmy's agent since 1972 or '73. While Jay was a star, Burrows is by any metric a supernova. He has now directed the pilots for over fifty-six series that have gone on air. Not failed pilots, broken pilots—on-air series. Fifty-six of them.

Jim Burrows: Since I come from a stage background, in comedy I kind of know what's funny. The first show I ever watched out here was *The Mary Tyler Moore Show*. It had four of the most powerful writers in television working on it—Jim Brooks, Allan Burns, Ed. Weinberger, and Stan Daniels. Powerhouses. The director was Jay Sandrich, who mentored me. I used to see Jay go after the writers, and Jay would say what he thought. He'd do that to protect his actors.

Writers want you to do the script, but sometimes what works in the writers' room doesn't work on the stage. Jay would say, "I'll do it your way, but I'm not sure it's the right way. Let's show you what we can do." That empowers the actors to feel like a larger part of the creative process.

Bob Broder: When you watch Jimmy shoot a show, he's fascinating. He's never watching. He's listening. He'll walk up and down behind the cameras, and all of a sudden he'll kick a camera dolly to change the angle. He has a quad split in his head. He knows what each camera is seeing.

Jim Burrows: The guys we pitched *Cheers* to knew a lot more about television than the guys we pitch to today. We got to pitch to guys who got it. We talked about a bar but not a romance. We might have mentioned Tracy/Hepburn. I don't remember. So many pitches under the bridge.

Bob Broder: I believe Abe Burrows, Jimmy's father, wrote on a radio show called *Duffy's Tavern*. The beauty of having set the show in a bar meant when the door opened, the story started, and any story could walk in that door. It wasn't like doing a family comedy where you had to figure out how you were going to service your six characters. Some pretty strange people came in that door.

Warren: I remember Jim Burrows and the Charles brothers told us the only show on television with adult relationships was *Three's Company*. "That's fine," they said, "but that shouldn't be the only one. There is so much more territory to cover." Charles/Burrows/Charles had a pedigree, and we, at NBC, didn't have one at the time. We had no sense of who we were as a network, and we were desperate for a hit show.

Bob Broder: Our offices were over a restaurant called Scandia. It was *the* dining spot in L.A. in the late seventies. The only advantage we had as an agency was "Come to lunch; we'll eat at Scandia." I called Irwin Moss, who was doing business affairs at NBC. I said, "Let's get lunch, and we'll discuss the deal." We do the deal over lunch on the back of an envelope. Series commitment. My partner and I had been in business a minute and a half. Good news: we had a series commitment. Bad news: it was NBC.

Warren: Being the smart agent that he is, Bob took the NBC offer and shopped it to Marcy Carsey and Tom Werner who were at ABC and were working with the team on *Taxi*, but ABC passed. It was too rich of a deal.

Bob Broder: I go to Paramount and say, "I have a series commitment." They want it, and we negotiate a deal. One of the better deals ever made in television. We set precedents there it took them thirty years to get rid of.

John Pike: We made the deal without having any concept of what the idea was. We really didn't know. We went into business with Charles/ Burrows/Charles. Typically, that's what I did when I ran Paramount Television. We let them make what they love, and we were there to provide support. We'd run interference with the network. I can recall over the run of *Cheers* that there was never an adversarial moment where it came to the principal talent of that show.

The *Cheers* relationship with Paramount was unique in the network world at that time. There was a pure partnership—Paramount TV and Charles/Burrows/Charles Productions. C/B/C didn't need Paramount. Everybody wanted to be in business with them. They had a series commitment from NBC. Paramount had a great distribution arm. We had a great track record with comedy—*Happy Days*, *Laverne & Shirley*, et cetera.

The deal was a fifty-fifty proposition, a true partnership. We'd produce the program for a certain amount of money, and there would be a distribution fee that was lower than most typical fees in the industry. My job was to manage the ball team. I had the three most-sought-after creative people that there were. Ours was a trouble-free partnership. We all had a common goal.

Bob Broder: The boys took this germination period—they were still doing twenty-two episodes of *Taxi*—and *Cheers* just started to percolate. They wrote a great pilot. Notes were easy, and then they did something that had never been done before. The boys came up with three pairs of actors to audition.

Jim Burrows: We had six finalists. Fred Dryer and Julia Duffy. Fred Dryer *was* Sam Malone. We had Billy Devane and Lisa Eichhorn, and Ted and Shelley. We got the *Bosom Buddies* stage, which had a bar. We fed the network, always good. We had the three couples each do a scene.

Bob Broder: Probably the most inhumane process in television is the casting process. There couldn't be a more demeaning way to treat people, even if they are actors.

The actors had been rehearsed for two days, and the boys made slight changes in the scene to accommodate each of the pairings. There must have been thirty people there. The actors were in wardrobe and makeup. We had lights. It was very nice.

Jim Burrows: I remember me and Glen and Les wondering how we could possibly say no to Bill Devane. But it was obvious it was Ted and Shelley. They were wonderful with one another.

Warren: From Burbank we drove over to the Paramount lot, and then we were taken in golf carts over to stage 23 next to Lucy Park. Yes, named after Lucille Ball, who with Desi Arnaz had started Desilu Productions there and had purchased the lot from RKO Radio Pictures. This was show business, and I was thrilled to be a part of it.

At the network, we were keen on Fred Dryer. He had a lot of upside. Former professional football player. Leading-man looks. His acting skills, however, were . . . evolving.

Bob Broder: Fred Dryer was the Howie Long of his time. He wasn't an actor, but every time he ran the scene, he got better.

Jim Burrows: Fred didn't have the comic chops at the time. Later, he was in two episodes of *Cheers* where he played the sports guy. "'I' on Sports." He was great.

Warren: Ted was great, but if it had been up to the suits, Fred Dryer would have had the job. That was a valuable lesson learned for me. When you get into business with talented, creative people, listen to them. Jimmy Burrows and the Charles brothers were convinced Ted

Danson was their guy, and they were right. We were too hung up on what Fred Dryer *could* be. Jimmy told us to put him in a drama. It wouldn't take us long after that, with the help of Steve Cannell and Frank Lupo, to launch the Saturday night staple *Hunter*.

Jim Burrows: Ted Danson is as far from an athlete as you can get. He's a farceur from Carnegie Tech. I took him to his first baseball game. Not a clue. So I told Ted, "You watch Fred. Watch how he moves. Watch how he preens. He's a peacock. That's who Sam Malone is."

Bob Broder: We even changed the character from being a football player to a baseball player so Ted would be more believable.

Jim Burrows: I've often thought about what would have happened with different pairs. Devane felt a little old. He dropped a glass when he did his scene and made a joke about it. He was wonderful, very creative, but we got the best two. That was obvious.

Bob Broder: I first caught wind of Ted Danson when I saw a busted pilot from the year before. He'd done a wonderful role in *The Onion Field*. He may have already done *Body Heat*.

Jim Burrows: Ted had read for *Best of the West*, a pilot I did in '79 or '80. He didn't get the job, but his name stuck in my head. We cast him as a gay hairdresser in *Taxi*. He was hilarious.

Bob Broder: We did the first five or six shows and were never quite sure if Teddy was going to be believable as a baseball player. But it worked.

Jim Burrows: If you can get the cast and a great script, you're halfway home. Then you have to make sure the network puts you in the right spot. We got lucky. People had been after Shelley Long to do pilots for years. She'd done a one-hour pilot the year before that was awful.

Bob Broder: Shelley Long was brilliant in the role but difficult. If you did a wardrobe change, she'd go up to the dressing room, and you'd lose her for thirty or forty minutes with an audience sitting there. It just killed it.

Jim Burrows: For Coach, we cast Robert Prosky, but he didn't want to move. He lived in Washington, D.C. We'd seen Nick Colasanto in *Raging Bull*. Nick was dying when we hired him, but he never told us. He had a bad heart.

It all goes back to *The Mary Tyler Moore Show*. Ed Asner, Gavin MacLeod, and Ted Knight all played heavies on *The Untouchables*. Bad guys. If you bring guys to television you've never seen funny and they are funny, you'll get bigger laughs. People just don't expect it.

Rhea Perlman we knew about from *Taxi*. The network didn't want her, wouldn't hire her without a reading. She played the nice girl on *Taxi*. John Ratzenberger came in to read for Norm. After we said "Thank you," he asked if we had a blowhard in the bar. He ended up doing every episode but for the first one.

I like people who've done stage before. You have to be able to play with the other actors and yet play for an audience. Everybody on *Cheers* had been onstage. Occasionally, you get a film actor, but you try to tell them to get on the level of the person opposite. If you underplay on TV comedy, you're dead.

Warren: In the pilot of *Cheers* the Charles brothers ended up adding a character called Mrs. Littlefield, a highly opinionated Boston Brahmin in a wheelchair, who was played by Elaine Stritch. I was honored that they used my last name. Sadly, while she was memorably funny, she was cut because the pilot was just too long. Many years later I got a copy of the rough cut with Elaine still in it and sent it to my mother for Mother's Day—way better than flowers.

Bob Broder: There was one other character in the show that never got any billing, and that was the set. Richard Sylbert designed the set. He'd won Academy Awards for art direction, most recently for *Reds*.

Jimmy Burrows directed one feature film called *Partners*. It was the best thing to happen to television. He hated the experience and said, "Don't ever show me another feature script." Jimmy had worked with Sylbert on *Partners*. Sylbert said he'd love to design the set, but he had to get a royalty. For the set! We gave him $250 per episode. When Michael Eisner found out, years later, that a set designer was getting a royalty, he went ballistic.

Jim Burrows: There are great nights when you run a show in front of an audience before there's anything at stake. Before there's film in the camera. A guy named Dave Davis, who started at *Newhart*, suggested an audience run-through, and I've done it on every show.

Cheers was a religious experience. For the pilot run-through, we had an entire audience of Seabees from Camp Pendleton. We were sweating bullets because there's a lot of sophistication in the show. But when Norm walked in and Sam said, "What do you know?" and Norm said, "Not enough." Never written as a joke, but the audience went crazy. They were laughing at attitudes.

Warren: I was asked to stay with the show by my bosses at the network and supervise it as it began its network run. It was the best education I could ever have had. My personal master's degree in comedy from the Charles brothers and Jimmy.

I had just begun to cut my teeth at NBC serving as the current executive on Steven Bochco's revolutionary drama *Hill Street Blues*. The show had been developed in NBC's comedy department, inspired by a Fred Silverman idea with a distinct comedy pedigree. "Why not,"

Fred had asked, "*Barney Miller* as an hour?" Fred's pitch was passed along to Bochco and Michael Kozoll, and *Hill Street* was born.

I started out as the junior member of the development team for *Hill Street*, but once the series got up and running, I was told to stay with the show, making me the current executive. While a development executive has to come up with the hits, my duty as the current executive on *Hill Street* was to keep the material on track and the episodes up to the standard that was established in the pilot.

Brian Pike: A current executive doesn't design next year's Fords. He just makes sure they come off the assembly line the right way. He's a brand manager. Every week he makes sure those shows have the proper vitamins and minerals, what the network thought it bought.

It's a completely unrewarding job. You didn't develop the show, and the people who developed the show take the credit.

Warren: My more seasoned colleagues at NBC had declined to take on the job on *Hill Street*. They were aware of Steven Bochco's fierce reputation. He had a quick temper and no patience for suits like us. So they knew better than to stick with the show, but I accepted the challenge in the spirit of learning as much as I could from whoever would teach me.

On *Hill Street*, I set about asking the traditional questions network executives ask when they read a script. What's the central story? Does it have a dramatic act-by-act build? Is there a sympathetic victim? Do we care about our central characters? Are they heroic?

Steven Bochco, as I was soon to learn, considered me a colossal pain in the ass.

Bochco told his boss at MTM Enterprises, Grant Tinker, that he wanted a meeting at the network. The purpose was to let NBC clarify what the network had in mind for his series and to let Bochco tell me, in front of my bosses, where I could shove my notes.

Looking back, it was a miracle I survived the meeting. I was way out of my league, but an interesting thing happened. While Grant Tinker was thoroughly supportive of Bochco, he and Brandon realized a guy had been put in the line of fire who wouldn't run away. Perhaps it was from the summer I worked with French-Canadian ex-cons who threatened to throw me from the roof of a high-rise or maybe the teamsters I trucked with in Paterson, New Jersey, but I wasn't afraid. I think they admired my unwillingness to budge because, at some level, they were just as leery of Bochco's wrath as everybody else.

In the course of the meeting, Brandon was wonderfully diplomatic in his praise of *Hill Street*, but he added that, as network executives writing the checks, we were trained to look for basic dramatic elements in every hour. If they were lacking, it was our job to raise warning flags, and that's what I'd done. Brandon suggested to Bochco that perhaps it was necessary to help the audience along as it went from a diet of *Quincy* and *CHiPs* into the brave new world of *Hill Street*.

Steven nodded, I recall. Point taken. From then on, Steven had a new level of respect for what I did and what I had to say. Of course, he still reamed me from time to time when the mood hit, but that was just Bochco. It was always worth it because *Hill Street* supplied me a hell of an education.

There were no such creative fireworks with *Cheers*. The show premiered on September 30, 1982. We loved it at the network. It was just what we'd hoped it would be, but the ratings were abominable. At the end of its first season, *Cheers* was the least watched show on prime-time network television. The chances looked good the show wouldn't have a second season, much less an eleventh.

In 1981, Grant Tinker had replaced Fred Silverman as CEO of NBC. By then, I was in charge of current comedy at the network. My first conversation with Grant began with him calling me into his office and asking me if I owned "a good heavy winter coat." Why? "I've watched the comedies on this network, and it's going to be a long cold winter for you!"

Grant's programming philosophy was simplicity itself. We were instructed and encouraged to make shows we'd run home and watch. At the end of *Cheers'* first season, when Brandon and I were agonizing over whether or not to cancel the show, Grant asked us a question: "Do you have anything better?" We didn't. We didn't have much that was half as good, so we stuck with *Cheers*, and our faith in the show (and in our taste) was rewarded. The audience found *Cheers* in summer reruns. We realized that a quality adult comedy audience had no reason to come to our network. Attracting those viewers would take time.

Jim Burrows: Nobody was watching the show when it first went on. There was no reason for the public to watch the show. No star in it. And nobody was watching NBC generally. The press loved us, and the guys at the network loved the show. Our first summer, we got all the way up to ninth. Everybody had seen *Simon & Simon* and *Magnum*, but nobody had seen us.

Warren: The Frasier Crane character was added in the third season of *Cheers* in the person of Kelsey Grammer. Kelsey would end up playing Frasier Crane for twenty years on network television, which hardly seemed likely in the beginning. Kelsey had been hired for four episodes. He'd driven out from New York and for a time was living in his car on the Paramount lot.

Jim Burrows: Frasier was a device to get Diane back in the bar in year three. She'd gone off with the artist, with Chris Lloyd, and had freaked out. She ended up in an institute, and her doctor was Frasier Crane. We offered the part to John Lithgow, but he turned us down.

John Lithgow: I just said, "No, I don't want to do Frasier." So they went out and found Kelsey Grammer for it. I barely even remembered that. It was like swatting a fly away. At that time, I just wasn't going to do a series.

Kelsey Grammer: I was doing *Sunday in the Park with George* with Mandy Patinkin. He had lunch with the casting director for Paramount, and she asked him if he knew of any funny leading men. He said, "Yeah, Kelsey Grammer. I'm working with him."

She called me in for *Brothers*, one of the first cable sitcoms. I read for the part, didn't get it, and she called me in for another part. She said it was very hush-hush. I got the sides, and I was reading for a character called Frasier Nye.

When I read it, I thought, "I can play this. I can get this part."

Jim Burrows: We started to see people, and we got a tape from New York with four actors. Up came Kelsey's face, and we all started laughing when we saw him.

Kelsey Grammer: I was told I'd be put on tape in a personality piece. This was something I'd never heard of. I went home and found a pair of yellow pants my mother had given me. I'd never worn them. They were Christian Dior, and I thought, "This is just what Frasier Nye would wear."

I went over to the Gulf & Western building in my yellow pants. I read the sides. I talked about who I was and where I was from. Burrows tells the story that they all saw this tape and started laughing. I don't know if that was a compliment or not. I thought I looked rather dashing in my yellow pants.

Jim Burrows: He was supposed to do four episodes. He played a pompous asshole, and when Diane left the show, Kelsey could do all the Diane jokes.

Kelsey Grammer: I remember saying, "Nye doesn't sound quite right to me," and they came up with Crane.

Warren: Writing for Kelsey's Frasier Crane required not just an ear for pomposity but a talent for witty, rapid-fire dialogue. The Charles brothers turned to Peter Casey and David Lee, who had impressed them with a *Cheers* script the pair had submitted on spec.

Peter Casey: We were working on *The Jeffersons*, and David and I would meet on the weekends or go into the office two or three hours before everyone else would arrive, and we'd work on a *Cheers* script. We'd read every episode from the first season and had studied the characters.

David Lee: We were producing *The Jeffersons* at the time, and we saw that the show was coming to an end. We also realized *The Jeffersons* wasn't in our DNA. We could execute it, but it wasn't what we aspired to. We tried to get hired on *Family Ties*, but Gary David Goldberg said he wouldn't read a spec *Jeffersons* script. So we said, "Uh-oh."

I went to the University of Redlands, where Glen and Les Charles also went, and the university had a TV seminar. We were invited, but Glen and Les were the big draw. We hit it off out there, and I remember the car drive on the way home. I said, "We have to write a spec *Cheers*."

Peter Casey: I had a little Honda Prelude we'd squeezed into, and we looked over to see Glen and Les getting into a stretch limo. I said, "Yes, I think we ought to write a *Cheers*."

David Lee: I was an actor, and I took a job in my downtime at a copy company. That was in the olden times, before Xerox. TV shows would send out their rewritten scripts every night to a company that typed them and mimeographed them. These days it's like being a blacksmith.

I was a proofreader and Peter was a typist. I'd never thought about writing, but I somehow convinced Peter that my expertise as an actor and my master's degree as a director would have some effect.

We had one of those "meteoric" rises—eleven spec scripts and three and a half years before we got our first meeting.

Peter Casey: We started writing hour dramas, but we kept putting jokes in them, so we decided to write sitcoms. We finally wrote a *Barney Miller* that the people at *The Jeffersons* read and liked. We brought in five ideas, and they bought one of them.

I was selling sandwiches for A Moveable Feast. I have a picture of me selling a sandwich to Stephen Collins during the filming of *Star Trek*. It was another six months before *The Jeffersons* called us and had us write another script.

David Lee: *The Jeffersons* was a great training ground. It was a good starter education. When we moved over to *Cheers*, we realized we'd only completed kindergarten.

Peter Casey: We wrote that first episode with a generic psychiatrist in mind.

David Lee: Les and Glen Charles wanted our take on who Frasier was.

Peter Casey: They ended up using a speech of ours in the casting process for Frasier.

Kelsey Grammer: I got called out to L.A. to read and meet people. I met Ted and Shelley, and Jimmy in his office. We read through the scenes once there, and then we went down to a table with twenty or thirty people above stage 25. We read through the scenes again, and there weren't many laughs. As I turned and left, I said, "Thank you. I'll go out on the street and see if I can get any laughs there."

I called my friend Lois, and I said, "Let's go to San Diego. I have a rental car, and I don't think I got this job."

On Monday night I got back to the Holiday Inn on Vine and Hollywood Boulevard, and I found a green box on the table when I walked into my hotel room. Inside was a bottle of Dom, and on a little card it said, "Welcome to *Cheers*."

Warren: Kelsey was one of several actors we saw at the network. It came down to Kelsey or John Bedford Lloyd, a handsome, leading-man type, who consistently works in film and television. Jimmy Burrows and the Charles brothers said of Kelsey, "This is the guy we want." We'd trusted Jimmy and Glen and Les with Ted Danson over Fred Dryer, so we trusted them again. Early on, it became clear to us that Kelsey was perfect for the part. The precision with which he could deliver his lines was like the creative blending of a surgeon and a concert pianist.

Jim Burrows: Our show was the most sophisticated comedy on television—with Kelsey and Bebe. They were playing Noël Coward. It was better than movies. I remember an executive said to me, "You can't do Schopenhauer jokes." But Schopenhauer was getting big laughs.

Warren: Kelsey, however, handled his success as Frasier Crane rather poorly. Things didn't go Charlie Sheen sideways, but they were certainly bad enough.

Jim Burrows: Kelsey came out from New York, and he had a six-month-old baby and was getting divorced. He had a horrible family history.

Peter Casey: It's just brutal, hard to believe that kind of tragedy has fallen on one person's shoulders.

Warren: Kelsey's father and sister were murdered in separate incidents. His twin half brothers died in a scuba-diving accident.

Peter Casey: Kelsey also had a terrible circle of friends. He was the sort of guy who could be driving up the Pacific Coast Highway and pick up a hitchhiker. He'd invite him home. The next thing you know, "Here's my assistant, Hacksaw."

David Lee: Or he'd see a stripper in a club and marry her.

Peter Casey: Kelsey would come in after an incredibly rough night, and his performances weren't good. It came to a head with John Ratzenberger. They had to be separated. Ratzenberger was getting fed up with Kelsey missing his lines and missing his marks.

David Lee: Kelsey was so smart and so talented that he could perform at a certain level when he was drunk or stoned. He was delivering everything you needed. But then his performance started falling below acceptable levels. When we were editing the show, it got to the point where we were having trouble cutting around Kelsey's performances. They were . . . enhanced.

Peter Casey: An intervention was called in Les and Glen's office. Everybody was there. Kelsey walked in, and he said, "What's going on?" The interventionist explained what was happening.

David Lee: Kelsey said, "Oh, okay," and it was over quickly. We found out later that part of what makes interventions successful is when everybody goes around the room and tells how they've been affected by the person's behavior. That didn't happen, and that intervention didn't take.

Peter Casey: He went to a facility here in town, and David Angell and

I went down to visit him. There was Hacksaw or one of his minions sitting in the room with him. I remember thinking, "I don't know if this is going to work." It didn't. The next one worked.

Kelsey Grammer: There were issues I had to deal with. I probably had some anger going on, feeling that my family should still be alive to enjoy this part of my life. I just had to work that out.

Warren: The second intervention, this one during the *Frasier* years, was held in Kelsey's house. Stupidly, we at the network had given Kelsey a Dodge Viper that he had flipped over and wrecked, a sure sign of trouble. I later learned that he'd been under the influence of alcohol and cocaine. The night of the intervention I remember going into Kelsey's kitchen to tell all the hangers-on, "Get out. The party's over." Somehow Kelsey couldn't believe he was worthy of his success. We spent a number of hours trying to convince him he was wrong.

As *Cheers* continued to thrive, the Charles brothers began pulling back from their day-to-day involvement. They were intent upon handing the reins to Peter Casey and David Lee. Les and Glen would still set up the goals for the season. The Charles brothers always had a great articulation for where the season would start and where it would end. They had character arcs for the core characters. This was a revelation to me. I'd never seen that at the network with any other show.

Peter Casey: For us, it was a very new concept. On *The Jeffersons*, we had twenty-four episodes, and they were twenty-four individual, stand-alone stories. The Charles brothers would say, "Here's the way we're going to tilt the season. First we had Sam chasing Diane, now Diane will get the hots for Sam. That'll be the arc." Then Frasier came in, so we had a triangle.

I think we spent the first year and a half learning at the feet of the Charles brothers, and then they handed the show over to us. When you're the show runner, you're the person who has the yes/no on the stories. You run the rewrite room. Do the casting. Supervise the editing. Les and Glen would come in a couple of times a month at most.

David Lee: When we found out we were going to be producing *Cheers*, we heard that Nick Colasanto died. So we started out having to replace the most beloved character on the show.

Lori Openden: Woody Harrelson came in and read against another actor. The producers expected to go with the other actor, but we liked Woody. Woody was an understudy in *Biloxi Blues* in New York. He was also in a Goldie Hawn movie called *Wildcats* as football player number 4. Those were all of his credits. Woody was reading for Woody Boyd. People thought we'd changed the character's name to suit the actor. Nope. That was a real meant-to-be kind of role. He did a film test the next day, and then he went to work right after that.

Jim Burrows: Woody came out here, and the second night he was here he was robbed, mugged, his car taken.

Lori Openden: When Woody got the part, he called his mother—single mother, raised three boys while Woody's father was in prison. He told his mother he got the part and wanted her to quit her job.

David Lee: Shortly after we'd solved the Coach problem, Shelley Long waltzed in and said she was leaving.

Bob Broder: Shelley was an award-winning television actress with movie aspirations. She had one or two children during the run of *Cheers*, and then she decided she wanted out of the show. She'd done five years, and she was finished. It was probably a good thing. At that point, if they'd continued the series arc, she and Teddy would have had to get married, and it would have been a different show.

Kelsey Grammer: I wasn't aware of the numbers for *Cheers* before Shelley left, but I did think, once she'd left, it was a huge opportunity for the show to catapult into legendary status. Because her story was kind of over when Shelley decided to leave. So a show that had built an audience had a chance to become a new show. I thought, "Boy, this could really turn out well."

Jim Burrows: When Shelley left *Cheers*, we hated her for that. We went back to the original concept of the show—Sam Malone working for a woman. We told Jeff Greenberg, our casting director, what we wanted, and the first name out of his mouth was Kirstie Alley. We brought her in. She was wonderful, but we said, "No, we can't buy the first house we've seen." So we went through this long process, but nobody could beat her. She was great.

She showed up for the first reading as Rebecca Howe dressed as Shelley Long. She came in a blond wig and a skirt. It was hysterical.

Bob Broder: We gambled and got Kirstie Alley, and that gave us another six years. She flipped the show.

Jim Burrows: The first run-through with Kirstie was abysmal. We wrote Rebecca Howe as a martinet. She wouldn't give Sam Malone the time of day. She was mean. It wasn't working. She had to exit to her office, and somehow the office door got locked. An accident. She started wrestling with it, and we cracked up. It dawned on us that we had to make her a woman of the eighties and the nineties who thinks she's empowered but can't get through the day. The minute we found her frailty and vulnerability, then we had it.

Warren: There was a lot riding on the decision, and I remember holding my breath that night on the *Cheers* set hoping that this show that I loved wasn't over. But the audience loved Kirstie. She got big laughs. I couldn't wait to tell Brandon and called him at home that night after filming. I told him Kirstie was funny and she was great—very different from Shelley Long but sensational—and *Cheers* was going to be all right.

Bob Broder: Then came Ted's decision in year eleven that he was done. We could have gone on for another two years. Everybody was disappointed but respectful. Ted had given eleven years of his life to the show.

John Pike: I can name very few actors as cooperative as Ted Danson. We never had a disagreement. He never held us up for money. Ted came and sat in this very room, and it wasn't about money. He was just tired and didn't want to do it anymore.

He was the highest-paid actor at the time without question. But he was tired, tired of coming to work every day. The leverage Ted had was unbelievable. The leverage Ted used was absolutely in the spirit of the partnership.

When you make a movie, you have a beginning, a middle, and an end. A television series is a living thing that doesn't really end. I went through a lot with Ted, so I knew when we sat down that it was over. Nobody wanted to believe it, but it was over.

Steve Levitan: As a viewer, I was completely invested in the *Cheers* characters. I thought it was the greatest place on earth. Who didn't want to go to a bar like that? Who didn't want to have friends like that? It was smart. It was Tracy/Hepburn. It was slapstick. It was everything all in one.

What I love is you're watching a show and laughing hard, having a wonderful ride, and then you have a profound moment that makes you feel something, and then you're laughing again. That's what works for me.

Jim Burrows: We ran eleven years. We ran more years without Shelley than with her. That's how good the cast was. When she left, we had to do shows about the rest of the people in the bar because we didn't want to do Rebecca and Sam in a romance. Woody came in. Bebe came in. We had a great time. It was a wonderful show.

Mike Mandelker: The real value of *Cheers* was that everybody used to watch *Cheers*. Everybody wanted to see their commercial on *Cheers*. The value of *Cheers* was far greater than its audience share. The magic of *Cheers*, just as it was the magic of *Seinfeld*, was that it was the show Madison Avenue watched.

John Pike: We put together a piece of paper called "The Value of *Cheers*." We calculated that net dollars to NBC for one year of *Cheers* was $75 million. The *Cheers* asset over the years was about three-quarters of a billion dollars of profit for the network.

Warren: It was worth more. *Cheers* was an absolute game changer for NBC. Successful both artistically and financially, *Cheers* validated our judgment and our taste and marked the beginning of our discovery of who we were as a network. It was a lesson I would remember and come back to.

2

Bill & Jack

Warren: *Cheers* was bumping along well enough by 1983 to make us hopeful of its eventual success, but it was no world-beater quite yet. The conventional thinking among the entertainment press was that the half-hour comedy was dead, and most of the print interviews I gave at the time took the form of comedy postmortems. Reviving the sitcom, both in the affections of TV writers and in the habits of the viewing public, would take an out-of-the-blue ratings champion, an unmitigated comedic success that hardly anyone who turned on a television could bear to miss. It would take, in short, Bill Cosby.

Following the airing of the first episode of *The Cosby Show* in September 1984, two years after the premiere of *Cheers*, I would never again be asked about the death of the sitcom.

Legend has it that Brandon Tartikoff proposed the idea for the show to Bill Cosby, a legend cultivated by Brandon, who as a network president knew better than anyone how to prolong his position. It's not true, of course. It's just as false as the legend that Brandon "created" *Miami Vice* by suggesting, "MTV cops." In response to Michael Mann and Tony Yerkovich's pitch for *Miami Vice*, Brandon said, "I get it. MTV cops." Not quite the same thing, but people don't always argue with network presidents.

The Cosby Show was developed by two former ABC executives

turned producers, Marcy Carsey and Tom Werner. They'd approached Cosby about starring in a TV series. Bill wanted to play a limo driver in an hour drama, but Tom and Marcy convinced him to do a family comedy that was an extension of Bill's stand-up. And Bill's stand-up was a brilliant comedic extension of Bill's life.

Tom Werner: Making *The Cosby Show* was a transforming experience for us. Marcy and I had been in comedy at ABC and had discovered some pretty talented people and put them in shows—Robin Williams, Tom Hanks, Billy Crystal. It was scary to leave that network, with corner offices and people calling you all the time to pitch ideas.

Marcy Carsey: I grew up at ABC with Leonard Goldenson instilling in us a really idealistic view of network television. Public trust. Public airwaves. Our job as programmers would be to deliver shows that not only were successful but shows we could be proud of. We should put together a schedule that serves everyone. It sounds really corny now, but that's how we felt about it.

I would have preferred to stay at ABC if the people I liked had stayed. There was no other job available in town that was like that. The only other choice for me was to go out and be as independent as possible as a producer. I always thought it was in the network's best interest to have strong independent voices out there along with the studios and big companies.

Tom Werner: At the time we were pitching the show, Bill Cosby wasn't as hot as he'd been previously. He'd been wildly successful on *I Spy*, and he'd done a variety show. He'd be white-hot later but not at the time.

People think *The Cosby Show*, because it was such an enormous hit, was always going to be an enormous hit. Not the case. We went to ABC, where we had a big development deal, and they turned us down.

Warren and Brandon liked the idea, but I didn't get the sense they thought it was going to be a big hit. It was more "Let's take a shot."

Marcy Carsey: I don't think Brandon believed in the show. He told the advertisers he thought it would come in a strong second to *Magnum P.I.*

Warren: I was getting a haircut early one morning on my way to work, and Brandon and John Agoglia called me to say they were passing on the Cosby deal. "What?!"

By now I was vice president of comedy programs, and they thought I had other strong shows in development and the *Cosby* deal was just too rich. I told them, "We have to have this show. Put a little more on the table." Thankfully, that's just what they did, and John closed the deal.

We had Bill, Marcy, and Tom, but we didn't have a writer yet, and it was getting very late in the development season. At the last moment, Tom and Marcy secured Ed. Weinberger (*Mary Tyler Moore*, *Taxi*) and Michael Leeson (*Phyllis*, *Rhoda*, *Taxi*) to write a pilot demo script. It wasn't a full pilot, because of the lack of time. It was written very quickly.

Brandon and I got together after reading it and decided for the first (and for me the only) time in our professional lives to deliver this message to the producers: "We have no notes. We love it!"

At that time little or no prime-time entertainment production was done in New York, so for simplicity's sake the plan was to make the demo in Los Angeles. We had the demo shot in less than a month, probably the quickest turnaround in network history. I remember thinking to myself as I watched the taping of the pilot episode, "This is a hit."

There's a scene in the demo where Cliff has to go to Theo's room and punish him for getting D's on his report card. Cliff grabs a baseball bat as he heads upstairs. The audience did not know what to expect.

Theo then passionately tells his dad, "I may not grow up to be a doctor like you or a lawyer like Mom, but you should love me for who I am." I remember the audience, led by the young people, really applauded Theo for standing up to his father. They were on his side.

Bill waited, and then he said, "Theo, that's the dumbest thing I've ever heard. You're going to study because I said so. I brought you into this world, and I can take you out." There was a roar from the entire audience. It was as if they were saying, "God Bless you, Bill Cosby, for taking back your role as a parent and telling these spoiled children to study." The energy from that laugh was explosive.

I was sitting in the audience. The younger members appreciated Theo's speech, but then when Bill said, "I can take you out," everyone in the audience was united, the place went nuts. At that moment, it felt like breakthrough television. I'd never known anything like it.

Marcy Carsey: We knew we had a hit on our hands from the pilot. We knew kind of before that, but the audience confirmed it.

Warren: Knowing what we had in our hands allowed us to go to the scheduling board and make changes on three nights of the week. The impact was enormous.

Tom Werner: Marcy and I were in favor of stripping away concept as much as possible. We adored Bill's point of view about family and about parenting and about humanity. Bill really was a stand-up genius. He had this ability to tell stories about his children or his parents, and he could do this for two hours. Most comedians run out of material after fifteen minutes. Bill had his own rhythm. It's not three jokes a minute, and we tried to emulate that rhythm in the show.

Bill's point of view was remarkable and unusual. People have said it had some effect on Obama's election. In 1984, everyone wanted to be a Huxtable. We stripped away the economic underpinning of the show and were just telling stories.

Warren: Creatively, Bill Cosby insisted on an enormous amount of control over the writing and the portrayal of his TV family, and, as with *Cheers*, putting our faith in the talent was well rewarded.

In series, the first head writer and show runner, Earl Pomerantz, couldn't handle Bill's creative process. I remember sitting beside Earl at the table reading of the second or third script. After Bill had worked a comic variation on a piece of dialogue, Earl muttered, "Just once I'd like to hear the words I wrote." After watching Bill's process at the read, I said to myself, "Boy, are you in for a lot of disappointment." Since it was Bill's show, and its success would depend on Bill's sense of comic invention, saying the words as written wasn't really in the cards.

Tom Werner: Earl had written a couple of scripts he'd given to Bill. Bill had a challenging time giving notes before he'd heard the script read on the set. Bill gave notes with the understanding he could give better notes once he'd heard the script read. The process on *The Cosby Show* was going to be radically different from what Earl was used to. Bill would say, "I admire that writing, but that's not me, and I wouldn't say it this way."

It got to where whatever the writer's first draft was, it was open to being thrown out on the table-read day. There are certain writers who realize a first draft is a thing to continue on or throw away. Earl just couldn't work that way. And we had a four-day workweek. Most shows are done in five days. After a table read on Monday, you had to get the show ready in basically forty-eight hours.

Earl came to me and Marcy and said we had to support him or support Bill. He put us in the position where, if it was Earl or Bill, we had to go with Bill. He wasn't only the star of the show; he was the vision behind the show. Earl quit.

Warren: Elliot Shoenman took over, and the show motored along just fine from there. A young playwright, Matt Williams, was also added to the staff, and he would go on and eventually create *Home Improve-*

ment. Before *Cosby*, we were getting test patterns on Thursday at 8:00. It was all about CBS. *Magnum. Simon & Simon.* That two-hour block owned the world. But with the premiere of *The Cosby Show*, everything changed.

Tom Werner: The first night the show got a 48 share nationally.

Warren: According to Nielsen's audience measurement, it was actually a 21.6 rating/39 share. That's still an incredible number. TV viewership is commonly reported in ratings points and shares. A single ratings point represents 1 percent of the total number of television households in the country (households with one or more television sets). A share is the percentage of those available sets tuned to a given program. The premiere of *Cosby* was watched by over thirty-four million people (Nielsen Media Research). The highest-rated series today is *American Idol*, and it is watched by just over twenty-five million viewers.

When Brandon saw the numbers for *Cosby*, he thought it was a printing error. We just weren't conditioned to think that positively.

Tom Werner: When the national numbers came in, Warren called and said it was the number one show in the nation for the whole week.

I went down to the set and told Bill the show was number one. Not just for the night but for the whole week, and Bill couldn't comprehend it.

Warren: We could barely comprehend it ourselves. While *Cheers* had been an artistic out-of-the-gate success, the audience was slow to build. Everybody showed up for *Cosby* starting from the premiere of the first half hour.

Tom Werner: If you read the scripts, they don't come across as funny as when you watch the shows. Part of what made that show so powerful was that it gave people the sense—and Bill said it—of "how did you get in my living room?"

At times it was like shooting a live sporting event. Bill was often not on his mark and having fun, and you just had to submit to the spirit of it. Bill was very willing to take lots of chances. He'd hire actors who'd never acted before just to give them a chance. He had Dizzy Gillespie play Rudy's music teacher just to give Dizzy a chance to be seen by the American audience.

We would do a taping at 5:30 and at 8:00. Bill would invite people into his dressing room between tapings, and it was an incredible party. Sidney Poitier. Jesse Jackson. Maya Angelou. I don't think he ever took the show as seriously as he might have. Bill never saw a rough cut. He trusted us.

I do think the fact we were an independent production company helped the quality of the show. Our finances were on the line, and we shot in Brooklyn because it was cheaper. We were at Fourteenth and Avenue M. It really wasn't show business.

Warren: The camera guys knew soap opera. They didn't know comedy. The room in the apartment building next door where the writers and producers worked every day was dowdy and smelled like cabbage. The stage was an antique. This wasn't Hollywood. They worked across the street from 20th Century Fish. This was Brooklyn.

The first season was produced at NBC's Studio One. When that building was sold, the production moved to Kaufman Studios in Astoria, Queens. Leaving the studio one evening during rush hour in a car with Bill Cosby and a driver, I had an amazing experience. I was convinced it would take us forever to get into Manhattan, but I was riding with Mr. Bill Cosby, who would lower his window and stick his head out when need be. Almost as if by magic, traffic cones were scooted aside. Police stopped cars and trucks to let us pass, an urban version of the parting of the Red Sea. It was all out of love for Bill. We arrived at his town house in fifteen minutes, just in time for dinner.

Marcy Carsey: There was a time after *The Cosby Show* went on the air when I couldn't pay my bills. There's a lag time, and we were truly independent, so we couldn't pay ourselves. We just weren't making any money. I mortgaged my house. I had no backup, no family I could borrow money from.

Tom left the business decisions to me because he knew I was a risk taker, so I took risks. As a result, I couldn't afford to get my dry cleaning out when I had the number one show on television.

Warren: Cosby ended that first season averaging over forty million viewers each week (Nielsen Media Research). With the success of *The Cosby Show*, we began to entertain ideas about building a "Night of Bests." We had momentum and measurable success; we were finally giving CBS's *Magnum P.I.* real competition for viewers. We believed if we shored up our schedule, we could actually win the night. In the fall of 1984, we shifted *Family Ties* out of its Wednesday slot, and our Thursday night lineup opened with *Cosby* at 8:00. *Family Ties* followed at 8:30. Then came *Cheers*, followed by *Night Court* and *Hill Street Blues*.

By the end of the season, *Cosby* only trailed *Dynasty* and *Dallas* in the ratings. *Family Ties* was the fifth most popular show on TV. We were handily throttling both *Magnum P.I.* and *Simon & Simon* on CBS. *Cheers* had vaulted from seventy-seventh to twelfth. *Night Court* was twentieth. *Hill Street Blues* was thirtieth. We had the makings of an evening that both viewers and advertisers might flock to for years to come.

Tom Werner: I always felt like Brandon and Warren were our partners. It's quite different today with networks and suppliers. They're often our adversaries. We had the same goal. To get the show right, get it to the audience, and hope they watch.

Warren: Boy, did they watch. From 1985 to 1990, *Cosby* was the most popular show on all of TV. Bill Cosby's successful transition from stand-up to sitcom would make a whole era of network comedy possible. And it was the engine for Thursday nights. It was the engine for NBC.

The follow-up piece of development from Tom, Marcy, and Bill was *A Different World*, a spin-off of *The Cosby Show* starring Lisa Bonet, who was leaving the Huxtable nest and going off to college. The show never had the power of *Cosby*, but it was a solid success and filled in very nicely (we still dominated the competition) in its 8:30 time slot on Thursday nights.

In the summer of 1987, Marcy and Tom and their chief creative executive, Caryn Mandabach, invited me to a show at Universal Amphitheatre. Louie Anderson and Roseanne Barr were performing. They were eager for me to see Roseanne because they believed that like Bill Cosby, she could be at the center of a family comedy.

I thought Roseanne's performance was vulgar and kind of gross. The women in the audience certainly laughed at her jokes and cheered her on, but of the two comedians I saw that night, I far preferred Louie Anderson.

Marcy told me, "Forget Louie. We want Roseanne." I asked what they were looking for, and she said, "Six episodes on the air."

The next day I discussed the situation with Brandon and shared with him my reaction. He had zero interest in Roseanne. "Tell them to fix *A Different World*," he said. I suggested we offer Marcy and Tom a pilot in case they were right and we were wrong. After all, they were producing the number one show on television. Brandon agreed, and that's what we did. Marcy turned us down, so we lost Roseanne. I seem to recall the show had a decent (nine years!) run on ABC. Whoops. Thank God I had *Cosby* and *The Golden Girls* as part of my comedy development résumé, or I would not have survived that screwup.

Years later when *Roseanne* was the number one show and she was appearing as a guest on *The Tonight Show* with Jay Leno, Jay called me at my office and asked if I had anything I wanted to say to Roseanne on air? I ran down to the stage, onto the set, shoved my hand into my pocket, and threw a big wad of cash at her and begged her to come to NBC. Roseanne kept her job and my cash.

Thanks to an invigorated and widely watched comedy lineup featuring *Cosby*, *Family Ties*, *The Golden Girls*, *Cheers*, and *Night Court* and a renewed emphasis on quality drama embodied by *Hill Street Blues* and *St. Elsewhere*, we had finally developed at NBC the sorts of shows that critics loved and audiences flocked to. For the television season ending in the spring of 1986, half of the top thirty shows were running on our network. NBC had flourished into a conspicuous success, a gaudy jewel in the crown of our parent company, RCA. People noticed. One guy in particular.

Jack Welch: I went after RCA in 1986 because we were being attacked by the Japanese on every front. I was looking for a long-term cash-flow business. A business that was secure with regulation, that foreigners couldn't take. A beachhead while we reshuffled the portfolio. I tried CBS and got turned down, but by trying CBS and getting the gossip out there that I was running around trying to do it, I got the call that RCA might.

I didn't think, "We must be in entertainment." Mine was a vision of raw numbers. We needed cash. The Japanese were coming after us in many areas—television sets, semiconductors. It turned out RCA was a much better deal than CBS would have been because we got all the RCA properties. RCA was the number one TV-set producer, which we merged with our number three or four, and that gave us a strong TV package, which we then traded with Thomson to get a medical business.

Our aerospace business was okay. RCA's was better than okay. We merged those and got their management to run it. We sold that business to Lockheed Martin for $3.5 to $4 billion. So we got our money back and still got a free NBC.

Warren: While RCA had been relatively benign and uninvolved, as corporate overlords go, our new relationship with GE promised to be something altogether different. "Neutron Jack" Welch had a reputation for ruthlessness where profits were concerned. All of the divisions under the GE umbrella made their quarters. Or else.

Brian Pike: Jack Welch flew into Florida for a management meeting. By accident, I was sitting at his table. He was very engaging. There was nothing about him that was officious or difficult at dinner. He was lovely.

In the corner of the room was a whiteboard, and we thought it was left over from an earlier meeting. But Jack walked up to this board, and he said, "I think I should explain to you what I do and how I spend my days. I've got all these companies, and I run the people who run the companies and figure out how it all fits together."

He draws a graph, an *x*- and *y*-axis graph. I remember this because I thought my life ended. He draws these boxes above and below the line. He says the companies above the line are cash-generating companies, and the companies below the line are cash-eating companies. They're profitable, but they need a lot of cash.

He said the reason he'd bought NBC was because we were throwing off tons of cash. I thought, "Oh my God, nobody ever explained it to me that way. I was just there to make TV shows."

John Agoglia: When GE came in, I just wanted to meet my budget. We had an annual budget, and I knew GE would beat the shit out of me if I didn't meet it.

Warren: Technically, the way it worked was this. In August you had to have a business plan that represented the next calendar year. You'd yet to premiere that fall's shows. You didn't know what was going to be a hit, what was going to be a failure. You didn't know what the spot sales were going to be, how much revenue you were going to have. We plugged in everything we did know, and we'd fill every single hour with a show.

It was a list of assumptions. We had to have a success plan and a failure plan, and it all had to work for the budget. In the course of an ordinary year during my tenure running NBC, we'd hear about 1,000 pitches for new series ideas. Of those, 150 might go to script. Of those, we might make a dozen comedy pilots and a dozen drama pilots (at approximately $1 million apiece for the comedies and $2 million apiece for the dramas). Of those, three or four comedies and the same number of dramas might make the schedule. If one comedy and one drama stuck and was worth renewing, we'd had a good year.

In many ways the TV business is all about managing failure. Failure is very costly. A successful show is a rare commodity.

John Agoglia: Jack Welch called me and Brandon up and flew down to L.A. to have lunch with us. We met him at a restaurant on Ventura at Coldwater. I didn't eat anything. I was like blubber. We were trying to figure out what he wanted to know, what he was going to do. We rode back with him in his limo, and he said, "Why don't you . . . ," and made some sort of programming suggestion.

As I was getting out of the car, I told him, "Jack, that's a great idea, but we just don't have the cash to do it. We won't meet the quarter."

About forty-five minutes later, the phone rings and it's Jack Welch from his plane. He screams at me, "If you were fucking smart, you'd know how to bury some money and make your quarter."

Warren: Jack Welch's reputation as a hard-as-nails businessman was well earned. I remember attending a conference at GE's Crotonville facility in Ossining, New York, in the early nineties. It's a university setting where you examine your business practices, study your competition, and hopefully come away with an enlightened game plan.

John Agoglia: We were talking about NBC's lack of success in development—we'd had a really bad year—and Jack had some numbers he put up. Perry Simon, an executive in development, raised his hand and said, "We don't have enough money." We'd spent $32 million on development that year, and *all* of it had failed. It was like waving a red flag in front of Jack.

Warren: Perry made the mistake of asking Jack Welch, "How would you do it?" The room got really quiet. Jack said, "It's not my job. I don't know how to do it. That's up to you."

Unfortunately, that was probably the moment Don Ohlmeyer decided Perry would not be in NBC's future.

John Agoglia: You can't blame your boss for your failures. You just can't do that. Shit doesn't flow upstream.

Warren: Fundamentally, the network's relationship with GE and Jack Welch was a pretty happy and healthy one, provided we continued to kick off cash as Welch expected. Bob Wright, formerly of Cox Cable, had been installed by Welch as president and CEO of NBC. His message was an incredible downer. Bob told us life would change, everybody would have more channel choices, and what we did wouldn't matter. It was icy water in our faces, but he was right.

Under Grant Tinker and Brandon Tartikoff, there was no strategy at NBC. There was a philosophy. Bob Wright and GE told us, "You must have a strategy, or you won't survive." Bob Wright forced us to think about who we were as a network and what we wanted to become.

I told Brandon the guys at Cap Cities and ABC knew right away if something was for them while we were still agonizing over it. They knew who they were and what fit their schedule. We were still a big tent with a very diverse lineup. That was fine for the eighties, when viewers had few choices, but things were changing. More homes were getting cable channels, and they wouldn't just run network repeats forever. Bob Wright helped us focus.

Bob Wright: People do want to see broadcast shows because, by definition, those are shows lots of other people are watching. I think that's broadcast's greatest strength. But it is the hardest form of television. It's easy to go narrow, but it's hard to stay broad and attractive. That's why the failure rate is so high.

The grading on broadcast shows is much tougher than the grading on cable shows. I use Fox as an example. People can go on Fox, and as long as they're bitter and sarcastic, the Fox viewers will watch them.

I feared we'd get into some kind of tailspin at NBC as our shows aged, and GE would just come in and clean house, get rid of everybody.

Warren: In the face of all this gloomy news, it was our job to continue to develop and air shows that would keep the audience glued to the peacock. We were having a good run, but by the late eighties our shows were getting old and shedding audience, and we weren't having much luck developing the next hot thing. We got conservative. Coming up with successful programming is anything but a science.

John Agoglia: I learned an enormous amount from GE in terms of management technique, but some of their ideas were absolute bullshit. They had a guy do a computer matrix, which would guarantee you how to pick hit programs. He worked on it for two years. I mean, come on!

Jack Welch: The news people would say I meddled a lot. Not entertainment. I wasn't that good at programming, but I quite frankly didn't think they were that good at it either. I thought it was a crapshoot.

I loved *The Tortellis.* I knew it was a home run. Total flop. And I hated *ALF*, and it was a hit. That's when I stopped mucking around in programming.

Warren: However, that didn't prevent Jack from pitching *Wall Street*, the series, after seeing Oliver Stone's new hit movie. Starring Michael Douglas as Gordon "Greed Is Good" Gekko. "I think *that* would make a great series," Jack told me.

To my mind, that was a pitch, and I responded instinctively as a programmer. "That's where you're wrong, Jack," I said. "Nobody gives a shit about those guys. All they care about is money."

I remember Jack Welch looked at me with his mouth hanging open. "I'm going back to the guys in electrical," he told me. "They listen to me."

A couple of hours later, my life flashed before my eyes. I'd shot down Jack Welch, my new boss. What the hell was I thinking?

John Agoglia: I gave a development report at the first GE board meeting I went to, and some guy from power systems or jet engines said to me, "What you guys have to do is pick the hit shows." Jack Welch just winked at me.

Warren: To give Jack Welch his due, network programming is part crapshoot, but it's part savvy and judgment as well, tempered with an awful lot of hard work. Computer matrix? Not so much.

Brandon Tartikoff and I had divergent views on the basics of program development. As I've said earlier, my preference was for turning talented people loose to shine. I reacted to the pitches that came through the door and tried to improve upon them where I could. I felt it was also my job to articulate to the creative community what our needs were—family comedy or medical procedural. Moreover, I aggressively preached to the entire TV industry the value of being at NBC—a network where a good idea could be nurtured into a hit show. That hit show would bring tremendous revenue to them beyond its network run. Brandon would send out word of ideas that were intriguing to him. Producers and writers would tailor their pitches to suit him.

Brian Pike: NBC was run by committee until Brandon. He had a point of view, a very strong point of view about what TV should look like.

When agents would call for meetings with heavy hitters, they'd call Brandon and ask him to give them ideas on what he wanted. So they would show up with some version of what Brandon had in mind.

People would call me and say, "What are you looking for this year?" and I didn't have a fucking clue. I wanted to know what *they* wanted.

Brandon saw himself as this idea guy. He'd have these nuggets, and then everyone's job was to get as close as they could to what Brandon had in mind. Because Brandon said it was blue with polka dots, you were always trying to figure out what that meant. It was like putting you in a dark room and saying, "I'm in here too. Find me." It was very frustrating.

Warren: The epitome of my approach to programming versus Brandon's arrived at NBC in the form of Dick Wolf in 1989. Dick showed up with more than a pitch. He arrived armed with a show called *Law & Order* that he'd sold twice already and had shot a pilot for. *L&O* featured a new and distinctive form of storytelling for TV, something no development executive—even one as talented as Brandon—would have known to ask for.

Dick Wolf: I think *Law & Order* was the only series ever sold to three networks. I sold a pilot to CBS, but before that I sold thirteen on the air to Barry Diller at Fox. He called me two days later and told me he'd made a mistake, that *Law & Order* wasn't a Fox show.

Warren: Barry Diller was right.

Brian Pike: I'd just taken over development when *Law & Order* was made. Dick Wolf wanted us to see his pilot that CBS had passed on.

We all went downstairs and watched it, and it was really good. It broke a lot of rules, but it was really compelling.

I remember the opening shot like it was yesterday. I'd never seen anything like it. It opened with a bizarrely high camera that was shaking. You heard this noise in the background, heavy breathing and a snort. I was like, "Why is the camera so high?" and the camera looks over, and there are feet behind a bush. Then you turn around, and you see a policeman on a horse in Central Park.

Dick Wolf: CBS had walked away from *Law & Order*. It was a dead pilot. Eight months later, we were losing all the actors, so we took it to NBC and screened it.

Brandon said, "This is very interesting, but how are you going to do that every week?"

I said, "Give me six scripts, and I'll prove it to you." We wrote six scripts, and Brandon ordered thirteen. I think there'd be a lot lower failure ratio if people wrote six scripts before there was a firm order.

Warren: Dick was given an opportunity, and he delivered. If I had learned anything from working with Steven Bochco on *Hill Street Blues*, it was that sometimes the things that scare you have the biggest upside. Dick's lack of convention was unpredictable and scary, but it was also compelling.

Coincidentally, as we were rolling out *Law & Order*, Bochco was about to premiere his own cop show on ABC, which was using up most of the available publicity oxygen. It was called *Cop Rock*, and the pilot was under wraps, held so close that I couldn't turn up anybody who'd seen it and was finding it impossible to get my hands on a copy. I worried that the show would be Bochco brilliant and create scheduling problems for us with *Law & Order* and *Hunter*, our vehicle for the talented (and meant to star in a drama) Fred Dryer.

I finally found a friend working at 20th Century Fox Television (who shall remain nameless) who agreed to supply me with a copy of the *Cop Rock* pilot. "Midnight," he told me. "Your mailbox." So I waited up, checked my mailbox at midnight, and discovered an envelope inside containing a VHS tape. I popped it in and started watching.

The opening of the show was riveting, a police raid on a house in L.A. to a pounding, urban beat. It was gritty and real, pure Bochco dynamism. Shit! ABC was going to have a hit drama. But then came the singing. First from a cop. Then from Barbara Bosson, playing a judge. There was a bit of dancing as well, and it was all very odd and exotic, but not in a good way. This couldn't possibly work, could it? Our answer would be to put *Hunter* up against it.

Dick Wolf: I had a mole at ABC. Mike Post. He told me he was doing a song an act for Bochco's *Cop Rock*. Four songs a week. So I said if the show ran for five years, he'd write 440 original songs.

Mike said, "Yeah."

I said, "Gee, that's more than Adolph Green. Nobody can do that." What were those people smoking and drinking and snorting? Four hundred and forty songs?

Warren: The show didn't work dramatically. Better still for us, it didn't work with viewers. It went on the air in September 1990 and was off the air in December. *Law & Order*, thankfully, was only just getting started.

Brian Pike: In *Law & Order*, the audience never knew anything before the characters did. You never went home with the characters, and there was this very daring thing at the half hour—a handoff from the cops to the lawyers. I remember it was better than our own shows.

I wanted to find out how CBS had made this mistake. It turned out the guy running CBS thought *L&O* was a cold, dark show, and he thought all of the rules they'd broken were insulting.

Dick Wolf: Most dramas make my skin itch because they give you personal stuff with a soup ladle. When you go into work and look around your office, how many of your colleagues' apartments have you been in? Ours is a workplace show. All we're interested in is what happens in the eight or ten hours when the characters are actually at work.

There's also no time. That's why there are no establishing shots, no driving shots, no people walking into buildings. Each half of the show is the equivalent to a normal hour cop show or legal show. You're essentially doing an hour's worth of content in half the time.

I grew up on *N.Y.P.D.*, the original, and *Naked City. Naked City* is much more the prototype for *Law & Order* than anything else on TV. The best pictures about conflict are the ones that almost look like news. Like *The Battle of Algiers*.

Warren: NBC's acquisition of *Law & Order*, which ran for twenty years, was the epitome of my approach to programming at the network. Dick Wolf came to us with his creative vision realized, and we embraced it.

Oddly—maybe inevitably—Dick Wolf's next pitch to NBC was the antithesis of everything I believed in as a development executive and a programmer. The show was called *Nasty Boys*, and the pitch was pure crack for Brandon Tartikoff.

Dick Wolf: I gave everybody in the room a manila folder with an eight-by-ten picture of a unit of the Las Vegas PD called the Nasty Boys. They wore black ninja outfits and masks and carried heavy weapons.

Brian Pike: It was ninja cops. All you could see was their eyes. A SWAT team in Nevada.

Dick Wolf: It said "Nasty Boys" in graffiti over their heads, and underneath them it said, "We make house calls."

I said, "Okay, open the folder."

Brandon looked at it and said, "Sold."

It was the only nonverbal network pitch I've ever given.

Brian Pike: Everybody was seduced by the image. We didn't know who the characters were, what the show was. Nothing. But Brandon couldn't get it on the air fast enough.

Dick Wolf: Unfortunately, the show was too expensive. We shot the first six episodes in Las Vegas, and it was damned exciting television. We moved the show to L.A., and it just wasn't Las Vegas. It didn't have the same octane.

In one show, we had a big gunfight on the strip, and the next week they were out in the valley. People said, "No, no. That's not what I saw last week."

Warren: *Nasty Boys*, starring Benjamin Bratt and Dennis Franz, first aired in February 1990 and lasted half a season.

By the end of the third season of *Law & Order*, it had become apparent to me, while looking at the performance data with Preston Beckman, that for all the show's strengths, it was being held back in the ratings by the fact that there were no female leads in the show. Women just didn't watch *L&O*, and I was determined to do something about that.

I called Dick Wolf and asked him to come see me. It was just the two of us in my office. I told him I was sorry but I was canceling his show at the end of the season. That certainly got Dick's attention. I didn't go into his restaurant and tell him how to cook. I didn't tell him whom to keep or whom to get rid of. I just told him we needed more women as series regulars on camera and more stories that featured women in critical roles.

Dick Wolf: Warren gave me a cancellation notice a year early. He said, "Dick, it's a really good show. Everybody likes it, but there are no women watching. You have to put women in the show."

That led to the worst phone call I've ever had to make, to Dann Florek. He was the only sane one in the front half of the cast until Jerry Orbach came in. I told him he'd done an incredible job, always showed up on time, never bumped into the furniture, was always prepared, knew his lines—you're fired.

It was terrible, but it changed the show. Epatha Merkerson is still there. It worked out great. The pilot was written twenty-two years ago, and the reality was that there weren't that many women cops at the time, and certainly not many women prosecutors. Now it's about fifty-fifty, but not then.

Warren: In 1998, when Dick came in to pitch me a show called *Sex Crimes*, my response was "Interesting idea, but we'll never be able to get advertisers on board." I advised Dick to spin the show out of the *Law & Order* brand. "Just go write it, Dick, and sometime in the next six months business affairs will figure out how to make a deal." Thus began the now commonplace network practice of procedural spin-offs (*CSI*, *NCIS*). The Emmy Award–winning *Law & Order: Special Victims Unit* just completed its twelfth season.

Brian Pike: I used to say I want to work at a network someday because I really don't understand how decisions are made. I learned it's crazy how decisions are made.

3

Yada Yada Yada

Warren: The long, slow birth of *Seinfeld* marked the transition from the end of Brandon Tartikoff's reign as president of entertainment at NBC to the beginning of my tenure in that job. I would be announced as Brandon's successor within weeks of the airing of the first regular episode of *Seinfeld* in May 1990.

Getting to that first episode was as unlikely a process as any of us could have possibly imagined. No one at the network had any inkling that we were helping usher into existence what would become one of the most successful half hours in television history. Here's how it all started.

Rick Ludwin: That first meeting was Jerry Seinfeld, Warren, Brandon, me, and George Shapiro, here in my office. I can still bring people in, and they can sit on the *Seinfeld* couch.

George Shapiro: I first saw Jerry Seinfeld on July 3, 1980. I saw him at the Comedy Store. I liked him right away. We started booking Jerry in clubs, and I wrote a letter to Warren and Brandon. Jerry had his first show at Town Hall in Manhattan, and nobody from NBC came to the show, even after the letter I wrote.

Then we had that first meeting with Warren and Brandon in Rick

Ludwin's office. They said if we had an idea, they'd be interested. Three days later, Jerry was in New York at Catch a Rising Star, where he met Larry David. Larry was doing stand-up at the time. They went for a walk, and Jerry said NBC was interested. Larry said, "This should be the show. Two guys talking."

When we left the NBC meeting, we didn't know what we'd walked out with. We walked back in and said, "Pilot!"

Brandon said, "Yes, and now you don't have to write me any more letters."

Warren: The reality was they had a script commitment and a little holding money for Jerry, but it wasn't actually clear who would write the script.

Jerry Seinfeld: Imagine you have this kid who's been on *The Tonight Show* thirty times and on the Letterman show thirty times. He's on your network *all the time*. Presentable fellow. Seems to do well. No one ever thought, "Why don't we talk to this young man. Maybe we can do some business. Do a show." That never happened.

Rick Ludwin: Jerry Seinfeld was known from being on some of our shows, but he certainly wasn't known to a wide audience. Jerry and Larry David had never written a sitcom. Our department (late night, variety, and specials) had never developed one. They came in with a story idea, and we approved the story idea and approved a pilot script.

There was no production company attached to it. George Shapiro called and asked how I'd feel if they went to Castle Rock. I told him, "Sure, that sounds like a good idea."

Glenn Padnick: We'd met Jerry when we brought him to ABC to star in a pilot there. He was rejected for the part. When NBC bought the pilot script for what would become *Seinfeld*, and NBC couldn't own the show, Jerry said, "Why don't we use those guys from last year. They seem nice enough." That was us, Castle Rock. That was our payoff.

Howard West: We took Jerry's act. That was the pilot. Nobody was thinking a hundred shows, or whatever. Then we wondered, "What happens when we burn up the act?"

Jerry Seinfeld: I knew what I wanted the show to sound like. I didn't know what it would be, but I knew the way I wanted the people to talk. Larry and I both felt there was a type of dialogue in the world that wasn't being shown on TV. A lot of it was New York. I knew whenever I talked with Larry that this kind of talking would occur. A style of talking and a superficiality of substance. What I've always enjoyed my whole life.

There were a lot of people at NBC and Castle Rock at the time who'd look at the stuff we were doing and say, "I don't really get this, but . . . go ahead." I remember Glenn Padnick told us our scripts were elliptical. I didn't quite know what he meant.

When we began, the number one show in America was *ALF*. We never thought we were going to be at that level of acceptance. We didn't think that was possible. We just wanted to do our thing.

Glenn Padnick: Warren told me I had to furnish a show runner because he didn't trust Larry David in that role. We brought in Gary Gilbert, who had been, oddly, the writer of the pilot Jerry had done for ABC. The one he'd been rejected for.

Howard West: NBC didn't approve Larry David. We sort of resented it, but we understood.

George Shapiro: Larry and Jerry didn't feel any creative compatibility with Gary Gilbert. They wrote separate scripts. Both scripts went to the Writers Guild, and the guild awarded Jerry and Larry a created-by credit. They had their own rhythm.

Glenn Padnick: I knew Larry David, not personally, but I knew of him. I was given a script he'd written early at Castle Rock. It was *Prognosis Negative*. The plot was about a man who can't commit, and he meets a woman who he hears is dying. He can commit to her because her prognosis is negative. Of course, the prognosis turns out to be wrong, and he has to live with her. It was a very funny script.

I didn't start to feel Jerry and Larry had something special until they'd written the first draft of the pilot. I said to myself, "Am I crazy, or is this really good?"

Warren: The script was very funny, totally unconventional but funny. It didn't sound like anything else on television. There was no historical precedent. We decided to make a pilot.

Jason Alexander: When I read the pilot script, I thought it was a glorious mess. It wasn't paying attention to the rules. There were many episodes early on when George and Jerry were in conflict with each other, and they'd never resolve it, just let it sit. I remember asking Larry if there was another scene coming to tie it up, and he said, "No. It isn't funny after that."

George Shapiro: I was in all the casting sessions, and George was based on who Larry was, but Larry wasn't ever going to play the part.

Jason Alexander: The elements that make George—the elements that make Larry—don't go together. This odd combination of an unbelievable ego that's convinced it's not ever receiving its due coupled with the knowledge that George has no innate ability to do anything. They just don't fit together.

Howard West: In Larry's head, he always wanted to be an on-camera star. When I was at William Morris, I was involved with *The Three Stooges*, and I got a picture of Larry David with a note from his agent. Larry was being submitted for Curly. At the bottom of the photo it said, "He must have script approval." I broke out laughing.

Jason Alexander: Larry and I had a special bond. I knew I was playing him, and he knew that I knew, but we never talked about it.

George Shapiro: Marc Hirschfeld was the casting director, and he did a fabulous job. Jason Alexander was doing a play in New York, *Jerome Robbins' Broadway*. Marc arranged for a videotape, and Marc read with Jason.

Jason Alexander: I was looking for film or television. It was all a happy accident. I was living in New York, and I had four pages of a script in a casting office with a casting director who'd been hired to put fifty people on tape. There was no Larry to talk to or Jerry to talk to, and *nobody* gets a job that way. Every New York actor knows that.

I remember thinking it read like a Woody Allen script, so I went out and bought some Woody Allen glasses, and I did a blatant Woody Allen impression. I was shocked when they told me they'd like to bring me out.

Lori Openden: Jerry wanted Larry Miller to play George Costanza. I was very vocal about not having one comedian who's learning to act with another comedian learning to act.

Jason Alexander: I flew to L.A. In my memory, the only other guy testing that day was Larry Miller. I didn't know Jerry Seinfeld, but I knew Larry Miller, and I knew he was good friends with Jerry. I thought, "This is a *fesso*. I'm here to keep Larry from negotiating."

I had nothing on it when I walked into the conference room at

NBC. I did my thing, and by the time I'd landed in New York, they called and said, "You've got it."

Warren: We knew Jerry was a great comedian, and we had a lot of respect for Jason's acting ability. Watching Jason bring George to life was wildly funny and seemed effortless to Jason. It wasn't a tough call to make.

Jerry Seinfeld: Larry and I saw Jason on a grainy VHS tape. We were standing there with our arms folded, and within twenty seconds we said, "That's the guy."

Glenn Padnick: Jason made George vulnerable and lovable and likable in a way that Larry David never would have, never could have. Jason made George palatable no matter what Larry had him doing. That was a great treasure for the show.

Lori Openden: Bob Wright was being honored at the Century Plaza hotel. There was no time for Brandon and Warren to see actors except right before the luncheon. I arranged a room for them to see two actors read—Michael Richards and Steve Vinovich.

Steve Vinovich came dressed in pajamas and a bathrobe. He was very good. Michael Richards came in, and he was Kramer.

George Shapiro: Michael Richards was standing on his head while he was doing his lines. A yoga pose. Brandon Tartikoff said, "Well, if you want funny . . ."

Lori Openden: He was born to play that part and can't really play much else. The part wasn't written for him, but when you think about it, it was written for him.

Warren: We had worked with Michael before, and regardless of the size of the role he was always a scene stealer. We were fans.

Glenn Padnick: Larry had worked with Michael Richards on camera. Larry objected to Michael because Kramer was based on a real person, but Jerry convinced him. Larry can be reasonable.

The real Kramer, jerk that he is, felt we should pay him for using his name. He was called Kessler in the pilot because Larry knew he'd make trouble. Then Larry decided he needed to call him Kramer. We paid him a moderate sum—$100 an episode or something.

Warren: I attended run-throughs for the pilot. The show was about Jerry pestering George to give him a ride to the airport. Jerry needed to pick up a girl who was staying with him, a girl whom Jerry was interested in but who would ultimately tell him she was engaged. Signals, Jerry! There were no big, dramatic scenes. Act breaks had jokes, not momentous decisions. In the coffee shop—very much about life. In the Laundromat—about laundry. No hugs. No great emotional stakes. And no Elaine. Not yet.

Glenn Padnick: We loved the script, and we loved it for the little stuff. Most shows go for big plots—Grandma's coming to visit et cetera. We filmed the pilot in the spring of 1989. We also filmed the Gary Gilbert pilot that Jerry had gone up for but with Howie Mandel. ABC didn't pick it up. It was sort of like *How I Met Your Mother*.

Jason Alexander: In the pilot, there was some famous Larry David bit where the line isn't funny, but he had a rhythm in mind. "No hand. No hand." That's all it said on the page. There's a million ways to interpret that. I did it one way at the table read, and then we rehearsed it. Then Larry came over and said, "We kind of heard that this way . . . I hope you don't mind a line reading."

I told Jerry as long as we were discussing this sort of thing, would it be okay if I told him how he might be missing the mark as the actor? We'd been doing a scene in the coffee shop where Jerry was arguing with George about what a girl's offer to stay over meant. The fun of the scene was that Jerry represented one position, I represented the other, and we switched over and then switched back. The only way that works was if he was adamantly advocating for his side of the argument, and Jerry doesn't do that. I was playing George with such force that the whole scene was out of balance.

I said, "If you don't push as hard in your way as I'm pushing in my way, then I'll have to back down, and that won't help you."

Jerry said, "That's good. That's good."

That became the *Seinfeld* way with all of us. What apparently was unique among us was when we started rehearsing an episode, we didn't leave the stage. We all watched each other work, and we'd all throw ideas to each other. I think that's what built that ensemble so quickly.

Jerry Seinfeld: I wasn't comfortable as an actor in the pilot, but after that I relaxed pretty quickly. I got better as it went along until eventually it was like a warm bath.

My main job, as I saw it, was executive producer. The acting was down my priority list. I'm here to make sure this scene works. People would say, "It looks like you're watching the scene." I'd say, "I am. Who cares if I'm a good actor. We pay these people to act. You want to see good acting, watch them."

Jason Alexander: Initially, Jerry wasn't comfortable playing any kind of real anger, and he wasn't comfortable playing any kind of real sexuality. Well, that's the bulk of a sitcom. I think after I'd kissed Marisa Tomei, he thought, "I could kiss Marisa Tomei!"

Warren: Once the pilot was completed, we handed it over to NBC's research department for testing. In typical fashion the episode was shown to test audiences, and the respondents were in four different locations across the country with a sample audience size of about six hundred people. It was also screened by a test audience of about a hundred people locally in Los Angeles, and then they participated in a lengthy discussion about the program's pros and cons. All of these responses were compiled in a research document. The test report that came back on the *Seinfeld Chronicles* pilot was, in a word, disastrous.

SEINFELD TEST REPORT: Jerry Seinfeld who was familiar to about a quarter of the viewers, created, on balance, lukewarm reactions among adults and teens, and very low reactions among kids. Jerry's "loser" friend, George, who was not a particularly forceful character, actually appeared somewhat more in charge, and viewers found it annoying that Jerry needed things to be explained to him.

None of the supports were particularly liked, and viewers felt that Jerry needed a better backup ensemble. George was negatively viewed as a "wimp" who was only mildly amusing. Kessler [Kramer] had low scores but was the best of the supports—he mildly amused some twelve- to thirty-four-year-old males and reminded some of their own weird neighbors.

PILOT PERFORMANCE: WEAK.

Glenn Padnick: I've had that happen to me too many times. A few years before, I'd done a show with Morris Day for NBC. It had a time slot and everything, and then the testing came in, and they hated Morris. The same thing seemed to happen with *Seinfeld.*

Jerry Seinfeld: I made this cartoon movie a few years ago for Dream-

Works, and I went through a brutalizing process of testing for that movie. I think in the end it was valuable. I test jokes every night. The Marx Brothers tested all of their movies. They performed the scripts in theaters before they shot.

Paul Reiser: The *Seinfeld* testing should put an end to all conversations about testing, ever. Please don't tell me my show is going to come down to twenty people in Sherman Oaks. Why not let those people create a show. I've never been to any testing that's any good. It's like waking up and seeing my liver sitting in a chair.

Jason Alexander: I remember after the pilot, Jerry asked me, "What do you think?"

I said, "There's no way."

"You don't think it's good?"

"I think it's really good. The problem is the audience for this show is me, and I don't watch TV. It's guys, not girls. Eighteen to thirty-two at the outmost. Every guy I know in that age group is either working or out trying to get laid. They're not watching TV, so this isn't going to play for anybody else." I guess initially I was right.

Warren: We screened *The Seinfeld Chronicles* along with all of our pilots for that year in the third-floor conference room at NBC in Burbank. In attendance were program executives from the West Coast, New York and Burbank members of the sales department, executives from the promo department, high-level management from New York, and the research department.

There were about sixty people in the room, and the overall reaction was positive. They laughed. They got it. My birthday is May 11, and usually that was right about the time in the May screening and scheduling process that the research department would deliver most of their results of the pilot season testing. The truth is most pilots don't test well. Television is not a science, and audiences do not respond well to things that are new or different or have had no previous promotional marketing. It was not a happy birthday. The research report killed *Seinfeld*'s hope for a fall pickup. The pressure to perform was tremendous, and we went with two other shows that had better test results. We picked up *The Nutt House*, with Harvey Korman and Cloris Leachman. It was on the air for two entire months. *Sister Kate*, starring Stephanie Beacham, was about a nun caring for orphan kids. One of these kids was Jason Priestley, but that show only lasted one season. In the summer of 1989, with minimal promotional push, the *Seinfeld* pilot aired.

4

---

*Master
of My Domain*

Warren: We loved *Seinfeld* at the network, the research report notwithstanding, and when we were in danger of losing our rights to the show because of the actors' contracts expiring, I got creative in an attempt to get *Seinfeld* on the air. I went to one of our budget and finance guys, Rick Lacher, to see if we could find some money—any money—to help us keep the show.

Since *Seinfeld* was Rick Ludwin's baby, and Rick was in our variety and specials department, Lacher suggested we take the money from Ludwin's budget, which was the only place that still had some available funds. In what would be a brilliant "rob Peter to pay Paul" finance move, he also suggested we make one less two-hour Bob Hope special and use the savings to pay for four episodes of *Seinfeld*.

And that's exactly what we did. I let Rick Ludwin break the news to Bob Hope, and I distinctly remember calling Jerry Seinfeld to tell him about the four-episode order. There was a long silence on the line. Jerry finally asked me, "Has any show, in the history of television, ever succeeded with four episodes?" I didn't know, and that's exactly what I told him.

Glenn Padnick: I was very surprised when Rick Ludwin called me to say he was ordering four episodes of the show. They'd burned off the pilot during the summer—fiasco theater. I thought that was it.

Jason Alexander: They ordered four episodes. The whopping four. The confidence four.

George Shapiro: They were four half-hour specials, and they had to go through the variety department. It was so much more fun to do the show without all of the notes from the comedy department. When we got the order for four shows, Larry David said, "That's all I got in me anyway." He ended up doing 137 episodes, I think.

Jerry Seinfeld: I was always pretty confident. I thought four episodes was fine. I thought, "If they let us make four of these, they'll get it by then."

Warren: At the network, I only had one note for Jerry: get a girl.

Glenn Padnick: Women especially hated the show, and the typical response is to add a person from the group who like the show least.

George Shapiro: Jerry, Jason, and Michael Richards were the only three regulars under contract for the pilot. Then we got a note that we needed a young lady. Rosie O'Donnell read. A whole lot of people read before Julia came in.

Lori Openden: I planted the seed for Julia Louis-Dreyfus with *Seinfeld*'s casting director so they wouldn't think the idea came from us.

Warren: Lee Garlington, a terrific actress who never stops working in both comedy and drama, was featured in the diner and could have easily been added to the series, but I thought that as the waitress she'd never really be one of the gang. She'd be relegated to pouring coffee, catching up. So I insisted they create a female character that they wanted to spend time with. I knew Julia from *SNL*, and she'd been the most memorable part of a not so memorable Gary David Goldberg comedy we'd done called *Day by Day*.

Glenn Padnick: Julia had a holding deal at Warner Bros. that was about to expire. Larry thought she was terrific, and she came in and read with us. I remember Larry chasing her out of the room and begging her to be on the show. She wasn't sure—the third lead, the money, only four episodes. Not the most promising start you could have.

Megan Mullally: I auditioned for Elaine. I was testing with two other girls, and then I got a call that day that they'd cast Julia, who I went to college with. My first boyfriend broke up with me to go out with her, and then they got married, and they're still together. Extremely happily married for thirty-some-odd years, with two sons, and the whole thing. So anyway, I knew Julia. I heard she had a development deal that was expiring that week with the network, and they thought, "Oh, wait a minute, we already have somebody."

Jerry Seinfeld: I knew when I met Julia that she was the girl. I don't think I could possibly have realized how perfect the chemistry would be.

Glenn Padnick: Much of the show came from Larry's life rather than Jerry's life. Larry had had a relationship with a woman named Monica Yates, Richard Yates's daughter. After they stopped dating, they remained friends, and Larry used that relationship as the model for what Jerry and Elaine's relationship would be.

Jason Alexander: Jerry told me, "There's going to be a girl on the show, but she's not my girlfriend."

"All right. Who is she?"

"She's like my best friend."

I said, "I thought George was your best friend."

I actually had a wary eye on Julia. I knew you didn't do a show with three guys and one girl. You did a show with two guys and one girl. In those first four shows, they made one that George and Kramer weren't in. That's when I famously went to Larry and said, "If you do that again, you'll have to do it permanently."

Glenn Padnick: I got a phone call from Brandon offering me Sophie's choice. He said he could either put us on in the spring on Wednesday nights after *Dear John*. Or he said he could hold off until the summer following *Cheers*, though we wouldn't be on the fall schedule. I accepted the latter proposal immediately, without calling anybody.

It was an easy decision. "Life is better than death" is one of the rules I operate by. And "life" in this instance was following *Cheers*. It was a no-brainer.

We went on the air on May 31, 1990.

Warren: Larry David thought NBC would never air the episodes. He tells a story where he envisioned a dinner party hosted by himself and Jerry. They invite all their friends over to eat and watch the episodes NBC never put on the air. They made those first episodes to make their friends laugh. But we did put it on.

The show did well enough with the benefit of a *Cheers* lead-in— even with *Cheers* in reruns—but Brandon was convinced *Seinfeld* was too Jewish to be widely successful. I called up our scheduling guru, Preston Beckman, and told him I needed the Jew/not-Jew numbers for the show.

Each morning at 6:00, I would get a fax of the overnight ratings from the research department in New York. Preston had worked there, and he'd routinely be my first call of the day. As we stared at the numbers, I'd ask, "What did we learn last night?" Preston would usually reply with a useful illustration of who'd been smart and who'd been dumb. If it were the middle of winter, for instance, and CBS had aired a movie set on a Caribbean island with lots of tanned flesh on display, that was a point for them. They'd done well.

In my new job I knew I would need Preston's insight and wisdom, so I had asked him—a hard-core New Yorker—to move with his wife and young kids to Los Angeles to be in charge of scheduling and strategic planning.

Preston Beckman: Interesting result with *Seinfeld*. Whether it was New York, Chicago, Seattle—it didn't matter. There was the same retention of the *Cheers* audience. I wrote a memo to say *Seinfeld* didn't skew to any part of the country. It was not about the Jews.

Warren: Those first four episodes of *Seinfeld* in the summer of 1990 were originals against repeat competition, and they didn't suck. Didn't go up, went down a bit from *Cheers*. But just a bit. The interesting thing was of those two million plus viewers (Nielsen Media Research) it was the young adult men, for whom *Cheers* was an anthem, who said, "Hey, I kind of get this show. These guys are as fucked-up as I am."

Better still, Brandon Tartikoff had been kicked upstairs, promoted to chairman of the NBC Entertainment Group, and I had been given Brandon's job. Now many of the programming decisions were mine to make, and I was nearly as confident in the potential of *Seinfeld* as Jerry himself was.

Jason Alexander: As Jerry tells it, he was supremely confident in the show from the get-go. As dubious as Larry and Julia and I were, Jerry could step back as an experienced comic and say, "I don't know if this is good storytelling, but it's funny. I've run enough funny material through myself to know this will make people laugh." He had the confidence to know if you put twenty-two minutes of television on the screen and say it's a comedy and people were laughing, that should work.

Steve Levitan: *Seinfeld* pulled off just being *funny*. That's a high-wire act, a very hard thing to do.

Jerry Seinfeld: I personally believe that what Larry and I brought to the sitcom format—a twenty-two-minute format—was a stand-up comedian's structural sensibility. We didn't really have time to tell what the characters were all about, because we had jokes to do. We weren't really storytellers—we became that—but only through that lens.

George Shapiro: Jerry would give the best lines to Jason or Julia. I called him the Magic Johnson of comedy because he would pass off so frequently. Comedy was the god, and I saw him so many times give lines to Jason and Michael and Julia when he could have gotten the laughs.

Glenn Padnick: Jerry was always writing himself out of the show. I said, "You're the star. It's called *Seinfeld*. Shouldn't you have a part in the show?" He so admired his co-stars that as a writer, he kept throwing stuff to them.

Jerry Seinfeld: We wrote the damn thing. There was no issue as to whose show it was, not just on the screen, but in the deal. It didn't matter to me. I just wanted the scene to be good. When someone plays a scene you've written, it's a very enchanting experience. You watch it come to life.

Jason Alexander: I thought the scripts were—as Hammerstein said to Sondheim—talented but terrible. You could see everything that was yummy about them. It was a new way of telling these kinds of stories that I didn't truly understand. I didn't quite know why the show was working, but I could see it was working.

Warren: We'd bought the pitch for *Seinfeld* in 1988. The pilot had

The cast of *Cheers*, from left to right, George Wendt (as Norm Peterson), Kelsey Grammer (as Dr. Frasier Crane), John Ratzenberger (as Cliff Clavin), Shelley Long (as Diane Chambers), Ted Danson (as Sam Malone), Woody Harrelson (as Woody Boyd), and Rhea Perlman (as Carla Tortelli).

Ted Danson and Warren Littlefield at an NBC event. In the fall of 1991, just as Warren assumed his new role as NBC president of entertainment, Ted Danson called to say that this would be his last season on *Cheers*. Panic set in.

From left to right, George Wendt, *Cheers* creators Les and Glen Charles, and Ted Danson on the *Cheers* set. As Warren tells it, NBC was so desperate for quality programming in the mid-eighties that it guaranteed Les and Glen Charles and Jimmy Burrows "thirteen episodes on the air even though they had never developed a show."

Ted Danson and Shelley Long discuss dialogue with the legendary television director Jimmy Burrows. Six finalists auditioned for the parts of Sam and Diane. "It was obvious it was Ted and Shelley," remembers Burrows.

Ted Danson and Kirstie Alley (as Rebecca Howe) on the *Cheers* set. Jimmy Burrows recalls, "When Shelley left *Cheers*, we hated her for that. We went back to the original concept of the show—Sam Malone working for a woman. We told Jeff Greenberg, our casting director, what we wanted, and the first name out of his mouth was Kirstie Alley."

(Below) From left to right, Grant Tinker (former CEO of NBC), John Pike (former head of Paramount Television), Warren, and Kerry McCluggage (chairman of Paramount Television Group) drinking at the *Cheers* bar. On May 20, 1993, the last night of *Cheers*, "we . . . had a massive celebration of the series that had meant so much to us," Warren says.

(Above) Marcy Carsey and Tom Werner, the powerhouse team behind the megahit *The Cosby Show*, among many others.

(Left) Bill Cosby (as Dr. Heathcliff Huxtable) and Malcolm-Jamal Warner (as Theo Huxtable). "Creatively, Bill Cosby insisted on an enormous amount of control over the writing and the portrayal of his TV family, and, as with *Cheers*, putting our faith in the talent was well rewarded," Warren recalls.

From left to right, Jerry Orbach (as Lennie Briscoe), Michael Moriarty (as Ben Stone), Chris Noth (as Mike Logan), and Richard Brooks (as Paul Robinette). Dick Wolf claims that "*Law & Order* was the only series ever sold to three networks" before it aired.

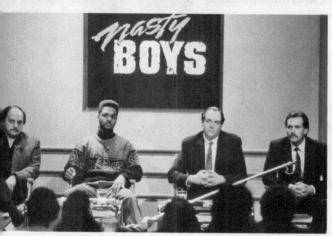

Dick Wolf (second from the right) next pitched NBC on a show called *Nasty Boys*, about a SWAT team in Las Vegas who wore black ninja outfits. It only lasted half a season.

The original cast of *Law & Order SVU*, from left to right, Dann Florek (as Donald Cragen), Mariska Hargitay (as Olivia Benson), Christopher Meloni (as Elliot Stabler), and Angie Harmon (as Abbie Carmichael). In 1998, when Dick pitched NBC on a new show called *Sex Crimes*, Warren advised him "to spin the show out of the *Law & Order* brand." That was the beginning of the now commonplace practice of procedural spin-offs.

Julia Louis-Dreyfus (as Elaine Benes), Jason Alexander (as George Costanza), Michael Richards (as Kramer), Jerry Seinfeld, and Warren (background) on the *Seinfeld* diner set during the shooting of the final episode. "The test report that came back on the *Seinfeld Chronicles* pilot," Warren reminisces, "was, in a word, disastrous."

Bob Hope, Warren, and Johnny Carson at the shooting of Bob's ninetieth birthday celebration. NBC decided to make one less two-hour Bob Hope special in order to pay for the first four episodes of *Seinfeld*. "I let Rick Ludwin break the news to Bob Hope," Warren says.

Larry David giving notes to the cast while shooting an episode of *Seinfeld*. Larry thought NBC would never air the episodes. Warren mentions that Larry "tells a story where he envisioned a dinner party hosted by himself and Jerry. They invite all their friends over to eat and watch the episodes NBC never put on the air."

(Left) An offstage moment between Jerry Seinfeld and *Seinfeld* co-creator Larry David in Jerry's dressing room.

(Below left) Jason Alexander and Heidi Swedberg (as Susan) on *Seinfeld*. Jason says, "It is the single coldest moment in the history of television when the doctor comes out to say Susan has died. George's reaction was 'Huh.' Like, 'How about that.'"

(Below right) Jerry Seinfeld reading over a scene while getting his makeup touched up on the *Seinfeld* set.

Jerry Seinfeld with cast and crew watching the monitor while Michael Richards films a scene in the background from the episode titled "The Burning."

Jason Alexander admits, "I actually had a wary eye on Julia [shown here in an episode from season 8]. I knew you didn't do a show with three guys and one girl. In those first four shows, they made one that George and Kramer weren't in. That's when I famously went to Larry and said, 'If you do that again, you'll have to do it permanently.'"

From left to right, Warren, Brandon Tartikoff (president of entertainment), and John Miller (executive vice president of advertising and promotion) pose for the camera. As Warren explains, "The long, slow birth of *Seinfeld* marked the transition from the end of Brandon Tartikoff's reign as president of entertainment at NBC to the beginning of [his] tenure in that job."

From left to right, Warren, John Agoglia (executive vice president of business affairs and NBC Productions), Bob Wright (chairman), Brandon Tartikoff, and Perry Simon (senior vice president) made up the main executive team at NBC during the Must See TV era.

Don Ohlmeyer and Warren. *(Below left)* Posing for a Must See TV promo. *(Below right)* Giving good face during a joint presentation. Warren confesses that "by 1996, Don's drinking and his behavior in the office and at numerous NBC 'off campus' events had become serious liabilities."

aired—almost surreptitiously—in July 1989, and the first four episodes had finally made the schedule a full year later. Now we had to decide—I had to decide—if we were going to pick up the show with some sort of proper commitment and put an end to our long, tortured courtship.

Perry Simon: It was the deadline for renewing the option after the first four shows. We had to do it by the end of the day, so we all went in a conference room and watched a couple of episodes to decide if we'd renew. We said, "It's too Jewish. Too New York. They don't tell stories, but the fucking thing is funny. Let's just try it." There was still great uncertainty about the show at that stage. It was right down to the wire.

Warren: My response after the screening was to walk up to the scheduling board and grab the magnetic card that said *Seinfeld*. I took it off the fringes of the board, where we had our backup shows, and put it right smack in the center. This is our future! Rick Ludwin smiled.

Preston Beckman: We screened a couple of episodes of *Seinfeld*, and Bob Wright was there, and he said, "Why hasn't this show been on the schedule?"

Warren: Brandon left NBC in April 1991 to become chairman of Paramount Pictures. With Brandon gone, there was no reason anymore.

Naturally, because it was *Seinfeld*, we ordered just thirteen episodes—half a season—and scheduled the show as a mid-season replacement in January 1991.

When Jerry told Larry the good news, Larry said to turn the order down. He said he was out of ideas.

Glenn Padnick: Warren called and ordered thirteen episodes for mid-season—two years after we shot the pilot.

Rick Ludwin: After a few episodes, we thought we had a nice little show on our hands, but that's about it.

Perry Simon: After we'd picked up the show for thirteen more episodes, we got Jerry and Larry in. They came into my office with Rick Ludwin. I tried to wing typical network notes—maybe we needed a little more story, little more of this, of that. They were incredibly gracious. "Let us work on this, and we'll come back to you." Then they walked out the door, and I knew they were like, "Fuck that." And now I think, "Thank God." Whatever they were doing, they were doing it right. It's a good thing they didn't listen to me.

George Shapiro: Larry and Jerry were ready to walk away after the four episodes—creatively. The network wanted Jerry and Julia to be married or dating. We had a meeting with Rob Reiner and Glenn Padnick and Jerry and Larry out in the parking lot. Jerry and Larry felt strongly that Jerry and Julia shouldn't have a relationship. They were ready to walk away.

Howard West: That was normal, network thinking. Fortunately, we had two creators who didn't give a shit.

Jerry Seinfeld: All creativity should be exploratory. If we know what we're doing completely, we're not in the right place.

Warren: While they clearly knew what they were doing with the scripts, Jerry and Larry had never run a sitcom before, and it showed. For all the brilliance of the episodes, the production schedule was a bit of a mess from the outset and never really improved.

Jerry Seinfeld: Larry and I wrote everything together. Sometimes the writers would figure out a story while I was rehearsing. Then we'd work on that, and once we had the story, we'd sit at our desks and work on the dialogue.

We used the Carl Reiner/Dick Van Dyke model. Most sitcoms would start on Monday and shoot on Friday. Carl Reiner figured out if you started on Wednesday and shot on Tuesday, you'd have the weekend to rewrite. We had no personal lives anyway, so that was okay with us. It was a lot of work—fifty- to sixty-page scripts—and Larry and I would turn them out in two days.

Howard West: George and I would read first drafts of scripts, and they'd be quite weak. Then Larry and Jerry would get ahold of it for the rewrite, and the difference was night and day. Larry and Jerry just needed a story.

Jason Alexander: We were a show that was shooting on Tuesday nights. That means you come in Wednesday for the table read. We'd get a call, "The ten o'clock table read is going to be at three." Then another call. "It'll be at ten on Thursday." Another call. "Take Thursday off." Eventually, it got to where we were coming in on Saturday at one. On Sunday at two.

They would hand us a schedule for the season, and we'd have three weeks off on the schedule, but it would soon be gone. Larry would say, "Sorry." I lost two movies that way. To that extent, I knew we were being afforded a treatment that was unusual, to say the least.

Warren: The treatment was unusual because of the unusual genesis of the show. *Seinfeld* had been developed not in NBC's comedy department but in the variety and specials department (which also reported to me) under the care and guidance of Rick Ludwin. Just as Larry David and Jerry Seinfeld had never run a sitcom, Rick Ludwin had never developed one.

Rick Ludwin: Neither Jerry nor Larry had *any* situation comedy writing experience. It's safe to say that the longest thing they ever wrote was a sketch. Most of the people that they hired for the writing staff were like themselves, nontraditional writers without any sitcom credentials. They mostly came from late-night television: *SNL*, *Letterman*, *Conan*, and *The Tonight Show*.

When they would pitch a story to me, I didn't have the background or experience to say, "You can't do that story." I just didn't have enough experience in scripted television to say no. I think that was a big factor in the show's success.

Warren: There is no better illustration of how *Seinfeld* played by its own rules than the celebrated "Chinese Restaurant" episode, where the cast spends the entire show waiting for a table they never get.

Jason Alexander: The first time I suspected the show might be a unique experience and something we could be proud of was with that episode. NBC very rightly said, "What the hell is this?" No story, just shenanigans in twenty-two minutes. We were just hanging around.

Rick Ludwin: The only time I can recall having an unpleasant conversation with Larry David was over the "Chinese Restaurant" script. It was too early in the run and too form-breaking an episode. The audience wasn't going to buy into it. We had a core audience, but we hadn't gone broad yet.

Jerry Seinfeld: I don't know where we got the confidence. I think a lot of it came from Larry. If Larry felt good about something and I got on board with it, we were like a freight train.

In the beginning, we were scared, but as we became confident with ourselves and with our audience, we felt like our instincts were good enough for them. We believed we could mold the clay any way we wanted.

Rick Ludwin: After the table read I remember walking around the lot and deciding what to tell Jerry and Larry. We debated shutting it down and telling them not to film that week. But we decided that would really be a provocation, too radical. What we said to them was "If you feel passionate about this—which you obviously do—go do it, and we'll hope for the best."

Then Larry David wanted to walk around the lot with me. He was very upset that we didn't like the episode. He felt it was in keeping with the style of the show, and he was very angry that we didn't agree with him.

Jason Alexander: The network could have said, "We don't get this. You can't do this." Instead, they said, "Do what you want to do." That, I think, is what made the show the show. There was no way Jerry and Larry were going to conform to what everybody else was doing. That turned out to be a really funny episode of television.

Rick Ludwin: That was one of the landmark episodes of the show. Viewers did embrace it. I still felt we had to express our opinion, but it turned out to be okay. I'm glad they stuck to their guns and glad we weren't stupid enough to try to start a war and shut the show down.

Warren: This is a critical difference between how we ran things at NBC and what some networks are like today. We took a risk, a leap with the creator and the show runner even when our instincts said, "This will not work." More often than not, taking that kind of chance served to strengthen our relationships in the creative community.

Glenn Padnick: Larry loved doing that stuff. Could he command a half hour with no plot or minimal plot? "The Chinese Restaurant" and "The Parking Garage" are two examples of that. He also liked having several stories converge. You think they're separate, and then they ping-pong against each other at the end. He does that all the time on *Curb Your Enthusiasm.*

Jerry Seinfeld: "The Chinese Restaurant" was one step, but with "The Boyfriend," when we took a movie and made fun of it successfully, I thought we were really in their house now.

Glenn Padnick: We filmed "The Boyfriend" before a single audience in one night. It was an hour show. It was a takeoff on Oliver Stone's *JFK.* The magical loogie. The second spitter. You could hear the laughter build as the audience began to appreciate what was going on. Suddenly we weren't just doing little things.

Warren: It signaled to us that they were in a new stratosphere of comedy. The show was satirical, sophisticated, complex, and brilliantly hilarious.

Jerry Seinfeld: "The Junior Mint" was transitional for me and Larry. The hinge was that me and Kramer go to watch an operation, get in a fight in the gallery, and a Junior Mint falls into the cavity of the patient. It was a completely preposterous situation. We'd never done anything that implausible.

We'd started out thinking we would be plausible, that the show would be about how life really is. That silliness. When we got to that story line and nobody questioned it, the horses were out of the barn. Then Kramer was hitting golf balls into a whale's blowhole, and we were just having fun.

Jason Alexander: We kept hearing about the masturbation show. "The what?" Larry had put me in some pretty precarious positions, so I thought, "The masturbation show. This is going to be a George story line." Then the script showed up, and it had all those euphemisms and the audacity of having a female character involved in the contest. It was brilliant. I knew it was going to be a great episode.

Rick Ludwin: We had the table read, and the word "masturbation" was never used. The script was so funny and so clever. Who would have thought they could deal with a topic like that in a way that was so funny?

Jason Alexander: That episode was the first time I was aware how much impact we were having. The next morning I was driving to work, and we were on the radio, every station.

Warren: It was another script that confirmed the extent to which the show was in a league all its own.

I had a memorable conversation about that episode, called "The Contest," with Dr. Roz Weinman, who was head of broadcast standards and worked at 30 Rock in New York. Based on the day-to-day negotiating that we were required to do with broadcast standards—you can't use the Lord's name in vain, you can't say "penis," priests don't do that to kids on our network, et cetera—I was worried that they might shut down the production of the episode. I knew we didn't have a backup script lying around, and Larry (of course) had never gotten the story approved.

But the response from the "censor" was thoughtful and surprising. I was told that *Seinfeld* was an adult show, that it had established a kind of pact with its audience, and that it was possible the episode didn't violate that pact. "We're going to keep our eyes wide open," I heard, "but this may well be okay."

Our sales department was a little less understanding. At first.

Mike Mandelker: I thought we had an episode that was worthless. But not a single advertiser objected to "The Contest." I think we might even have raised the rates. Different rules for *Seinfeld*.

Warren: A few objected but, trust me, we raised the rates. We ended up making leather-bound copies of the script and gave them to advertisers who supported the show. Collector's item.

Jason Alexander: I've been on other shows where the cast believed the magic of the show was them. On *Seinfeld*, we believed the magic of the show was what was on the page. They kept throwing us these gems that we'd be hard-pressed to screw up.

Jerry Seinfeld: My biggest regret is that I didn't try to enjoy the show because I felt like I'd have time afterward to enjoy it. I was obsessively working and focusing on the show. It wasn't easy. Larry and I either wrote or rewrote every script. We never shot a draft handed to us by our writers. Good as they were, theirs wasn't our sensibility exactly.

Paul Reiser: I think people miss what *Seinfeld* did in terms of production on TV. Shorter scenes. Smaller sets. Scenes that don't have to play out beginning, middle, and end. That it's not all proscenium. You've since seen people imitate it badly, but *Seinfeld* really led the way.

Jerry Seinfeld: To my knowledge, people didn't seem to realize that we took the sitcom apart. They never talked about that. We oftentimes did more than twenty scenes in a twenty-two-minute show. Twenty locations. It was necessary to tell the stories and bend all those narratives. We liked getting the narratives to dovetail. Once we started doing that, we liked doing it. You always needed other locations to get people to bump into each other.

Glenn Padnick: I grew up with and worked on the classic Norman Lear structure—two acts, seven scenes. I tried to wheedle Larry and Jerry into having a plot at the beginning, and then it got to *how much plot can the show possibly hold?* I'm not sure Larry and Jerry knew they were throwing traditional comedy structure out the window. They were just writing stories.

Jerry Seinfeld: We were also very good at casting. When somebody came in who was good, he did not slip through the net. Since Larry and I were comedians, our tuning forks were pretty good. When John O'Hurley came in, Wayne Knight, Jerry Stiller—we knew it. We'd say, "Him."

Jason Alexander: The show was theater. There were four pesky cameras between us and the audience, but that show was more theater than what I think of as television performance. It spoiled me. My kids were little, and it was like a nine-to-five job. And they were paying me a ridiculous amount of money to do very little actual work.

The thing you love as a theater actor is the ability to work on the material over and over, but it's also the thing that kills you. Six months into *Hamlet*, and you're saying, "Who wrote this shit?" You get tired of it. Here was an opportunity to work on this character, but the material changed every week. It was a dream job.

Jerry Seinfeld: Once the standard got set and the audience was expecting something every week, we couldn't let up. Then it was *Little Shop of Horrors*. You feed it, and it keeps growing.

Glenn Padnick: Larry worked his ass off on that show. Once the production began and Jerry was no longer by his side co-writing the scripts, Larry did it all in terms of the writing function of the show. Jerry was not only acting on the show but also going to clubs and trying out material. So he was working day and night and didn't have time to write.

So many scripts with other people's names on them I know the final draft was rewritten by Larry. One of the great episodes was "We're not gay! Not that there's anything wrong with that" ["The Outing"]. Larry Charles has the credit on that script and had written the first draft. The table reading was a disaster. It was awful.

I came calling on Jerry and Larry that afternoon and proposed that we drop the script altogether. I told them it wasn't very good and the audience already knows Jerry and George aren't gay. We've certified them as heterosexuals through several seasons, and they're howling about something we all know—the audience included—isn't true.

They responded by rewriting the script and adding "Not that there's anything wrong with that," as if they were saying, "Not that there's anything wrong with that, Glenn."

Jason Alexander: I don't believe the four of us ever truly appreciated the iconic impact the show was having while we were doing it. Jerry made this great observation in an interview once. He said, "We think of ourselves as the world's most successful garage band. We're just four idiots banging away in the garage, and the neighbors are saying, 'You know, these guys aren't bad.'"

Warren: At the network, we finally demonstrated the smarts—I think it was in the third season—to accept Larry David as the official show runner, though he'd been doing the job from the beginning. Once Ted Danson had announced he was leaving *Cheers* and 1993 would be the show's last season, we knew we didn't have a lot of time to find the replacement for *Cheers* and the new tent pole of Thursday night. At the time, *Seinfeld*'s following was enthusiastic and loyal but not terribly large. *Home Improvement* was opposite us on Wednesday nights at 9:00, and they were averaging a 28 share while we were hovering at about a 17 (Nielsen Media Research). The future was *Seinfeld*, and I announced the plan to move it to Thursday nights at 9:30 following *Cheers*.

Preston Beckman: The great thing about *Seinfeld* was that nobody had seen the first twenty episodes. We'd repeat them, and they got big rat-ings because they played like new.

George Shapiro: I saw Ted Danson about three weeks after we'd learned that Ted had quit and we were replacing *Wings* after *Cheers*. I hugged Ted and said, "Thank you."

"For what?"

"Quitting."

Warren: Richard Zoglin at *Time* magazine made this assessment of where we stood at the time: "NBC, the onetime kingpin of prime time, has seen its fortunes turn sour almost overnight. Its biggest hit of the '80s, *The Cosby Show*, took early retirement last spring, while several other veterans—*The Golden Girls*, *Matlock*, and *In the Heat of the Night*—were given their unconditional release. (All were later picked up by rivals.) The network's last remaining Top 10 hit, *Cheers*, will call it quits at the end of this season; highly regarded younger shows like *Seinfeld* have not lived up to ratings expectations . . . The network is desperately in need of a miracle."

George Shapiro: When we moved to Thursday night, Larry said, "I don't want those people." That's why we love *Curb Your Enthusiasm*. Larry puts all of his human defects right on the screen.

Glenn Padnick: I once told Larry that when I first met him, he was a lifelong bachelor, never married, a failed stand-up. Today—married [now divorced] with two lovely daughters, rich beyond anybody's wild-est dreams, and one of the most respected writers in television, and as unhappy as the day I met him. But he was a sensational show runner.

Warren: Early on story was something that didn't seem all that impor-tant to them, but the more episodes they made, the more complex their stories became. As Larry and Jerry gained more experience at the helm of *Seinfeld*, they began to look ahead, just as the Charles brothers had done with *Cheers*. They started thinking of seasons not just as a string of episodes but as a potential narrative arc.

Jason Alexander: Larry called me over the summer and said, "We've got a great arc for George. He's going to get engaged."

"To what character?"

"Susan."

"Who's playing Susan?"

"Heidi."

"Who's playing George?"

I love Heidi Swedberg [who played Susan], but I could never figure out how to play off her. Her instincts and my instincts were diametrically opposed. If I thought something had to move, she'd go slow. If I went slow, she'd go fast. If I paused, she'd jump in too early. Loved her. Hated Susan.

Larry said to me, "Don't you understand how perfect she is for you? You've driven her to lesbianism. You burned her father's shack down. You've practically shit on her, and nobody feels bad for her. They're all on your side. She's the greatest foil for you."

But every week, it was the same thing. I didn't know how to play off her. I didn't know what I was doing. Larry had no idea how this was going to end, and finally I realized I was the only guy on the show working with her.

Seven or eight episodes in, they write an episode where Jerry and Elaine spend a lot of time with Susan. After the taping, we were all at Jerry's Deli in Studio City. And Jerry said, "You know it's hard to figure out where to go with what she gives you."

I said, "Don't even talk to me. I don't want to hear your bullshit."

Julia said, "I just want to kill her."

And Larry said, "Wait a minute."

It was at that moment that the notion of killing Susan got into Larry's head.

It is the single coldest moment in the history of television when the doctor comes out to say Susan has died. George's reaction was "Huh." Like, "How about that."

Warren: My kids' pediatrician wouldn't talk to me, but I thought it was the boldest comedy move I had ever seen. Knowing *Cheers* was leaving, we placed our bet on the network's comedy future with *Seinfeld*. It was a huge bet, but we used every weapon we had to promote it. In January 1993 we had the Super Bowl on NBC, and we used our on-air promo time to tell America *Seinfeld* was moving to Thursday night. The cover of *TV Guide* that week opened up accordion-style with a big picture of Jerry and then the rest of the cast. This was it; we had no plan B.

By the time the *Cheers* finale aired in May 1993, *Seinfeld* had overtaken *Cheers* in the ratings. It was astonishing. To surpass *Cheers* when they were taking their final victory lap? No one predicted it.

Jim Burrows: We didn't want it to end, but I think the audience was trying to tell us something.

Warren: Given the steadily growing popularity of *Seinfeld*, the audience was trying to tell it something too.

When Tim Allen negotiated a new deal for *Home Improvement* in the mid-nineties for $1 million an episode, it was a big story in the entertainment press. Tim declared himself "the highest-paid actor in television." That boast prompted a call from Jerry Seinfeld, who dialed me up one day to tell me, "I'm calling Tim Allen."

"Why?"

"I want to know if he really thinks that the co-creator, executive producer, and star of the number one comedy on the number one network on the number one night makes less money than he does."

"Jerry," I said, "don't make that call. You've said it to me instead, and doesn't that feel good? Let's keep how much you make to ourselves, okay?"

"Well," Jerry told me, "okay. I could call Tim, but I guess I won't. Thanks, Warren."

"No, Jerry. Thank you."

Glenn Padnick: I didn't feel I was working on something extraordinary. It was just another TV show at the outset. I knew the show was popular, but I didn't appreciate, until the end, how enormously influential the show was.

Jason Alexander: We were in our third season, which was our first full season, and I was walking in my neighborhood, and a black family drove by. A little girl rolled down her window and said, "We love you, George." And I thought, "Why?" I guess because the show was funny. It was slavish to funny.

5

King of the Hill

Warren: President of entertainment at NBC—the position I'd been elevated to in June 1990 when Brandon Tartikoff became chairman of the network—was about as close to king of the world as a suit could get in the TV business at the time. Now who and what got on our air would be largely up to me.

Brandon had taught me well. In particular, I learned an invaluable lesson from him in talent relations: talent needs to be loved. An actor's career is largely about rejection. Auditioning is a way of life, and the odds of landing a role that brings success and security are incredibly small. Brandon taught me that I should never underestimate an actor's hunger to be appreciated.

I had that thought in mind as I watched Madonna's meteoric rise as an actress and a musical artist in the eighties. In the nineties she launched Maverick Records, her own label, and would make the occasional surprise appearance on *SNL*. The audience loved her, and the live format fit her well.

Though I was based in Burbank, I would make regular trips to New York, where I also had a modest office on the fourth floor of 30 Rock. On such a trip in 1992, I arranged through Madonna's manager to meet with her to "discuss television." Our relationship with Garth Brooks provided Garth and NBC with highly popular specials and ultimately helped to sell over thirty million copies of Garth's albums. I thought, why not tell Madonna how much I love her music and her *SNL* appearances and see if there is any kind of a relationship to explore.

Her manager told me she was in the studio working on a new album, that her schedule was very unpredictable, but that the meeting would definitely happen. I didn't hold my breath but received an afternoon call at my New York office telling me the meeting was on for that evening at 11:00 at Madonna's place. At the time, she was living in the Dakota, the storied, Gothic building on West Seventy-second Street made famous by *Rosemary's Baby* and John Lennon's death.

In all my twenty years at NBC, regardless of the talent I was meeting with, my wife, Theresa, was never jealous or voiced concern until this meeting with Madonna. And that was before she knew the name of the album Madonna was working on—*Erotica*—which would go double platinum in the United States and sell over six million worldwide. What time? Where? Who else was going to be there? Just me . . . and Madonna. Eleven o'clock. Her apartment. Silence.

One of the Dakota's doormen escorted me to an elevator. The door opened directly onto the entryway of Madonna's apartment. The place was dimly lit, and Madonna greeted me with a weary hello.

She was dressed in a loose black T-shirt, rolled up denim shorts, and black Doc Martens. This was the pre-sculpted Madonna. She offered me something to drink, and when she went off to fetch it, I looked around and noticed a painting on the wall. It was a Salvador Dalí, and of course it wasn't a reproduction. I stared in awe. Madonna told me she'd just bought it for $5 million. Apparently, she was doing quite well.

She then asked me why I was there, and three things quickly became clear to me. She was exhausted from endless days at the recording studio. Her manager had done a poor job of explaining who I was and why I wanted to talk to her. And she had zero interest in pursuing any kind of relationship in television.

I thanked her for her time. I left. I phoned home. It was just 11:30.

I had a similar experience with John Hughes in Chicago. I flew out to court him. We had dinner together and a lively conversation about the show John would create for NBC, something along the lines of *The Breakfast Club* meets *High Fidelity*. I was wildly excited about landing John Hughes. I guaranteed him thirteen episodes on the air, and nothing ever came of it.

So I've long had Madonna and John Hughes as proof of the limits of the seductive power of network television. Even when the president of entertainment himself comes courting, that doesn't mean a hit show will follow. In these cases, it didn't even result in a script.

In 1990, when I replaced Brandon, the cable universe was growing but still modest in scope, while the big three networks commanded the attention and loyalty of viewers on an enormous scale. Fox was still an infant network. I was suddenly responsible for prime-time programming on a network watched by tens of millions of viewers, and my success would depend almost entirely on my judgment and taste. My new job gave me the chance to succeed while the nation watched or fail with all eyes upon me. It was potent stuff, and I welcomed the challenge.

In the 1990–91 season we dropped to number two in adults eighteen to forty-nine. In the 1991–92 season we dropped to number three. The pressure was mounting. At the press tour in June 1991 one new series we highlighted was *Sisters*. It had premiered with a short run in May and was returning in the fall Saturday nights at 10:00. This really was my first press tour flying solo without Brandon, and early on I got a question about the appropriateness of the opening scene of *Sisters*, where they sit in a steam bath and discuss orgasms. "Warren, is this acceptable for network television?" I thought about that for a second and said, "Corporately, we believe in orgasms." Big laugh.

Newsweek put the quotation in bold print the next week in the Perspectives column, and the über–feature producer Kathleen Kennedy had the line engraved on a Tiffany clock and sent it to me with kudos.

For the 1991 season, *Cheers* would be NBC's lone entry in the list of top ten TV shows. *The Cosby Show*, in its final year, had fallen to eighteenth. Its spin-off, *A Different World*, was seventeenth in the ratings, while *Wings*—written and produced by former writers for *Cheers*—held the nineteenth spot.

Compare that with the 1986 season, when *The Cosby Show*, *Family Ties*, *Cheers*, *The Golden Girls*, and *Night Court* all held top ten spots for the season. This wasn't just a matter of bragging rights. The financial health of the network depended on the popularity of our shows. Many hundreds of millions of dollars were at stake.

I knew it was a long road ahead of me to put NBC back on track. But I felt pretty good about my ability to do the job. Unfortunately, Bob Wright (president of NBC) and Jack Welch (CEO of GE) didn't share my confidence.

Bob Wright: Brandon and Warren were very fortunate to have each other. Brandon became a glorified figure. He was a great self-promoter. We wanted other people in there who could perform when Brandon couldn't play anymore.

We wanted to put Warren in the position where the world wouldn't piss and moan that Brandon wasn't there any longer. While Warren was well regarded, all of the glory was going to Brandon.

Jack Welch: As I recall, we didn't think Warren had enough gravitas and maturity, and we thought we needed a bigger player. More voice. More lunches at the right places. More of that to help us.

Warren: The guy Jack and Bob decided they needed was Don Ohlmeyer. Don was a larger-than-life personality in the business. He had an excellent track record as a producer and director in sports and had particularly made a name for himself in the glory days of *Monday Night Football*. He'd had a chance to invest in ESPN in the beginning—a bet that had a huge payoff and helped to cement his reputation for business acumen. At Ohlmeyer Communications, Don developed both reality and scripted programming for networks and cable.

The position of president of West Coast operations was created for Don, and I couldn't help but take his hiring as a vote of, if not no confidence, then severely limited confidence in me. Don had the authority to clean house when he came in, but to his credit he chose to give me my shot. I am grateful for that.

Jack Welch: We hired Ohlmeyer because we needed a bridge to absorb some of the pain. Somebody who wasn't unwilling to talk to the press and express opinions about all kinds of things.

Brian Pike: The best way to get the job of network president is to not need and not want it. Ohlmeyer was already rich, so he could have always turned to Bob Wright and said, "I don't want to play your way."

Patty Mann: There was a rumor going around that Bob Wright was bringing in Don Ohlmeyer. It seemed that Bob Wright didn't think Warren was up to the job without somebody above him.

Warren: The third-floor dining room and kitchen that hosted the *Cheers* pitch was turned into Don's executive suite. It was one floor above me. "On top of me" might be the better way to describe it.

Patty Mann: Warren and I were at the office on a Saturday, and Don walked in a side door. I looked up and saw him. Big guy. Big, booming voice. I grew up in a family where my father yelled, so I was used to that sort of thing. Don was a yeller. He yelled a lot. It was such an anomaly in our office.

John Miller: Don came in to relieve Warren of East Coast headaches and allow Warren to do what he did best, which was focusing on the programs and dealing with producers. Particularly in concert with

Preston Beckman. Preston as programmer and Warren as developer was a good combination.

Warren: One of Don's first comments to me was "I don't think our scheduling is very good." I told him scheduling wasn't the problem; it was the shows. They'd gotten old and tired. "Get to know Preston," I suggested to Don.

Preston Beckman: I was Warren's consigliere. My job was to help Warren look good. I didn't care how I looked as long as I got rewarded. My job was to strategize short term and long term. Long-term strategy—how do you build a schedule so even Jeff Zucker needs four years to destroy it?

John Miller: Don was a good leader. Warren could execute what Don said he wanted to do, but there tended to be friction. Warren was the program guy, and Don was the business guy, but Don had done some programming, and Warren had done some business stuff. So each felt he could do what the other did. Maybe better. Friction. A fair amount of butting heads.

Warren: Some of that friction was simply due to differences in temperament and style between me and Don, but Don was also drinking heavily at the time.

Patty Mann: You knew when Don was hungover. He'd wear these blue satiny jogging outfits with loafers and no socks. Loafers! Just couldn't be bothered to get dressed. You could also tell Don's condition by the way he parked. A friend of mine who could see his spot would call and say, "Don's not feeling too well today."

Preston Beckman: Don would show up in his sweat suits and be drunk. He'd stand in the back of the screening room, pissing on everything.

Jamie Tarses: We stopped having as much fun when Don came. He changed the whole tenor of the place.

Lori Openden: I knew Don was an only child before I knew it. He was always the center of attention. Big personality.

John Wells: The great thing about Don was he'd always tell you what he thought. You didn't have to like it, but he'd always tell you.

Preston Beckman: I thought Don was a really smart guy and businessman. He was extremely loyal to the people he considered his friends. To a fault.

Harold Brook: Ohlmeyer was a conflicted human being but probably one of the smartest guys in broadcasting. Don was respectful of talent. If you look at the current executive suites at NBC today, nobody has any appreciation for talent, and it makes a big fucking difference.

Lori Openden: Don changed the parking so the suppliers coming in to pitch could have the good parking spaces. He went around to all of our offices to explain what he was doing and ask our permission. I thought the philosophy of making people welcome was a good one. Don didn't know it wasn't about the parking.

Warren: Don sought out some premier writer-producer talent and invited them to bring their ideas to NBC. Steven Bochco got a call and joined Don at our executive dining room, called the Hungry Peacock. Same lousy food as our commissary but served on tablecloths.

Steven is kind of a health nut, and he called me right after his lunch with Don. First to complain about the food: "If Don wants to encourage people to work at NBC, he ought to pick a better restaurant." And then to tell me that given Don's diet, he probably wouldn't be around for long. Don had eaten a hot dog with a side of mashed potatoes and gravy and a Coke chaser. Then he'd hustled outside for a smoke.

"The man's a walking time bomb," Bochco assured me.

Steve McPherson: Ohlmeyer was an interesting character. His desk was a foot and a half raised, and then it was a pedestal desk. When you were talking to him, you were about three feet lower than he was. It was like he was from another world. Sometimes he was very vocal about what we were doing, but then other times he couldn't be found.

Max Mutchnick: Don Ohlmeyer called us to his office, and I remember not knowing who he was. I thought the world stopped at Warren.

David Kohan: He was wearing a sweater. He told us, "It's always sixty-eight degrees where I am."

Max Mutchnick: He had this judge's desk. It was very high. There was no humor there. Everything about that meeting was uncomfortable. I came in, sat down, and immediately kicked over a sculpture. I was intimidated by the guy and in an uncomfortable sort of way.

I didn't like the machismo bullshit he put out. We were writing a script that was filled with humanity, a love story, and Ohlmeyer was a guy who I thought was from another time. I only softened toward him when I saw him with Jimmy Burrows. He loved Jimmy.

Lori Openden: Don kept his office at near sixty degrees, and he wore cashmere sweaters. You'd go in his office and freeze. His office chairs swallowed us. They were made for giants like him—he was six four.

Perry Simon: Don just shocked me. When he'd come in and give Jamie Tarses back rubs in the middle of meetings—inappropriate massages—I remember wondering what kind of alternate universe I'd stepped into. To this day, I've never seen anything like it in a corporate work environment.

Harold Brook: Don was a bully, but he was a bully who did his job well. He gave everybody the ability to do his own job, and that helped us. But we had a bunker mentality. The rest of us got closer because of Don.

Warren: I had a conversation with Don in which he looked at me and said, "We have to learn to love each other more. We don't have to vacation together, but we have to learn to love." Very Khalil Gibran. I thought maybe this means he wants me to agree with him more often.

David Nevins: I'd frequently clash with Don when it came down to choosing shows. We had Mommy and Daddy—Don and Warren— and if I didn't get an answer I wanted from one, I'd go to the other.

There was an atmosphere where not everybody had to love everything. I don't think you want to create a business where everything funnels through one sensibility.

Jamie Tarses: There was an autonomy that we didn't know we had. Don was noisy, but he didn't actually stop anything from happening.

Lori Openden: He was argumentative for sport.

Patty Mann: Warren and Preston had to push so much stuff through Don that they were frustrated. Don was drinking at the time, and he couldn't remember much. So they'd say, "Yeah, you approved that yesterday," and that's how they got a lot of stuff through.

Harold Brook: Don's first words to me would often be "What did you fuck up this time?" or "What's the bad news?" I don't know if it was paranoia or just anger.

Preston Beckman: He had a serious drinking problem, and then there was the murder trial. That made our job tough.

Warren: That murderer would be O. J. Simpson. Don was one of O.J.'s best friends coming out of their years together on *Monday Night Football*, and he was one of O.J.'s most conspicuous supporters. Simpson was arrested in June 1994, charged with killing his wife and her friend Ronald Goldman, and he was acquitted in October 1995. Don Ohlmeyer was by Simpson's side throughout, often to the detriment of NBC.

Don spent countless afternoons in prayer sessions with O.J. and Rosey Grier. He was at the L.A. County jail far more frequently than he was in his office. I thought it was fairly bizarre, but I was also happiest when Don wasn't around.

One afternoon Bob Wright called me and said, "I can't find Don." I asked him if he was still in his office at 30 Rock, and he said he was. I then told him if he put on the live news feed, he'd probably be able to catch Don exiting the detention center in downtown L.A. after his daily visit with O.J. Silence from Bob.

On a nightly basis Jay Leno's monologue would hilariously recap the proceedings of the trial, and *SNL* delivered some of their all-time greatest sketches thanks to O.J. In our current programming sessions (which Don sporadically attended) we were forbidden to discuss any of those antics.

Preston Beckman: We made a pilot starring O.J. with the knife he used to kill his wife. It was called *Frogmen*. We used to say if we were ever in a tough situation, we'd put on *Frogmen*. I threatened everybody [competing networks] with *Frogmen*.

Warren: By 1996, Don's drinking and his behavior in the office and at numerous NBC "off campus" events had become serious liabilities. I remember one episode in particular at an NBC retreat. Don, in his cups, was hitting on an NBC female executive, an openly gay executive. When she told him, "Don, you know I'm gay," Don shot back, "Doesn't matter to me."

Shortly thereafter, I approached Bob Wright and encouraged him to get help for Don. Don was clearly sick and needed our help and support. Turning a corporate blind eye was only making things worse. With Bob's encouragement, and in the wake of a full-blown intervention, Don checked into the Betty Ford Center in 1996. I later heard that initially Bob suspected I was just angling to get Don fired.

Don dried out, but he only managed to become more insufferable.

Harold Brook: Here was my normal workday. Don was getting up early. This is sober Don. I'd get a phone call every morning on Don's drive in. Don would call me about deals, and he'd go off on them. I'd have to pull files once I got to the office, and there was always an e-mail to Don laying out the deal. And there would be an "Okay, D.O." So I'd have to go up, and he'd say, "What idiot signed off on this deal?"

"You did."

John Miller: The business Don—pre-intervention—was a little easier to deal with. Whatever anxieties he had, he seemed to get rid of them through drinking. When he didn't have that outlet, the demons festered, and he brought them to work. Don was far more difficult sober.

Preston Beckman: Don was like an abusive dad. At his 2:30 meeting, there were a couple of people who would always say something stupid, and Don would go after them. David Nevins was the worst. I wanted to say, "Just shut up!"

John Miller: You know those National Geographic documentaries where the lion takes a wildebeest, takes one down, rips its neck open, and kills it? That was Don. Once he'd savaged somebody, you could deal with him for the next few hours. He'd had his wildebeest.

Karey Burke: Don was a different person after he got sober. Don was less distracted sober, so he paid a lot more attention to what we were doing. Warren was a buffer for us. Don tried to love us to death, paid too much attention to us.

Preston Beckman: We often thought about leaving a case of vodka in Don's office.

Warren: I tried, but I didn't like Don. He just didn't leave a lot of oxygen in the room for anybody else, and he made life a lot more difficult than it needed to be at NBC. Don was first a drunk bully and then a sober bully, but always a bully. He ran effective interference for us with the network suits in New York, and when Don was on your side, he was a great asset. But he was an abusive impediment far too much of the time.

Throughout my tenure as president of entertainment at the network, when we were airing the Must See shows no one could bear to miss, executives at the other networks openly coveted what they called "that Ohlmeyer/Littlefield thing." Until now, I doubt anybody outside of NBC knew what a tumultuous, dysfunctional *thing* it was. It's a wonder we got shows on the air, much less the iconic programs that made us the Must See network.

6

Voilà!

Warren: The Cosbys' ratings juggernaut had lost quite a lot of altitude by 1990. At Fox they sensed an opening and moved the animated hit *The Simpsons* to Thursday at 8:00 to hasten the inevitable end of Huxtable dominance. Once *Cosby* finally left the schedule, in September 1992, we moved the *Cosby* spin-off, *A Different World*, into the leadoff position against Bart. Behind it we aired a show called *Rhythm & Blues*. It was about a white DJ at an all-black radio station in Detroit.

I don't know what we were thinking, certainly not about quality. *Rhythm & Blues* was a one-joke premise. It wasn't very good, and America quickly told us as much. What was once a Thursday night of great television and huge audiences was suddenly in rapid decline. After I dumped *Rhythm & Blues*, the only palatable option was to open Thursday night with *Cheers* repeats at 8:00 and move *A Different World* back to 8:30 with *Cheers* originals at 9:00.

Cheers was certainly a known commodity. By 1992 it had been around for ten years, and the research department estimates for how the repeats would perform were decent. Networks didn't use multiple runs of their hits back then and I wasn't particularly proud of the fix we were in after years of going gangbusters on Thursday night, but I was desperate. Surprisingly, *Cheers* repeats at 8:00 did much better than any of us expected or research had predicted. The audience was telling us there was an opportunity for high-quality adult comedy prior to 9:00 p.m. That was a bit of a revelation, a revelation we would ultimately act upon with the Paul Reiser/Danny Jacobson comedy *Mad About You*.

Jamie Tarses and I had heard the pitch for *Mad About You* in the fall of 1991. Though compelling, it wasn't terribly elaborate or involved and was delivered by Paul and Danny.

Jamie Tarses: The pitch was basically "It's the car ride home. When you leave the party or the dinner, it's you and your wife in the car." Paul did some riffing from his stand-up, but it wasn't much more than that.

Paul Reiser: The show came out of my stand-up. I'd started writing and performing relationship stuff, and everything else felt more trivial. I'd started to get laughs of recognition, and that's a better laugh.

Before I was in *My Two Dads*, I'd written a pilot for Gary David Goldberg called *Wonderland Trucking*. I'd worked hard to get out of my father's business, and there I was going into the pretend trucking business in pretend New Jersey. It didn't work, and suddenly this pilot came up—*My Two Dads*—and I did it.

That was my ambivalent step into series TV. It was presented to me as a show with the possibility of being adult, but it didn't turn out that way.

My Two Dads had taught me what I didn't want to do. I used to hear from fans, "My little daughter loves your show!" That was okay. I wasn't making napalm, but that wasn't what I wanted.

I knew if I did a new show, it would be something small, a couple. Part of our pitch was "It's *Thirtysomething*, but it's shorter and funnier." Adult, smart, introspective. Perhaps overly introspective. The show was simple. It was about simple things. We wanted to keep the show small. I think Cosby had said, "The smaller you make it, the more universal it is."

Warren: Danny and Paul looked at me as if they were confessing something to a priest and said, "We're both married men now . . . and it doesn't suck! That's the show."

We liked the pitch, and we liked Paul and Danny. Paul Reiser, like Jerry Seinfeld, was a stand-up comedian, but Paul also had some serious acting experience, particularly his wonderful turn in *Diner*. In a sense, then, we were working an improvement on the *Seinfeld* equation by going into business with a comedian who could already act.

Paul Reiser: Part of what sparked the process for us was that the very people we were pitching to responded to what we were saying. It helps if the people you're pitching to actually care. Somewhere along the line, it was thought our show might be a good companion to *Seinfeld*.

Glenn Padnick: Paul Reiser was a very good friend of Jerry's, and he very much admired Jerry's show. *Mad About You* was sort of the domestic version of *Seinfeld*.

Warren: Paul's manager pushed very hard for it to be called *The Paul Reiser Show*. I told him no, the show was about this couple. Don't ask me again.

Paul Reiser: I don't think I had anybody in mind when we were casting, but in December, when I was writing the pilot, I met Helen Hunt at a dinner party. She was sharing a house with a good friend of my wife's. That evening we were talking about couples, and I turned to my wife and said, "She'd be great."

Helen Hunt: By the time *Mad About You* happened, I had done much more television than movies, and at that time if you did TV, then you weren't invited to the party of being in movies. I had just started to get into movies. I had done this movie called *The Waterdance*, which I was very proud of, and this movie, *Mr. Saturday Night*, which wasn't so successful, but it was a big movie. It was a big deal for me to finally be in that club, so the last thing on earth I thought I would do was a TV series, particularly a sitcom, because at that time you were even further from having a serious film career if you were in a four-camera show.

Paul Reiser: Helen was doing a lot of movies, and I asked her to read the script. She read it. She called and said, "I like it. What do we do now?" She came over to the house, and I think I put her at ease.

Helen Hunt: I met with Paul and Danny, and I asked them, "Where is it going?" I assumed the show would get bigger and wackier, because one would need to tell stories, one would have crazy neighbors, and the sister would do things. I remember Paul saying, "The hope is to get smaller and smaller and smaller."

That *really* interested me. That, to me, felt new. It's what I like. I just did the production of *Our Town* in New York, and it's all about smaller and smaller. There are no lights, no costumes. It is spare, and I'm often interested in what kind of truth you can get out of how little.

Paul Reiser: With *Mad About You*, we fought to keep it from becoming "she's X and he's Y."

Helen Hunt: I loved Paul's comedy, and I knew he was a good actor too, which I think is a pretty rare combination. A lot of comedians pull it off, but they're not really actors. He's a real actor, not just accidentally a decent actor. But I was pretty sure that I didn't want to be the wife on the "Untitled Paul Reiser Project," which is what showed up.

But then I read it, and I thought, "They've written at least as good a part for her as they have for him. It really is a two-hander. I would have to wait a long time to get to look at a relationship the way that this does." The only reason I took it was the writing.

I went to Paul's house, and I knew, for me, who wasn't a jokester, that I would have to find my way, and I intuitively felt that my way was to be physically busy all the time. Paul has this goal, this is the show that happens after you leave, after the company leaves, or after you drive away from the people's house, what happens then.

So to really do that, I rarely sit in my living room and talk to my partner about our day without doing something. I'm emptying the trash, or checking the mail, or making lunch. So I intuitively knew that for me to pull off this kind of out-and-out comedy, I would have to be physically busy. That just seemed right. So I started doing dishes at his house. We rehearsed in the kitchen. He got an actress and a housekeeper all at once.

Paul Reiser: When we went into final casting, it was Helen Hunt and Teri Hatcher. I remember getting a phone call from the network—thirteen on the air if you use Valerie Bertinelli. She wasn't right. She was just coming off a sitcom, and I wanted something fresh.

Lori Openden: Teri Hatcher tested the last day before Helen came in. She was good, but she wasn't magical like Helen.

Jamie Tarses: Teri Hatcher gave Helen a run for her money. She was good, but Paul and Helen were great in that room together. It was the idea of the minutiae of that relationship. Picking out a couch, being in the kitchen and having inane conversations about everything. It was that.

Lori Openden: Paul wanted Helen for the part. They were friends. Helen's was one of the best comedy readings I've ever seen.

Warren: That was the moment it went from a promising script to green-lighting the pilot. I looked at everyone in the room and said, "Let's go!"

Helen Hunt: It was an audition for me and for the show, kind of all at once. Paul was so nervous. I remember giving him a back rub. It was supposed to be my audition, and I was rubbing his shoulders. I didn't feel nervous, maybe because I felt comfortable with the material. Also, to sign up for seven years of anything, or five, whatever we had to sign before you walk in, I was so ambivalent about that that I thought, "It's a win-win for me either way." So I had that luxury of not being terrified.

Me and Paul could see the same thing in the show—the three of us, in fairness, Danny too—we could see: they should try to get pregnant, it shouldn't be easy getting pregnant, one of them could almost have an affair, or have an affair. There should be a time where it gets incredibly hard. Whether there's an affair or not, there should be a baby, ultimately. We could both look down the road that didn't exist yet and see that. That's a lot. When I meet with people now and ask what a series is going to be, they say, "Well, we're going to explore the way the law . . ." There's no good answer, because there are very few subjects that should be given seven years to be played out. Very, very few. So those were the elements for me.

I remember when we shot the pilot thinking there must be something here, because there's so little, so low on concept here. What is this show? It's two people, a little bit of a funny thing around them. So if that's working, something's happening because it wasn't a big hook. There must be something to it, or else everyone wouldn't be laughing this hard at so little.

Jamie Tarses: When the show went on the air, it didn't instantly work.

Paul Reiser: For the first six shows of *Mad About You*, we tried it with an audience and without one. I was afraid I'd be reaching too hard with an audience, but I'm glad I got convinced out of that. I found it could be electrifying. We were putting on a play, and those laughs could really spark the show.

When I heard the audience say, "Awwww," that really shriveled my spine. I hated it. I remember saying, "I'm going to talk to the audience," but somebody stopped me. We just started taking the "Awwww's" out of the track, and it trained the audience. "Oh, you don't do that on that show."

Preston Beckman: We had a show called *Monty* that was supposed to be our 8:00 show, and it sucked. We were all saying, "We're fucked. Now what are we going to do?" We wound up putting *Mad About You* there and took a lot of heat for it. Paul and Jamie had sex on the kitchen table or something. You don't do that at 8:00.

Warren: In press interviews and in discussions with affiliates, our strategy was challenged. Is this appropriate for 8:00 p.m.? I argued that the world was changing. There were plenty of kid and family choices available on network and cable. The conventional thinking had long been that you couldn't run "adult" material at 8:00. That was the family hour kickoff and called for much tamer fare. No one had ever tried the grown-up stuff this early before, but I was desperate, and Thursday night needed to work. Hey, at least they were married. Sex on the kitchen table? Why not?

Lisa Kudrow: I did a guest star at the beginning of the first season on *Mad About You*. I played Karen, and I was a blind date for Paul. It was a flashback to the night he met Jamie. I was always trying to find little things that wouldn't take up too much time or go off the dialogue to make scenes more interesting or funny or another level of stupid.

Paul Reiser: Lisa had two lines in that first show. I said, "I'm a documentary filmmaker." She said, "That's so funny. I work in a bank." That was her line, but it was all in the way she delivered it, the way she connected the two.

Lisa Kudrow: Then my agent called me one morning, and I was almost out of money. I was about to get a day job. And my agent said, "Okay, *Mad About You*, Danny Jacobson has this part. It doesn't even have a name. It's called 'the waitress,' and they want you there in an hour. I can't even show you anything. You'll see it when you get there. I say pass, because they can't treat you like this." And I was like, "Treat me like what?" I needed money, and they were offering me a job. I thought it was the best show on television, so I said, "I'll do it."

There's no such thing as "You're better than this." You have to show up and do a good job. So I just drove down there, and I thought, "Whatever it is, just listen and respond and make it funny. That's it. That's all you have to do."

I say you do everything, if it's not porn. Do anything. Work begets work. I always thought that. You never know who's watching. By the end of that week, Danny said, "Would it be okay with you if we brought you back for five more episodes, because you're really funny?"

My agents at the time—and maybe I'll be nice and not say who they were—one of them said, "Hey, my daughter watches *Mad About You*, and she said she saw you on it." I thought, "Why don't *you* know I'm on it?"

Paul Reiser: Then Lisa told us she was going to audition for a new show. We told her good luck, but pilots never get picked up . . . *Friends*.

Warren: In the course of its seven-year run, *Mad About You* got shifted around the schedule quit a bit. It was a strong show for us. We found we could play it almost anywhere, and it would draw an audience, so the show became a kind of utility fielder for the network.

As a programmer, I have found that a utility fielder like *Mad About You* is a rare and valuable commodity, but I'm sure Paul Reiser took a different view altogether.

Paul Reiser: Then we got tossed out of Thursday. That was the tough part. Wednesday, Monday, every day but Friday. That was hard. Then Warren put us on Sunday afternoon at 4:00. That seemed ill-advised.

Warren: It played Sunday night at 8:00 in the fall of 1995 until the summer of 1996.

Helen Hunt: All I remember is it being so horrible for Paul. Each change was like a knife at his throat, and I was blissfully unaware of what each change meant.

Preston Beckman: At one point, we exiled *Mad About You* to Saturday night. We just didn't know what to do with it.

Paul Reiser: That was a very tough time for me. I knew all I could do was what I could do. It's a gorgeous painting, and that's going to look great in our garage. It's your painting, if you want it in your garage, God bless.

The show lost its moment of heat when it was moved to Sunday. It was viewed as a lesser show because of the move. The audience never really found us again. We had a long run, and we all did very well, but in the context of what *Mad About You* was able to do . . . Somebody has to get moved around, and we were the show that moved around.

Helen Hunt: Sometimes people ask me, what would be today's version of *Mad About You*? I guess it would be *Modern Family*. People are still not putting the toilet paper on the toilet paper roll, and interrupting each other, and trying to change each other, and unable to change each other, and having trouble getting pregnant, and having parents that make you crazy. So I don't know that it would be so different.

It was really in love with love, that show.

7

Tossed Salad
and Scrambled Eggs

Warren: In the mid-eighties NBC's *St. Elsewhere* may not have drawn as many viewers as CBS's *Murder, She Wrote*, but the demographics of the *St. Elsewhere* audience were right in the sweet spot for advertisers—predominantly eighteen- to forty-nine-year-old upscale urban viewers—while the audience for *Murder, She Wrote* was older and rural. CBS may have had more eyeballs, but we made the money. It was a critical difference between the two networks—one I would embrace. Because of the quality of the show and the nature and size of its audience, *Cheers* had been minting money for a decade for NBC and Paramount, and now we had to replace it.

We were determined to salvage what we could from the show. We'd already tried the disastrous *Tortellis* spin-off and briefly entertained the notion of a show centered on Cliff and Norm. But it soon became evident that the only *Cheers* character who could conceivably carry a quality show on his own was Kelsey Grammer's Frasier Crane.

As incentive, I offered John Pike at Paramount Television thirteen episodes on the air for the new Frasier Crane show. We knew the creators must be Casey, Angell, and Lee, the team that had created the Frasier character for *Cheers* before going off to create, write, and produce *Wings* for NBC.

David Lee: People criticized *Wings* as *Cheers* in an airport. If only we could have lived up to that.

Peter Casey: When you live in the sheltered environment of a hit show like *Cheers*, all you have to do is come up with stories and keep the thing going—and then we stepped out of it. We had our offices, and that was about it. Everything else we had to come up with.

We debated if we should create interesting characters and put them in an environment or create an environment and populate it with characters.

David Lee: One Labor Day, I went to Nantucket, and we landed at this airport. We'd thought about various other airports, even the Grand Canyon.

Peter Casey: We learned we should have moved the show farther away from Boston.

David Lee: We picked the model of what we knew and translated it. A public place where anybody could walk in the door. *Wings* allowed us not to be safe on the following show. The next show would be the show we wanted to do. *Wings* was like middle school.

Peter Casey: We learned a lot doing *Wings*. Everything was in place at *Cheers* for us, and we could always call the Charles brothers. There was nobody to call with *Wings*.

David Lee: We wrote a *Wings* script, and Tartikoff said no. The mistake we made in the first one was doing scenes that showed who each character was. What we learned was to come up with a great story, and the characters would be revealed in the course of that story. We needed a great through-line.

Peter Casey: We pitched the show to Brandon, and he said he kept seeing ticket counters and big jets and the backs of people's heads. We literally had to show him a picture to give Brandon an idea of the sort of airport we were talking about.

David Lee: *Wings* was not the Zeitgeist express. We couldn't cast the female lead. We wrote her as a sultry Greek beauty. We wanted Peri Gilpin.

Peter Casey: But she wasn't ready for prime time.

David Lee: Somebody said, "How about Crystal Bernard?"

Peter Casey: We read her, and she was a lot better than we'd thought she'd be.

David Lee: She was supposed to have grown up on Nantucket, but she had that southern accent.

Peter Casey: We took our first casting trip to New York, and that's where we found Steven Weber.

David Lee: Trying to find a handsome, sexy, great actor, funny, and thirty-two years old isn't easy. And we had to find two of them.

Peter Casey: Thomas Haden Church came in to read for Brian. We thought he was wrong for the part, but we knew we had to get him in the show. So we created the Lowell character for him. I think he never got over the idea that he came in to read for Brian but he was this Lowell guy.

We were seven episodes in, and Tom said he wanted to leave the show. We had to get our producer backbones up and tell him he wasn't leaving.

David Lee: He left the minute he could. It was never acrimonious, and Tom has done quite well and has the career he wanted.

Warren: *Wings* was referred to at the network (on the sly) as *Cheers Lite*. It was a solid show and performed well for us, but it couldn't really kick off an hour. It was a satellite show. It needed a lead-in.

The bar that Glen and Les Charles and Jimmy Burrows first walked in and said, "This is the place," was the Bull and Finch in Boston. On May 20, 1993, on the last night of *Cheers*, we took over the Bull and Finch and had a massive celebration of the series that had meant so much to our network. The cast and producers were all there, live feeds went out to all of the stations with interviews and hype. The entire Thursday night was dedicated to *Cheers*. *The Tonight Show* hosted live from the bar, and I put on an apron and tended bar, serving Boston legends like Red Sox pitcher Roger Clemens. It was an amazing and emotional event and is still in the top twenty list of highest-rated nights in broadcast television history.

Reality came crashing in early in the evening when Suzanne Wright, Bob's wife, greeted my colleague Perry Simon and me with one panicked question: "Where are the hits?" With the new Kelsey Grammer show, we knew we needed a bona fide hit and just not another *Wings*. Not only was the pressure on me; it was also on John Pike and the writers to deliver one. Only recently have I learned how rocky the birth of *Frasier* was.

John Pike: NBC wanted to be in the Casey/Angell/Lee business. They created the Frasier Crane character on *Cheers*. David Angell was a former priest. David Lee was gay. Peter Casey was straight and white-bread. They were wonderful together. Fortunately, we owned Casey/Angell/Lee.

Also, NBC smartly said they wanted to be in the Kelsey Grammer business. I had a great relationship with Kelsey because of the things

I'd gone through with him for a number of years. The one thing we knew for sure was we weren't going to do *The Frasier Crane Show*. Kelsey didn't want to play the character again, and Casey/Angell/Lee didn't want to be the spin-off guys.

Peter Casey: We had always felt if there was any character to spin off that show it was Frasier. The best character. The most depth. The most complicated. Our biggest concern was, "Do we really want to be the guys who try to spin a character off of *Cheers*?"

John Pike: Frasier Crane was the only person in the *Cheers* cast you could pluck out. He had an occupation. He was a psychiatrist. On the series, he was already in a state of flux. You could take that character and put him anywhere in the world.

Peter Casey: *Cheers* was America's favorite show. We thought we'd pale by comparison.

Bob Broder: Now it's four years into *Wings* and the end of *Cheers*. There was a whole ensemble concept on *Cheers* that worked effectively. Kelsey was fucked-up at the time. We'd spent a year with him in an orange jumpsuit picking up trash on the side of the road.

Brian Pike: An enormous amount of money and effort went into replacing *Cheers*. People like Bob Wright had no idea what development was. He thought replacing *Cheers* was like making next year's refrigerator. You change the handles, you change the color, and you go to the market.

Warren: Bob's full appreciation of how difficult it really was to produce a successful spin-off of a hit show would not come until years later with the *Friends* spin-off *Joey*.

John Pike: I knew I had the actor, the writer-producers, and a time period commitment. Time period in those days was really important.

Warren: He had thirteen episodes but no time period guarantee. If I learned anything from *Seinfeld* it was you had to be "master of your domain."

Kelsey Grammer: In the eighth year of *Cheers*, Paramount had approached me about doing another show. When Ted finally said he was done, that's when I started talking to people. I talked to Casey/Angell/Lee, and they hatched this idea about a guy who'd been in a terrible motorcycle accident and runs his empire from his bed.

John Pike: We'd have meetings, and then I'd send them away, and the writers would go away for a long time. I don't know what they'd do, but they'd go away for a long time. I mean it's a goddamn sitcom. Twenty-two minutes. It's real easy. Finally, I get a call one day from Peter Casey. They want to come see me. They've got an idea.

It was the worst idea I'd ever heard in my life. They preface it by saying, "Kelsey is totally on board." There's a self-made man, very wealthy, arrogant, think Ted Turner when he was young. He's stricken with an illness and is bedridden. Basically, he runs his empire through his household, and that's the series.

Warren: I would call John constantly and ask for a progress report, and his answer was always "We've got something great. We'll lay it out for you in a few weeks."

Kelsey Grammer: It was interesting, and I thought some parts of it were funny.

John Pike: We let it percolate for a couple of days and brought them back. I said, "Guys, this is gold. You've got a giant idea here, but I don't think you have a giant idea that's going to be commercial. You've got great stuff, but I don't think it's a home run." In other words, I lied.

David Lee: I still think the original pitch would make an interesting cable show. Kelsey was going to play a Malcolm Forbes type of guy. Big motorcycle. Really rich guy. He becomes paralyzed, and the relationship would be between him and his physical therapist. In retrospect, you can see hints of what was to come.

Peter Casey: Him trying to run his empire from this incredible penthouse in Manhattan. John Pike, when we pitched it to him, said, "I think it's a better idea to do a spin-off of Frasier."

John Pike: The boys said I'd never get Kelsey to do it. I said, "Let me talk to Kelsey." I remembered when Kelsey used to live on the Paramount lot, lived in his Cadillac. I'd been through a great deal with Kelsey. I'd visited him in jail. We're close.

Kelsey Grammer: John Pike invited me to dinner at Toscana in Brentwood. He looked at me and said, "Kelsey, I think a sitcom should be funny. This isn't funny." He said, "I do have an idea. Why don't we go with Frasier?"

I said, "I get it, but it has to be different. I don't want to still be married, and there can't be any kids around." That was the deal we made at that moment.

Peter Casey: The whole point of having Frasier move to Seattle was to make it hard for the network to say, "Can we have an episode with Carla?" We only felt we could bring Lilith. That was organic.

David Lee: I think part of our original deal was no Carla, no George.

Peter Casey: No visiting crossover stuff. Even the structure of the show—the idea that we didn't have music in the show, or didn't show exterior shots, brought the black cards in. That was all purposely designed to make *Frasier* different from *Cheers*.

The cards were in the pilot, designed to alleviate exposition. "The Job." "The Brother."

David Lee: So you don't need the dialogue "Well, Niles is my brother and . . ." Our resistance to doing a spin-off served us all well—in our creative process and in the way we approached the piece.

John Pike: I said, "Either put a dog or a baby in it, and it pops." So that's how the dog got on the show.

Peter Casey: We'd been trying to break a story on *Cheers* where Frasier had been a guest host on a radio show, but we could never quite get it right. So when we had him move to Seattle, we decided to give him a whole new job. It left him off balance a little. You get fun with Frasier when he's not quite sure what he's doing. Then he could become a local celebrity like Sam was a local celebrity in Boston.

We were thinking of it as a workplace comedy. The key to the whole show was David Lee coming in one day and saying he thought a lot of people were going through what he was going through. David's father had suffered a stroke, and David is an only child, so he was helping his mother take care of his father. David said people our age are going through this, and *Cheers* never delved into Frasier's life in that way, so we had this incredibly fertile field.

Warren: After countless calls, negotiations, and cajoling, the day finally came when Peter, David, and David came into my office to pitch *Frasier*. Jesus, it was late in the development season. Could this be pulled off?

Perry Simon: I had been pushing those guys from my end to create a family show. When they came in for the pitch, Peter Casey said, "You're not going to believe it. We're going to give you a family show." I fell out of my chair onto the floor and prostrated myself. I literally got on my knees and bowed to thank him.

David Lee: At the pitch meeting, we laid out the story, and the network guys said that sounded great. We said we'd like somebody like John Mahoney. They said if you can get John Mahoney, he's preapproved. David Hyde Pierce—preapproved. Jane Leeves—preapproved. This was like getting free money.

Perry Simon: I remember being struck that *Frasier* was one of the first times I'd ever seen a show where they knew every actor before they pitched the show.

Lori Openden: *Frasier* was the most well-crafted show and well-put-together pilot I've ever worked on. They wanted John Mahoney. He was living a quiet life in Chicago doing theater, and he had to get talked into it by the producers. He'd done *The House of Blue Leaves* on Broadway and *Moonstruck*. He didn't have to audition.

We knew David Hyde Pierce. There wasn't a brother in the original plot of the show. One of the casting directors who was working with the producers brought a picture of DHP to the producers and said, "Look at this guy. He looks just like Kelsey." He never auditioned either.

Jane Leeves came in to read. She'd been on *Murphy Brown* as one of the secretaries. She'd scored in that.

Peter Casey: Frasier had this perfect life, and then his father moved in and had a home care worker. So you had conflict. Then our casting director walked in and asked, "Are you guys thinking of having a brother on this show?" She showed us a photo of David Hyde Pierce. "Doesn't he look like Kelsey ten years ago?"

We had a meeting with David Hyde Pierce. We gave him a basic outline of who the character was, and he said he'd love to do it.

David Hyde Pierce: When I went in, I knew it was guys who had written on *Cheers* and Kelsey. I knew his theater work, and I knew what a wonderful actor he was. I also knew John Mahoney's work onstage.

All they could tell me was that Frasier was a Freudian and Niles was a Jungian. Frasier had gone to Harvard, and Niles had gone to Yale. I went home and called my agent. I told her it seemed to have gone well, and she said, "It must have gone well because they offered you the part."

I was stunned and immediately concerned. I thought, "Oh, great, I have a part, but I haven't seen a script." *The Powers That Be* had been a mixed experience for me because I loved it, but for whatever reason it got thrown all over the schedule and then tanked and went away. And I'd been in plays that had closed, so I knew what that was like. So I was quite gun-shy about the whole thing.

Peter Casey: We decided Niles would be Frasier if Frasier had never walked into Cheers.

David Hyde Pierce: My character in *The Powers That Be* had no lines. The script would just say, "Theodore: Mutter mutter." I had read for Norman Lear in L.A., had read for Peter MacNicol's role. Norman said, "You're great but not in this part. Have you ever thought about directing?"

One of the strengths of *Frasier*, in the writing and the performance, was that the characters were three-dimensional so you could build on them. That certainly happened with the brothers. On the page, they were in conflict. We both instinctively as actors brought the other side of that as well. I think that's why the show had such legs, why it was such fun. Frasier and Niles could go at each other hammer and tongs, and yet they still loved each other as brothers.

Peter Casey: We start writing, and we're starting the casting process, trying to get everybody. We're on this deadline, and John Mahoney wanted to meet with us . . . in Chicago. So we flew to Chicago in February. We had dinner with John. We pitched him. He said it sounded interesting and that we should send him the script once we'd finished.

Jim Burrows: The only reason John Mahoney played Kelsey's father was because we had a *Cheers* episode about a man hired to write jingles for the bar. We hired Ronny Graham for the part. He was crazy. We had the dress rehearsal, broke for dinner, and Ronny drove off the lot and never came back.

We were trying to figure who to cast for Ronny's part, and I said I'd seen John Mahoney in *The House of Blue Leaves*, so he must play the piano. We hired him. He came out, and we shot a few scenes. Then I said, "John, now you have to play the piano." He said, "I don't play the piano."

Kelsey Grammer: We'd killed Frasier's father off in the ninth year of *Cheers*. I'd walked in with a stuffed owl and said my father was a famous professor and the owl was his prized possession. I asked Sam if he wanted to keep it in the bar. Sam said, "Hell, no." So Frasier tells him, "Toss it." The end of his sentiment about his dad.

When Sam visited *Frasier*, he said, "You told me your dad was dead." I said, "I lied."

David Lee: The only character we didn't have a good idea about was Roz. We eventually cast Lisa Kudrow, who lasted four days.

Peter Casey: We had Lisa read and Peri Gilpin. John Pike wasn't a fan of Peri's. When it came time to decide, John said, "Not Peri."

Lori Openden: Lisa Kudrow got the role of Roz. She'd done a number of guest shots on *Mad About You*. She didn't audition. We just hired her.

Peter Casey: Lisa gave us the laughs. She was really funny. We hadn't totally developed the character, but in that radio station she was going to be the top dog.

Lisa Kudrow: I know originally they wanted Peri Gilpin. All along they kind of wrote it for Peri, because they loved her and had worked with her before. So order was restored ultimately for *Frasier*. But it was devastating for me, because I had always thought, "I'm going to do a sitcom." And I had originally thought that I would do a guest star and it would go well, and then I would get a recurring role, and that's how I would be on a show. So when *Frasier* happened, it exceeded my expectations, because it wasn't how I saw it happening. But getting fired was devastating, because that was the best pilot.

Lori Openden: After the run-through, the only thing that wasn't quite working was Lisa's character. She had a hard time with long speeches. Jimmy said she was the only thing that wasn't really working.

Jim Burrows: Lisa Kudrow was wrong for the part of Roz. She just didn't have the authority she needed. For a while she didn't like me. Then *Friends* came along. We're good friends now.

Lisa was on a *Cheers*. She played an actress with Woody. They were doing *Our Town*. Peri Gilpin was also on *Cheers*. Peri isn't as comedically skilled as Lisa, but she had that "don't fuck around, Frasier" quality.

Lisa Kudrow: At the table read, I tanked. Then at the rehearsals Jimmy would say, "It's not working, don't worry about it, don't even try." And I didn't, which I think was a mistake, because you always need to do your best. But it wasn't working anyway. I think the character, the choice I made, was too snarky.

Lori Openden: At the time we fired Lisa Kudrow from *Frasier*, she was dating Conan O'Brien, who was our rising star. So we also had to break the news to Conan.

Warren: Naturally, Jimmy Burrows directed the pilot of *Frasier*. He certainly knew the character from his years at the helm of *Cheers*, and we needed Jimmy's magic. We needed a hit.

David Hyde Pierce: When I got the script for the pilot episode, I knew it was clearly a huge mistake because they had written two of the same characters in Frasier and Niles. I thought, "Why would they do that?" which is why I don't run a network and make programming decisions.

At the first table reading, I went, "Oh." From the first moment, it went gangbusters.

Jim Burrows: In the pilot of *Frasier*, the character of Niles only had one scene. I told the boys they had to go back to Niles.

David Hyde Pierce: Jimmy was legendary, of course. I'd heard he was a great director and fun to work with, so I was looking forward to it. Then Jimmy came into the conference room for the first table read, and he said, "All right, let's read." I thought, "This is what we've all been waiting for? This is God's gift to directing?" It turned out that that was one of the key elements of his directing: he doesn't waste time.

Mathilde DeCagny trained the dog on *Frasier*, the very first dog, Moose. Moose was this tough little dog, very smart, but if he learned a trick too soon, he got bored with it, and he wouldn't do it anymore. Mathilde had to figure out how to train him just enough so that on shoot night he'd do the trick and move on. That's how Jimmy treated us.

He'd see me and Jane working on something across the way, and he'd yell at us, "Stop rehearsing." Jimmy recognizes when you spend too much time on something, especially in that format, you kill it.

Peter Casey: Near the end of *Wings*, we had nine people in the cast and just twenty-two minutes to tell a story. With *Frasier*, we decided to keep the cast small and give everybody more material. The story of the pilot was very simple, and it gave us all this room to maneuver.

David Lee: We sat down to write the pilot without an outline. We did all sorts of things you're not supposed to do to write a TV series.

Warren: This took a lot of trust—no story document, no scene-by-scene outline. The first thing we saw on paper was the first draft of the script. This just isn't done anymore.

Peter Casey: I remember when we edited the pilot, we were seven minutes long. We cut it as much as we could, and we were still a minute long. NBC gave us the extra minute. They took fifteen seconds off every other show that night.

The day we shot the pilot, we did a dress rehearsal at 3:00 in the afternoon. At the end, the audience spontaneously gave us a standing ovation.

The first scene with John Mahoney: "Dad, your chair doesn't go with anything."

"I know. It's eclectic."

I looked up in the booth and could just see the soles of Warren's shoes because he was leaning back, laughing. That's when I knew we were in.

Warren: I loved that pilot, but once again there were a number of people who were afraid of it when we screened it. They thought the battle between Frasier and his dad, while dramatic, was maybe too rough for a sitcom. I thought the show was real and had great texture, and that was all part of the evolution of not simply being a *Cheers* spin-off but becoming its own show.

Jamie Tarses: *Wings* never did that well, and nobody particularly liked it. *Frasier* went on and worked right away.

Jack Welch: The only spin-off that worked was *Frasier*. When we wanted Michael Richards to go the next step to be Kramer on a spin-off, he didn't want to do it. We finally got him, but it bombed.

Bob Wright: Ninety-one and '92 marked the first advertising drop since World War II—all advertising. It was tough.

Warren: A strong advertising marketplace can cover up a lot of scheduling weaknesses, but when both the ad market is weak and your schedule is weak, that's the worst double whammy you can have.

Bob Wright: We drifted down from '89 into '92, and then the advertising markets were collapsing. We had a lot to lose. We lost 50 percent of what we had, and we still had as much as everybody else. But we were 50 percent down.

The breakthrough of that whole ugly period from '91 to '93 was *Frasier* coming out in '93. Seeing the show at the upfronts was a very big deal.

Warren: In 1993, President Clinton launched his new economic strategy that embraced budgetary discipline while investing in education and science. It paid off with a reduction in inflation and unemployment and a record 116 months of economic growth. Our creative surge could not have come at a better time. Just as the advertising market started to come back, so did NBC.

Frasier was a hit right away. We started it out on Thursday nights at 9:30 following *Seinfeld*, a blockbuster pairing. *Seinfeld* was the number one comedy in television, but *Frasier* was right behind it. Amazing for a freshman show. It was a dynamite hour of television, and any other network president might have left well enough alone. In the overall network ratings we were a strong number two (behind ABC). But the criticism that we were a one-night network (Thursday) was accurate and a little stinging.

For years we had been defensive in our scheduling strategies because we didn't have the weapons to attack our competition. Looking at *Frasier*, we knew what we had. It wasn't *Wings*. It was a self-starter, a hit show. So Preston Beckman and I decided, for the fall of 1994, to move *Frasier* to Tuesday night at 9:00. Frasier would go up against ABC's *Roseanne*, a wonderful family comedy (damn it!) but getting older and, we thought, possibly vulnerable to quality adult competition. That's what we hoped anyway.

We believed it was critical strategically for us to plant our flag on a night other than Thursday if we ever wanted to be the number one network. We told Don what we thought, and he agreed with us. At *Frasier* they felt a little differently.

Peter Casey: We were furious. We felt we deserved a couple of years behind *Seinfeld* to get fully entrenched. And then we learned we'd be opposite *Roseanne*. Then ABC blinked, and we went up against *Home Improvement*!

Warren: Word leaked of what we were doing, and before I got on the plane for New York to announce the schedule, I got a number of threatening calls from Paramount and agents representing Kelsey. I was told, "You can announce whatever you want in New York but don't expect Kelsey to show up for work!" Shit. I called Kelsey and told him why I believed in the move. He responded to me with "Lots of people will tell you many threatening things, but I'm telling you we have the best comedy on television and it will continue to be that no matter where you put us."

David Lee: I remember going into Don Ohlmeyer's office to protest the move to Tuesday night. We'd just aired an episode that ran in real time—Niles and Frasier in a coffee shop. And Don said, "About that episode that was just on—you guys were pretty self-indulgent."

Peter Casey: He said, "I hope you liked your little art film."

David Lee: My thought bubble was "You just wait."

Preston Beckman: We were screening pilots, and we still hadn't come up with the full Tuesday/Thursday schedule. We were thinking *Unsolved Mysteries*. I got a call from New York, and a woman in sales from the network told me, "If you put *Unsolved Mysteries* on Tuesdays, I'll fucking kill you." I think she would have.

Warren: The sales department was thrilled by our bold and aggressive move of *Frasier* to Tuesday at 9:00 and *Wings* was used at 8:00 to kick off the two-hour comedy block. But then one morning in August 1994, a month before the premiere, ABC made an announcement. They were moving their highest-rated comedy, *Home Improvement*, from Wednesday at 9:00 to Tuesday at 9:00 to go up against *Frasier*.

Clearly they were looking at some of the same data we were, and they knew *Roseanne* was vulnerable. In the chess game of network television this was their "we'll show you" countermove to hold on to their Tuesday supremacy.

Don called Preston and me into his office. "We have to move *Frasier* back to Thursdays, it was a good try, but now we'll get killed." Our response was unified and clear: no. We knew ad sales had cleaned up on this move throughout the summer, and we reminded Don this was never about being number one on the night. It was about attacking the dominant player with a quality adult alternative. We couldn't abandon that strategy, at least not yet. We had to play it out in the fall. Don told us we were nuts.

David Hyde Pierce: I was never convinced the show was going to stick around. Once we were on, we got moved to Tuesday night in the second year. So whatever confidence I had went away. We were up against *Home Improvement*. You have a certain amount of security, but things happen all the time. Contract negotiations come up. Things change.

David Lee: With *Wings* we felt we had to claw our way up the mountain, and with *Frasier* it felt like we'd stepped on the Zeitgeist express.

David Hyde Pierce: Kelsey's approach is very cavalier. He calls it "requisite disrespect." He would be running the lines in the makeup room the night of the show, and you'd watch the color drain out of the guest star's face, because it seemed like Kelsey didn't know anything. But he'd get it in his head. He believed firmly in the spontaneity and an actor thinking as a real human being, which is what happens when you're coming up with what you're going to say in real life as opposed to having memorized it.

In some shows, the actors are only allowed to talk to the director, and the director talks to the writers. That's a weakness of the director, but Jimmy Burrows was completely confident. As the seasons went on, everyone realized the gifts and abilities of each other. Then the writers knew if an actor asked for a new line, it wasn't because they couldn't act it. Similarly, if the writers asked an actor to do a particular line, it wasn't because they couldn't come up with another one.

David Lee: We knew we could do things and the writers and the cast would deliver.

Warren: It was the first and only series to earn a record five consecutive Emmy wins for Outstanding Comedy Series. At a total of thirty-seven Emmys, it surpassed *Cheers* and won more than any series in television history.

Frasier had a remarkable run. The quality of the show never flagged, and the audience was large and loyal. *Frasier* represented an 84 percent improvement in the time period, and Tuesday night was up 39 percent (Nielsen Media Research). ABC remained number one on the night but at significantly reduced levels. NBC was a solid number two for Tuesday, but by the 1995 season it catapulted us to number one each and every week, season after season. The bet paid off.

After four successful years on Tuesday night, the show returned to Thursdays in 1998, and the series ended with a two-hour finale in May 2004.

David Hyde Pierce: When the writers told us that they were going to end the show and shape the whole last season, we were stunned, but it felt right. It had been a decade, and we weren't sick of the show. We said, "Let's go when we're not sick of it."

John Pike: When it came to *Cheers* and *Frasier*, both sides of the equation really needed each other. It was an interesting marriage of network and production. Very collaborative. Non-adversarial. It wasn't everybody trying to kill each other. I think that's one of the reasons Must See TV worked.

David Hyde Pierce: *Frasier* was important for me. The people I got to work with, the time we spent. I don't want to mess with that. That's why I don't ever want to do a reunion. I don't want people to see us and say, "Wow. What happened?" It's bad enough when people see reruns and ask me, "Wow. What happened?"

8

Six of One

8

Six of One.

Warren: NBC's pilot season of 1994 is legendary in the business. In a world where failure is commonplace, we midwifed the births of both *Friends* and *ER*. While *ER* came essentially out of the blue, we'd been casting around for a *Friends*-like show for some time at the network.

One morning while I was studying the overnight ratings from the major markets, I found myself thinking about the people in those cities, particularly the twentysomethings just beginning to make their way. I imagined young adults starting out in New York, L.A., Dallas, Philly, San Francisco, St. Louis, or Portland all faced the same difficulty. It was very expensive to live in those places as well as a tough emotional journey. It would be a lot easier if you did it with a friend.

Addressing that general idea became a development target for us. We wanted to reach that young, urban audience, those kids starting out on their own, but none of the contenders had ever lived up to our hopes. Then Marta Kauffman and David Crane showed up with their pitch for a show called *Six of One*.

Karey Burke: I remember reading a Kauffman and Crane play when I was a secretary at NBC. We tracked them, me and Jamie Tarses. Jamie always wanted Kauffman and Crane to develop a show.

Jamie Tarses: That was a great pitch. Marta and David finished each other's sentences. We'd been hearing so many of those pitches. The six friends was a concept that was around. But that was a great pitch.

Karey Burke: The pitch was like two old friends telling you a story. The jokes were already there. They performed the pitch. The pitch was total entertainment. It was theater.

Warren: The craft of buying comedy pitches (or any pitch actually) lies in being able to see beyond a timid presentation. People often get nervous before a pitch, but Kauffman and Crane were magnetic. They owned it. It was their story.

Jamie Tarses: I remember there being no question about the show.

David Crane: *Dream On* was our very first show. We'd never worked on a TV show, and we were running it. It was madness. Here's the pool. Swim or something.

Marta Kauffman: We got to *Friends* in a roundabout way. We'd just come off of *Dream On* with one actor who was in every scene, and it was brutal. So we told ourselves, "We want to do an ensemble comedy."

David Crane: Not that long before, we'd been living in New York not doing TV. It was only three years later that we were pitching *Friends*, so we'd just been living it—that point in your life when your friends are your family.

Marta Kauffman: And we wanted to write something we would watch.

Warren: At the time, David and Marta were coming off the cancellation of *The Powers That Be*, a show they had created—largely by accident—for Norman Lear and CBS.

David Crane: *The Powers That Be* is a crazy story. It was *The Producers.* We got a job developing with Norman Lear. It was amazing for two theater writers from New York. "Wait, we're going to *each* get paid that?"

Marta Kauffman: The first script we did for Norman that the development people liked, Norman hated.

David Crane: TV for us was you write a show and nobody makes it.

Marta Kauffman: Norman came in. He took my hand. He said, "It's shallow and superficial."

David Crane: For six months, that's who we were to each other—Shallow and Superficial.

We decided to come up with a show nobody would buy, and that would get us out of this deal with Norman. The show is set in Washington, and we decided to make all the characters repellent.

Marta Kauffman: The wife is a lesbian who slaps the maid. The daughter is bulimic. The son is suicidal.

David Crane: We're actually having a very good time because it's dark and funny and we love it. It's very superficial. Broad and shallow. Super superficial. We go in to pitch it, and it's the first time we've heard Norman Lear laugh. We're thinking, "Oh no." We go to pitch it at CBS. *Dream On* has been on for a season, and the exec buys the show. We start casting, and we end up getting this brilliant cast. David Hyde Pierce. Peter MacNicol. John Forsythe. We need to cast the illegitimate daughter. Norman says, "I've got the daughter. Linda Hunt."

Brilliant actress, but not funny. You don't put her in the middle of a four-camera comedy. She made it clear we could do jokes about her height. So we start writing them, and she's very uncomfortable with them.

Marta Kauffman: We loved it. Linda Hunt. We thought, "They'll never do this." Perfect.

David Crane: We shoot the pilot, which is actually very funny but for Linda. It was dead at CBS. The network does not pick it up. Then we get the call. NBC wants it . . . if we replace Linda Hunt.

Warren: I loved the writing in that script, deliciously dark. I had to try it.

Even without the comic stylings of Linda Hunt, *The Powers That Be* lasted but one season on the network, its final episode airing in June 1993.

David Crane: We pitched *Friends* to Fox and sold it to Fox, and then we pitched it to NBC. Then there was some finagling, and somehow we were doing it at NBC.

Warren: Les Moonves, who was president of Warner Bros. TV at the time, said you have to make a pilot commitment, not a script. I loved the pitch. I said that was fine. Les understood the value of owning a successful comedy on NBC. What this meant financially was that if I got the script and wanted to get out of the commitment, it would cost me $250,000.

David Crane: We did the pilot for *Friends* and another show at Fox called *Reality Check*. Sometimes scripts feel absolutely right, and sometimes you just want to kill yourself.

Marta Kauffman: Every word is excruciating.

David Crane: Our Fox pilot was like that. One thing we're working on is this delicious, wonderful, fruitful thing, and at the same time we have this other show that's not working. Every scene is torture. It's not funny. It's not good, and we know it.

Marta Kauffman: We'd get notes from the network: "Make it more adult." It was a high school show.

David Crane: And we got the note "It's funny; it's not Fox funny." I don't know what that is.

If you read the *Friends* pitch now, the show was incredibly true to the pitch. Basically, we just memorized it and said it. We used to go in and read our pitches, which doesn't work.

Marta Kauffman: We finish each other's sentences anyway, so we never scripted who said what.

David Crane: We left no air.

Warren: David and Marta's script was just as wonderful as the pitch. Smart and funny. I called Jimmy and told him I had a script he had to read.

Marta Kauffman: When we finally started doing the show, the writers were so much younger than us that we felt like anthropologists.

David Crane: We were thirty-three or thirty-four by then.

Marta Kauffman: It was a fascinating casting experience. We saw a countless number of actors, but things happened as they were supposed to happen. One of the first actors on our list was Matthew Perry to play Chandler, but he was doing a show called *LAX 2194*, so he wasn't available. We brought other people in.

David Crane: We brought *everybody* in. We were so sure that would be the easiest part to cast. It's got the most joke jokes. It's sarcastic and kind of quippy, but no one could do it. No one.

Marta Kauffman: The person who came closest was Craig Bierko, and we found out later that Matthew had coached him.

Lori Openden: The producers wanted to go with Craig Bierko instead of Matthew Perry for Chandler. Bierko read the *Friends* script and passed.

Warren: Thank God! There was something snidely whiplash about Craig Bierko. He seemed to have a lot of anger underneath, more of a guy you love to hate. The attractive leading man whom you love and who can do comedy is very rare.

Karey Burke: We kind of talked Craig Bierko out of being in *Friends*. Ultimately, he made his own decision, sort of. He took another pilot where he could be the lead and the only star.

David Crane: We offered the part to him. We didn't have anything better. He's a really good actor and a lovely guy, but wrong for Chandler.

Marta Kauffman: We took Matthew in second position.

David Crane: He was doing a show about baggage handlers in the future, but not that far in the future. And somebody said, "Has anybody seen this thing?"

Marta Kauffman: We originally offered Rachel to Courteney Cox, but she said she wanted to do Monica, not Rachel.

David Crane: Courteney had just come off a terrible Bronson Pinchot show where she played the wife.

Marta Kauffman: There was something about Courteney that was adorable.

Lori Openden: Nancy McKeon from *The Facts of Life* also read for Courteney's part. She gave a terrific performance. Warren let Marta and David make the call. They went off for a walk and came back and said Courteney.

Warren: When I auditioned for my first job at NBC in comedy development, I had to watch episodes of *The Facts of Life* and evaluate them before the series had ever gone on the air. Then later, when I had current comedy reporting to me, I had the opportunity to watch Nancy McKeon grow up on that set and on that series. She was wonderful, and America loved her. It was a tough call because she gave a great reading for Monica.

Jamie Tarses: It was a very split room when Nancy McKeon and Courteney auditioned. Many of the executives at Warner Bros. wanted Nancy.

Marta Kauffman: Because we were casting an ensemble, there was something appealing about not Nancy McKeon.

David Crane: When we originally wrote the role, we had Janeane Garofalo's voice in our head. Darker and edgier and snarkier, and Courteney brought a whole bunch of other colors to it. We decided that week after week, that would be a lovelier place to go to.

Marta Kauffman: And more maternal.

David Crane: We brought in two actors for Joey, and everyone preferred Matt LeBlanc. We were told he was an actor who'd get better every week.

Matt LeBlanc: I got the script, and it was Jimmy Burrows's new project and the producers from *Dream On*. I think I had seen a couple of episodes of *Dream On*, not enough to know the show. I knew it had clips from old movies in it, and I thought that was a cool idea, but I never really watched it enough to get into it. I knew it was funny. That was all I really needed to know; the guys are funny. I'd done two series for Fox. *Friends* was my fourth series.

I was practicing lines with an actor friend of mine, and he said, "This show is all about a group of friends, so we should go out tonight and get drunk, as though we were friends. We should just keep that in mind." So we went out, and I fell down and skinned my nose really badly. I went to the audition with this huge scab on my face, and Marta said, "What happened to your face?"

I said, "Aw, it's a long story." She thought it was funny and laughed, and that kind of set the tone for the room. Who knew? I would never suggest, "You know what you do before an audition? You go out and face-plant on the sidewalk, and then go in all bloody."

David Crane: Joey was never stupid when we pitched the show. He wasn't stupid until we were shooting the pilot and somebody said, "Matt plays dumb really well."

Marta Kauffman: And he had so much heart. Down deep, you just wanted to take care of him. You knew that at some point, he'd fall in love.

Matt LeBlanc: I had some sitcom experience. I knew my way around a joke a little bit. The time on *Married with Children* and with Joe Bologna, I learned a lot. I watched how they did things. I learned the process—where the joke is, how to set up a joke. I learned a lot. So it went well. I got laughs.

Then I got a callback and had a studio test. I think Courteney was in the room when I came to read. It was between me and this guy—his last name was Yeager, I think. He was dressed in a denim jacket, jeans, cowboy boots. I think he had a cowboy hat with him, but he didn't have it on. I looked at him and thought, "One of us is *way* off the mark. God, I hope it's you."

David Crane: An exec at NBC called to say she'd offered the part of Rachel to Jami Gertz. We didn't have a Rachel, and Jami Gertz is a really talented actress, but not Rachel. So we held our breath for twenty-four hours until she passed.

Warren: Jennifer Aniston had been in our weak attempt to do *Ferris Bueller* as a series. (We did not have the services of John Hughes.) She played Ferris's sister, Jeannie, and we liked what we saw. We cast her in a few more pilots, but none were very good. One night while gassing up my car on Sunset Boulevard in Hollywood, I ran into Jennifer, and she asked me, "Will it ever happen for me?" God, I wanted it to. I didn't care what it would take—this was the role for her.

Marta Kauffman: Rachel was the part that was hardest to cast. Jennifer came in, and she was in a show that was on the air—*Muddling Through.*

David Crane: We had a meeting with the guy who created *Muddling Through* and asked him if he'd let her go. What chutzpah.

Lori Openden: Jennifer Aniston and Matthew Perry were technically not available. We had second position; we were taking a gamble that the show in first position wasn't going forward.

We auditioned other actors for Jennifer's part, but nobody else was good enough. It was a pretty big risk. Her show was a comedy for CBS. They'd shot eight episodes and had them on the shelf for six months. They still had the rights to air it.

Jamie Tarses: Then we had Jennifer Aniston crying to Les Moonves to let her out of the CBS show she was on.

Preston Beckman: I put Danielle Steel movies on opposite the Jennifer Aniston show on CBS. I killed it.

Warren: I remember watching *Muddling Through*, Jennifer's show. It was bad. I thought to myself, "They won't pick up this horrible show just to fuck us, will they?"

Lori Openden: When Lisa auditioned for *Friends* as Phoebe, she owned it. There was no debate on her.

Lisa Kudrow: I thought *Mad About You* was the best-*written* show I'd ever seen, and I always liked talking to writers, because I always wanted to understand how they got their ideas. Jeffrey Klarik was one of the writers who was always really friendly and complimentary, and I didn't know his boyfriend was David Crane. David saw me, because he paid attention to everything Jeffrey did. And I think that's how I got called in for an audition for *Friends*.

I read for David and Marta, and then I had to go back and read for Jimmy Burrows. That scared me a lot, because of *Frasier*. He's kind of who fired me.

So I was nervous to go in, thinking I'm about to read for the guy who doesn't get me and doesn't think I'm funny. My audition was a monologue, so there was no reacting off of anybody. Jimmy said, "No notes . . . Okay, thank you, Lisa." And I thought, "All right, so that's it." "No notes" either means "it was so great I don't have anything to say" or "why do they keep putting this girl in front of me?"

Marta Kauffman: Phoebe was easy to cast.

David Crane: We knew her from *Mad About You*.

Lisa Kudrow: I'd gotten good at auditioning, because I was taking a class where the guy was fantastic. His name was Ian Tucker, and he told us, "It's a business. All you guys want to do is act, and you finally get an audition, and all anyone is asking you to do is focus and act for two minutes, because that's about how long an audition is, and none of you can do it. You jump into their laps and wonder if they are paying attention. Do they like it? What are they thinking? Forget it. Just perform." So I got good at doing just that.

He told us, "They are dying for you to blow them away. They're on your side. What do you think, they want to go through hundreds of people and settle? No. Just do what you do. Either you're right for the part or you're not—let them decide. They're eating lunch while you audition because they're hungry. It's not because they don't like you."

Warren: Speaking as someone who's spent a professional lifetime watching talented people collapse at auditions, that advice is as valuable as it comes.

Lisa Kudrow: Those other actresses were falling apart. A lot of them really couldn't cope with the auditioning process, and I could. That's why I got the job, because I'm good at auditioning.

At one point I even said, "You know, I'm more like Rachel." And they told me, "No. You're this quirky girl." And then once I knew that I was going to the network—and that's when you work out the deal— that's when I was like, "Thank God it's on NBC. Pilots work and don't work, but we have to protect *Mad About You*, please." That was the only thing I cared about, so that I could still do that show. I thought since it was on the same network, maybe it wouldn't be a problem.

David Crane: When we got our time slot, we were following *Mad About You*. It was weird, so that's when we said, "What if Phoebe and Ursula were sisters." We called Danny Jacobson, and he said, "Okay." I'm not sure I would have.

Harold Brook: With *Friends*, the last actor to sign was David Schwimmer. Everybody loved Schwimmer, and his agent knew it. We were $2,500 apart [per episode]. We both dug in our heels. Lori Openden came to me and begged. I hated it, but we gave it to them.

Marta Kauffman: Schwimmer had auditioned the year before for a pilot we were making, and he just stuck in our heads. That was an offer. No audition.

David Schwimmer: I had auditioned for a pilot called *Couples* that Marta and David had written, and it was one of the few that I had tested for. It had come down to me and two other actors, one of whom was one of my oldest and dearest high school friends, Johnny Silverman. So, Johnny got the part. They made the pilot, I think, and then it never went anywhere. I got this other show called *Monty* with Henry Winkler.

I *adored* Henry and working with him, but I did not have an enjoyable experience as an actor on the show. I didn't feel like I had a voice on *Monty*. I didn't feel like the writers were interested in my opinion or my ideas or what I could bring to the table. I felt fairly stifled creatively and not a part of the process. I was just expected to be quiet and say the lines.

I was acting, writing, and directing ensemble theater for years. I was already twenty-seven when I was doing *Monty*. I had such a negative experience on that show. We actually shot twelve episodes. I felt like, "I can't believe I signed a contract for five years." I wanted to kill myself.

As soon as we were canceled—I think they only aired six episodes and then they stopped—I thought, "For the first time in my life, I have money in the bank because of *Monty*." And I said, "Good. I'm going to go back to Chicago and doing theater. I am never going to do TV again."

Eric McCormack: I went out for Schwimmer's role on *Friends*. Years later I told Burrows the story, and he said, "Honey, you were wasting your time. They wrote the part for Schwimmer."

I was already a full-on *Seinfeld* freak, so I was very upset when I didn't get past the studio level with the *Friends* part.

David Schwimmer: I told my agents not to send me anything. I moved back to Chicago, and I was in Chicago doing a play with my company. We were doing *The Master and Margarita*—this book that we had adapted—and we had just opened Steppenwolf's new studio space with this play. I was playing Pontius Pilate with a very short Roman haircut, which is why Ross eventually had this haircut.

I got the call from my agent [Leslie Siebert at the Gersh Agency], and she said, "Look, I know you told me not to send you anything, but there's a show I *really* think you should take a look at. It's by Marta and David, who—if you remember—had done that show *Couples*." And I go, "Oh yes. I remembered *loving* the writing." And she said the magic words to me: "It's an ensemble show. There's no star. There are six people, all similar age." And I say, "Okay, I'll read it, but I'm not going to do it."

Then I got a phone call from Robby Benson in Chicago, who is friends with Marta and David. I was a huge fan of Robby Benson, and I had never met him. Out of the blue, I get this phone call from Robby Benson. He said, "Look. I really think you should consider doing this. At least go and meet Marta and David and talk about it." And then Jim Burrows called. Jim is my idol. I just think the world of him.

The combination of a few things—to have those two people call, and then to understand, which I didn't realize at first, that Marta and David had written Ross with my voice in mind from the *Couples* audition. It was hugely flattering, and I thought, "Well, it's quite disrespectful with all this talent asking to meet and just consider it. I'd be an idiot not to go."

Lisa Kudrow: I'd be at *Mad About You*, and other guest stars would say, "I'm reading for Joey, will you help me with it?" And I was like, "Yeah, I'll help you learn your lines, but I don't know what they need or who they want." And I just thought, "Wow. Everyone wants to do this show. I wonder why?"

The drama people really wanted to do *ER*, and the comedy people really wanted *Friends*. The whole thing is such a crapshoot, and just because the script is good doesn't mean much.

Marta Kauffman: The first day we went to a run-through and the six of them were together for the first time, onstage in the coffee shop, I remember the atmosphere being electric. A chill ran down my spine. I knew we had something special.

David Schwimmer: I felt that it was something special immediately in the first rehearsals. Even the first read-through, I thought, "Oh." You could feel it. The energy. There was something *really* special about the six different voices and the energy of the six of us. There are six pieces of a puzzle that happen to click *just* right because of casting and because of the particular energy of the six people. I think luck had a great amount to do with it.

The miracle is the casting. Having been on the other side of it now in terms of directing and producing, to find *one* magical actor who is just right for the role is difficult enough, but to find six and then to have them actually *have chemistry* with each other is just kind of a miracle. I think we were just lucky. I looked at the five of them, I watched their work, and I thought, "Everyone is just so talented and perfect for their character." And they grew into their characters and enriched them and deepened them.

David Crane: We had absolutely no idea what this show was going to be. For us, it was just another pilot. We'd just had a series canceled. We were thinking we'd never work again, so we were scrambling. You pitch a bunch of stuff. We were doing this thing at Fox and at NBC. *Friends* was feeling good, but it was just another pilot. Or it was just another pilot until Jimmy Burrows wants to direct it. Excuse me, James Burrows. We thought, *"That's crazy."*

Marta Kauffman: I was most surprised by how good he was dramaturgically. He had such a good sense of structure and story.

David Crane: And he really embraced what we wanted to do. In the pilot, the structure is really loose. We started out doing a much more traditional story. It still had to do with Rachel leaving a guy at the altar, but we had an original version where her parents came, and the act break was her parents showing up. It wasn't good.

We approached it again and made it much looser. The structure is loose and unconventional. There's no event at the act break. Ross and Rachel are each looking out at the rain. In a pilot, that seems crazy. You couldn't do it today, and I'm surprised we did that then.

Marta Kauffman: Jimmy had a way of making a moment with a small action. You realize very quickly that Ross has a terrible crush on Rachel, and there's a scene at the end where he says, "Do you maybe want to go out maybe on a date sometime." And Rachel says, "Maybe." There was one Oreo cookie left. I will never forget Jimmy said to David, "Try the cookie in your mouth when you say that line."

David Crane: Rachel says, "Maybe," and David says, "Maybe I will," and pops the cookie in his mouth.

Marta Kauffman: It was such a victory for him. It made the moment.

David Crane: The first four minutes of the pilot were just the group sitting in the coffeehouse talking about nothing. Chandler has had a dream. Ross comes in, and he's mopey. It's just talk. There's no movement. There's no story. When Jimmy read it in our first meeting, he said, "It's great. It's radio." The fact that he got that and embraced it made all the difference.

Matt LeBlanc: I was this kid who got this gig, and here I am with the guy—Jimmy Burrows. I remember thinking, "Every episode of *Cheers*? I love that show! And almost every episode of *Taxi*? Wait a minute. I love *that* show!"

He had this air about him that I had never seen. At that point, I had worked with a handful of different directors, and I had never come across anyone who had such an ease to him. Like, "it ain't the cure for cancer" kind of thing. I'm sure he understands the value and importance of it all, but he never let the actors worry about that. "That's not your job to worry about that. All of that happens after we shoot it, so let's not worry about that. It's all about these little moments. We're all in it together. And also, I want to be out by 2:00."

Lisa Kudrow: I was terrified that first week. It was Jimmy . . . again. The great thing about Jimmy is that he wants to try different things, and the bad thing is that he wants to try different things. He was really open about what the potential problems were. He was collaborative and inclusive of the cast, not keeping us separate from all of the writers.

So Jimmy would say, "Why are *they* friends with her?" Meaning me. "We have to figure that out. She doesn't fit." And I was like, "Oh my God, here we go again. Well, if everyone just acts like they like me. If Monica acts like she likes me . . ." And at one point, he thought it would be funny if I deliver my monologue under the table. They're all sitting around the table. Rachel is about to cut up her credit cards. Instead of being with them, I'm under the table, because I'm "quirky."

I thought, "This is the run-through where Marta and David are going to say, 'This character doesn't work. We have to reconceive it.

She's just not part of the group.'" And I really thought that was gonna be what came out of that run-through. And thank God, they said, "Um, Lisa, not that it's a bad choice, but I don't think that's a good spot for you, under the table." I didn't know how to answer. I would never put myself under the table. Jimmy said, "No, that was me. We were just trying it." I was afraid they'd think, "Wow, this girl did a great audition, but she has the worst instincts about where to put herself." I was really wondering if I was going to be fired. Again.

David Schwimmer: What I was most struck by was the spirit of collaboration. I expressed to them my fears of what I had just experienced, and they made it clear to me that it was going to be a collaborative effort and that I would have a voice. And I thought that that was worth the risk of being in a situation and signing your life away for five or six years, not knowing the other five actors.

Lisa Kudrow: Courteney Cox was the best known of all of us, and she had done a guest star on *Seinfeld*. She said, "Listen, I just did a *Seinfeld*, and they all help each other. They say, 'Try this' and 'This would be funny.'" And she said, "You guys, feel free to tell me. If I could do anything funnier, I want to do it."

There's a code with actors. Actors don't give each other notes under any circumstances. So she was giving us permission to give her notes, and we all agreed that that would be great. Why not? And she also said, "Listen, you know, we all need to make this thing great." She just set the stage with "I know I'm the one who's been on TV, but this is all of us." She was the one who set that tone and made it a real group that way. And I thought that was a real turning point.

David Crane: We were the last pilot to deliver, and we got one note from Don Ohlmeyer: "The opening is too slow." The word came down that Don said if we didn't trim it, we weren't on the air. We fucking loved the beginning. It's right. We don't want to change it. We cut a ninety-second opening title sequence to REM's "Shiny Happy People." We didn't cut anything, but it started with energy. Don said, "Now it's right."

Warren: It may seem hard to believe today, but in 1994 we were playing in core conceptual territory that hadn't been explored that much on network TV—young adult relationships. We wanted these characters to feel real, and we knew they had to be likable. We thought Marta and David were navigating that well, and of course we had Jimmy, TV's best barometer. Don didn't see it that way.

Marta Kauffman: We were doing the network run-through with an audience, and Don said that when Monica slept with Paul the wine guy, she got what she deserved—that's how he rationalized it—fire began to come out of my nose.

They handed out a questionnaire to the audience: *Do you think Monica sleeping with wine guy makes her (a) a slut, (b) a whore, (c) a trollop.* And even with the deck stacked that way, the audience didn't care.

Jamie Tarses: The questionnaire for the audience after the run-through—that was completely Don. He didn't like the casual sex. It was just one guy worrying about this.

David Crane: Overall, the network notes were almost nonexistent. Don objected to a Maxi Pad joke. Ross couldn't throw out his ex-wife's Maxi Pads. He was using them as arch supports. Okay, Don was uncomfortable with Maxi Pads.

Jim Burrows: Based on the audience for the *Friends* pilot, I knew how popular that show would be. The kids were all pretty and funny, so beautiful. I said to Les Moonves, who was head of Warner Bros., "Give me the plane. I'll pay for dinner." I took the cast to Vegas.

Matt LeBlanc: Who goes to Vegas on a private jet? And Jimmy gave me five hundred bucks to gamble.

Lisa Kudrow: On the plane he showed us the first episode of *Friends*. None of it had aired yet.

Jimmy took us to dinner, and he gave us each a little money to gamble with. He said, "I want you to be aware that this is the last time that you all can be out and not be swarmed, because that's what's going to happen." And everyone was like, *"Really?"* I thought, "Well, we'll see. Maybe. Who knows? We don't know how the show's going to do. Why is he so certain?"

Jim Burrows: I told them they had a special show and this was their last shot at anonymity. They wanted to gamble, and I was the only one with money. They wrote me checks. Schwimmer gave me a check for $200, and Jen did. I should have saved them.

Matt LeBlanc: We went to Caesars for dinner. We sat at the big round table in the middle of the room. Jimmy said, "Look around." Nobody knew us. People kind of knew Courteney from that "Dancing in the Dark" video.

He said, "Your life is going to change. The six of you will never be able to do this again." It was almost like Don Corleone talking. He's not going to be wrong. He's Jimmy Burrows.

9

I'll Be There
for You

Jamie Tarses: I remember sweating the ratings of *Friends* the first few weeks. It was falling off more than anybody wanted it to. Outside of development, there was a lot of doubt about *Friends*.

Warren: *Mad About You* had successfully slugged it out with *The Simpsons*, and Fox had moved that show to Sunday at 8:00. Now we were leading off Thursday night in first place, so a big falloff with *Friends* was not going to be acceptable.

Preston Beckman: The *Friends* pilot didn't test great.

Warren: True—a "high weak"—but we loved it! Even though we still only had Jennifer Aniston in second position—CBS had yet to cancel *Muddling Through*—I decided to take another multimillion-dollar bet and shoot episodes with Jennifer in them.

Karey Burke: *Six of One* was the name of the show during the pilot. Then Kauffman and Crane came back with *Friends*, which we thought was such a snore. Some people thought the show was too Gen X, way too narrow. There was much more buzz about Fox's version of the same concept, a show called *Wild Oats* with Paul Rudd.

Matt LeBlanc: I remember seeing the test audience results for the pilot. It didn't test well, I don't think.

Karey Burke: Between *Friends* and *NewsRadio*, I couldn't have told you which one would be a hit. The *Friends* cast came to the pilot taping of *NewsRadio*. Jimmy Burrows was directing it, and the *Friends* cast was jealous.

Jamie Tarses: The first couple of scripts after the pilot, we were struggling with scripts and struggling with story. Then it was a soap opera, and it was hilarious. The Ross and Rachel thing set the tone for that, and you got thrust into a sort of soapy storytelling.

Warren: For me, we were about six scripts in, and each time I'd read one, I saw tremendous emotional resonance. I thought, "This is a Shakespearean soap opera. It's a drama that's really, really funny, and with a complex architecture." Unlike *Seinfeld*, which lived to be funny but not to feel.

David Crane: That's why we were always surprised when people compared us to *Seinfeld*.

Matt LeBlanc: In between all the jokes, there was this emotional thread. You cared about these people. You were invested in these relationships. You can't get enough of these people. Why? No one could describe their passion for it. An emotional soap opera is a great way to describe it. That emotional through-line threaded the whole season.

Marta Kauffman: One of the surprising things to us was when Monica and Chandler revealed themselves under the sheets in London. We had to stop. For minutes, the audience was screaming. It was so surprising to us how invested the audience was in these characters, how desperately they wanted them to be happy, how putting them together made some kind of weird sense.

David Crane: The fear was that we'd jump the shark. We only had six characters. When we brought Monica and Chandler together, I don't think we thought it would last. They'd just sleep together.

Marta Kauffman: One crazy lesson from the show was that everything was better with the six of them. Sometimes it was better to hear them talk about something that happened rather than see it dramatically. What the audience wanted, we had to learn, was the six of them in the room.

David Crane: Apparently, what they really wanted was two of them in the bed.

Jim Burrows: Ross and Rachel were the guts of that show. Everybody was good-looking on that show, so the critics didn't realize how funny they were.

David Crane: We sort of let rules go away in terms of how to tell stories and traditional television structure. They don't have to live together. We don't have to put it all in one set. We can spread it out.

Marta Kauffman: I think it was Warren who said, "Can you at least put them across the hall from each other?" Good idea.

David Crane: Warren also suggested we call it *Across the Hall*, which we did not do. One for two. Once we got into making the show, I don't think we'd realized how important having them across the hall would be. We just hadn't done that much four-camera television.

Marta Kauffman: There was an NBC note after the pilot that maybe we needed an older character, a guy who owned the coffeehouse.

David Crane: We tried a pass at this character, but it was like as you're writing, you're going, "Hate myself, hate myself, hate myself." We ended up bringing the parents in instead.

Warren: It was a really smart move on the producers' part. The core of the show remained the same, but the show became more relevant to a larger broadcast audience when those young characters had stories that involved their parents and not just other young adults. It became generational comedy that invited the older audience in, and once they got there, they never left. Eventually, almost 25 percent of the audience was over fifty. Advertisers didn't necessarily pay us for them, but it became a broad-based hit. We learned from that audience that they didn't have to still be twentysomething but they once were that age and *Friends* was a wonderful reminder of that time in their lives.

Jamie Tarses: The way we did everything was so different from the way networks do things now. It's astounding what executives think their jobs are today compared with what we thought then. I can't imagine micromanaging creators you supposedly respect and admire. I don't know why they don't produce the shows themselves.

We used to get on the phone, Marta and David would tell us the area, and then we'd get a script.

Marta Kauffman: The cast was very astute, very smart, and when things didn't work for them, they didn't work for a reason.

Lisa Kudrow: I can't say enough about David Crane and Marta Kauffman. And just Marta on the floor when we would do camera blocking, we would say, "Did that seem like it worked?" And she would say, "I think we can play with that . . . Okay." And then she had it, and it was something that made the scene better, drove home the point with a joke. She was unbelievable on her feet with the actors.

David Schwimmer: I would give so much credit to David and Marta and the other writers, because they *really* invited our ideas. They created an atmosphere in which we could play *and fail* and pitch stuff, and because of that it wasn't about any individual, it was about all of us trying to come up with the funniest and the best and the most emotional material we could.

I had never experienced it outside my theater company in Chicago with people I'd known, like brothers and sisters, for twenty years. I had never experienced it, and not to that level. It even exceeded that because of the caliber of the writing and the ideas from the writers and the direction from Jimmy and others. It was thrilling to be part of, and it was hands down the best creative experience I've had professionally as an actor. That kind of collaboration with your director, with those writers, and with the other actors—it's a huge high, and it spoils you for life. It does.

Matt LeBlanc: There was a conversation I had early on, when the show was just starting to take shape, and I remember standing back and being as objective as I could about Joey and thinking, "This thing could go a long time. Does my character fit if it goes a long time?" Because in the beginning, I was hitting on the girls all the time.

Strictly out of self-preservation, I went to Marta and David and said, "Can I ask you guys something? I have an idea."

They said, "Yeah, sure."

I said, "What if Joey hits on every girl in New York but these three? What if I'm like a big brother to these three?" Of course, I didn't say, "Because I'm afraid that you're going to run out of stories for me. I'm gonna have to move out from across the hall."

We went in that direction, and then my guy fit in more. He became this sort of big brother to the group.

Lisa Kudrow: When we started shooting that first season, Jimmy said, "Use my dressing room to hang out." Because it was bigger. We would all hang out playing poker and bonding because I think we all understood that the point of the show was that we were family and best friends. We needed to hang out, get to know each other, and bond as quickly as possible, because that's the only way that the show was going to work.

Matt LeBlanc: It wasn't like we were in college together. We were on a giant fucking television show together. Everybody worked really hard. Lisa Kudrow said it best. She said that she worked harder on these relationships than she did on her marriage.

We really spent a lot of time if someone's feelings got hurt. "Oh, let's drop everything and fix that. And I'm sorry." Rule number one: get along. Everyone knew the importance of getting along the whole way through.

Lisa Kudrow: I was a little older, one year older than the next cast member. I got engaged during the first season. To me there was life, and that had to stay on its course. And then there was work. My husband, Michel, really got what the priorities had to be. He was the one who said, "Go to Vegas." And anytime I told him, "You can't be part of this," he would say, "Absolutely, I should not be part of this. You guys need to bond." He was unbelievable in getting that and why it was important.

David Schwimmer: We were all approximately the same age. We had a natural chemistry, creatively and professionally. We spent an *enormous* amount of time together those first several years. We wouldn't want to leave each other. We'd go out to dinner after work, or we'd go to lunch together, or play poker, or just play games. I think we were genuinely having the time of our lives, and also there was something very bonding about how scary the whole experience was. We had the other five, like a very protective cocoon.

Warren: One way in which *Friends* did resemble *Seinfeld* is that it really found its audience over the summer of 1995 in reruns. That's when the main title song, "I'll Be There for You" by the Rembrandts, exploded too.

Matt LeBlanc: It was that first season of reruns that did it. We were like number twenty-seven in the big grand scheme of things. It was that summer that we broke the top ten, or top five.

Warren: On January 28, 1996, after a particularly compelling Super Bowl (Dallas vs. Pittsburgh) that delivered a whopping 46.1 rating and 68 share, we played a special one-hour episode of *Friends* featuring guest appearances by Brooke Shields and Jean-Claude Van Damme.

Despite the fact that most of the country had already been eating, drinking, and watching television for hours, the *Friends* special delivered a 29.6 rating and a 46 share. No network had ever accomplished that. For the night, NBC averaged a 42.0 rating and a 62 share. It was the most watched night in television history, with approximately 140 million Americans tuning in (Nielsen Media Research).

David Schwimmer: For whatever reason, I was "the breakout." I was the guy who had the movie offers; everyone since then has had their time, their moment, but I was the first when the show started. And my agents were saying, "This is the time when you go in for a raise."

I knew—because all of us were friends at this point—that when we started, each of us on the show had a different contract. We were all paid differently. Some had low quotes, some had higher. So I knew that I wasn't the highest-paid actor on the show, but I wasn't the lowest. And I thought, "Okay, I'm being advised to go in for more money.

But for me, it goes against everything I truly believe in, in terms of ensemble. The six of us are all leads on the show. We are all here for the same amount of hours. The story lines are always balanced."

Matt LeBlanc: David was in the position to make the most money. He was the A-story. Ross and Rachel. He could have commanded alone more than anyone else, and David Schwimmer quoted the idea of socialist theater to us. Did he know ultimately there would be more value in that for all of us as a whole? I don't know. I think it was a genuine gesture from him, and I always say that. It was him.

David Schwimmer: They usually had three story lines going on at any given time. So I said to the group, "Here's the deal. I'm being advised to ask for more money, but I think, instead of that, we should all go in together. There's this expectation that I'm going in to ask for a pay raise. I think we should use this opportunity to talk openly about the six of us being paid the same.

"I don't want to come to work feeling that there's going to be any kind of resentment from anyone else in the cast down the line. I don't want to be in their position"—I said the name of the lowest paid actor on the show—"coming to work, doing the same amount of work, and feeling like someone else is getting paid twice as much. That's ridiculous. Let's just make the decision now. We're all going to be paid the same, for the same amount of work."

John Agoglia: We convinced ourselves that we'd be better off with the cast if we recognized their success early instead of waiting until their contracts ran out. Chemistry was crucial to that show, and it was important to keep the cast happy. We started giving them raises as they were going along. At one point David Schwimmer's mother convinced the cast to negotiate as a group. She's a prominent divorce attorney. Her license plate is "Ex Barracuda."

David Schwimmer: I thought it was significant for us to become a mini-union. I was pushing for it. A union of the six of us. Because there began to be a lot of decisions that had to be made by the group in terms of publicity.

That was actually a by-product of how the impulse originated, which was from my ensemble theater. We all paid dues. We were all waiting tables and doing other jobs, but we all paid the same amount of dues, and we were all paid out equally. That idea was really important to me.

Harold Brook: The problem was how *much* they wanted to be treated the same. The numbers were insane when it came time to renew their contracts. The night before we were going to announce the schedule, I was in the bathroom at a restaurant and got a call from Warner Bros. "It's starting," they said. The negotiation started around 10:00 p.m. and closed around 3:00 a.m. We had two promos made—one was the season finale, and one was the series finale.

Dick Wolf: When they made the *Friends* deal, the $100,000 apiece deal, I was pretty upset. What I would have done was come out the first day, say I was disappointed the cast had chosen to negotiate in the press, and I had the unpleasant news that Matt LeBlanc wouldn't be on the show next year. I guarantee that you'd never have gotten to a second name.

Harold Brook: We didn't say "pass" a lot. It's a ploy, and a lot of times we couldn't back it up. You do it once, maybe it wins. You do it twice, it isn't really a pass. Also the actor could be in another show at another network in a heartbeat.

David Schwimmer: That negotiation made us realize that the six of us *should* be making decisions as one and looking out for each other.

It's just like a union, that's all. We're all equals, and by the way every decision was a democratic vote.

I didn't want to come to work feeling like people are resenting me for earning more, or me resenting anyone else for earning more. It's just not the environment I want to work in. I think everyone feels that way.

Warren: An odd by-product for me of the success of *Friends, Frasier,* and *Seinfeld* and our other shows was that I found myself called upon to give more and more depositions. Our lawyers explained it this way: "That's because you finally have successes, so people want to sue and claim that they own part of those successes. You never did depositions before because no one watched your shows, and no one cared to sue." I said, "Oh, okay, so this is a good thing."

Along about that time, I also discovered I had an impersonator in New York. One morning when I was sitting at my desk in Burbank, my assistant Patty walked in with a great deal of attitude (even more than usual). As she dropped a stack of mail on my desk, she told me, "You should be ashamed."

On the top of the pile was a handwritten note from a woman in New York thanking me for a wonderful evening the week before. She had also sent along a necktie as a gift. The trouble was I had absolutely no idea who this woman could be, and—as I explained to Patty—I hadn't been in New York the previous week. Apparently, there was another Warren Littlefield out there.

Patty tracked the woman down. Her Warren Littlefield was tall and dark with a mustache. Not me at all. Along about this time, David Letterman was routinely defacing photographs of me on air, so it wouldn't have been all that difficult to figure out what I looked like. Fortunately, the phony Warren had been a perfect gentleman.

We got wind of him again a year or so later when he stood up the legendary agent Mike Ovitz for drinks in Manhattan. The grief came my way. I remember thinking to myself, "It must be nice to be president of NBC without any of the responsibilities."

Paul Reiser and Warren at a *Mad About You* wrap party. As Glenn Padnick remembers, *"Mad About You* was sort of the domestic version of *Seinfeld"* in NBC's eyes.

Paul Reiser (as Paul Buchman) and Helen Hunt (as Jaimie Buchman). Paul reminisces: "When I was writing the pilot, I met Helen Hunt at a dinner party. She was sharing a house with a good friend of my wife's. That evening we were talking about couples, and I turned to my wife and said, 'She'd be great.'"

Helen Hunt, Paul Reiser, and Lisa Kudrow (as Ursula, the waitress) on *Mad About You.* "Lisa told us she was going to audition for a new show. We told her good luck, but pilots never get picked up . . . *Friends,*" says Paul Reiser.

Kelsey Grammer (as Dr. Frasier Crane) and David Hyde Pierce (as Dr. Niles Crane). As NBC head of casting Lori Openden recalls, "There wasn't a brother in the original plot of the show. One of the casting directors who was working with the producers brought a picture of DHP to the producers and said, 'Look at this guy. He looks just like Kelsey.'"

"*Frasier* was important for me. The people I got to work with, the time we spent," says David Hyde Pierce, shown here with Jane Leeves (as Daphne Moon).

John Mahoney (as Martin Crane) with Moose (as Eddie the dog). As Kelsey recollects, "We'd killed Frasier's father off in the ninth year of *Cheers*. When Sam visited *Frasier*, he said, 'You told me your dad was dead.' I said, 'I lied.'"

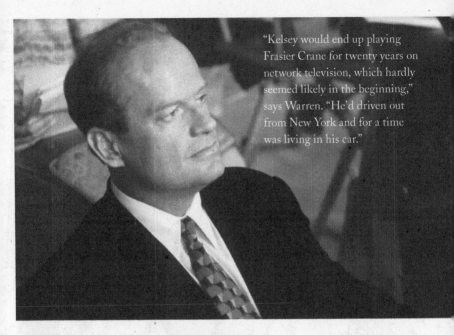

"Kelsey would end up playing Frasier Crane for twenty years on network television, which hardly seemed likely in the beginning," says Warren. "He'd driven out from New York and for a time was living in his car."

One morning Warren showed up at a table reading for an episode of *Frasier* and tried to make himself useful. As John Pike says, "When it came to *Cheers* and *Frasier*, both sides of the equation really needed each other. It was an interesting marriage of network and production."

(Right) Frasier creators David Angell, Peter Casey, and David Lee. Casey recalls, "When we edited the [*Frasier*] pilot, we were seven minutes long. We cut it as much as we could, and we were still a minute long. NBC gave us the extra minute. They took fifteen seconds off every other show that night."

The cast of *Friends*, from left to right, Courteney Cox (as Monica Geller), Matthew Perry (as Chandler Bing), Jennifer Aniston (as Rachel Green), David Schwimmer (as Ross Geller), Lisa Kudrow (as Phoebe Buffay), and Matt LeBlanc (as Joey Tribbiani). NBC's pilot season of 1994, which included both *Friends* and *ER*, is legendary.

David Schwimmer (shown here directing an episode) remembers that he could feel that *Friends* "was something special immediately in the first rehearsals."

Friends co-creator David Crane, pictured here (on the right) with fellow co-creator Marta Kauffman and executive producer Kevin Bright, says the show was about "that point in your life when your friends are your family."

Lisa Kudrow remembers her audition: "At one point I even said, 'You know, I'm more like Rachel.'" And they told me, 'No. You're this quirky girl.'"

Once when gassing up his car on Sunset Boulevard, Warren ran into Jennifer: "She asked me, 'Will it ever happen for me?' God, I wanted it to. I didn't care what it would take—Rachel was the role for her."

On getting the part of Joey, Matt LeBlanc says it was between him and a guy dressed like a cowboy. "I looked at him and thought, 'One of us is *way* off the mark. God, I hope it's you.'"

(Right) Marta Kauffman recalls, "The Ross and Rachel thing was fascinating. My rabbi, when I dropped my daughter off for Hebrew school, would stop me and say, 'When are you going to get them together?'"

Writer and executive producer John Wells (front center) with the cast of *ER*, clockwise: George Clooney (as Dr. Doug Ross), Eriq La Salle (as Dr. Peter Benton), Gloria Reuben (as Jeanie Boulet), Julianna Margulies (as Nurse Carol Hathaway), Sherry Stringfield (as Dr. Susan Lewis), Anthony Edwards (as Dr. Mark Greene), and Noah Wyle (as Dr. John Carter). Warren explains, "The original *ER* script was what is commonly known as a trunk job. By the time it came into our hands at NBC—in 1993—it was already a good twenty years old."

During the casting of the *ER* pilot, John Wells recalls, "George Clooney begged me for a part. George was the first person to audition. He came after me for it."

"There I was, thirty years old, and I considered myself finished. And then I had the best acting experience an actor could have on *ER*. I fell in love with acting again because of *ER*," says Anthony Edwards of his experience playing Dr. Mark Greene.

At the time his agent sent him the *ER* pilot, Noah Wyle only wanted to do movies, but, as he says, "A funny thing happened on the way to my film career."

The *ER* cast during a table read for the live episode "Ambush." Noah Wyle admits, "We were absolutely merciless on each other in terms of the quality of the performances we were giving. We would be brutally honest, and it galvanized us into a really tight ensemble."

Anthony Edwards, Julianna Margulies, George Clooney, and Warren at the May 1994 upfronts in New York. At the time, Anthony Edwards remembers, "Ohlmeyer was saying, 'Nobody will watch *ER*. There are too many characters, and it doesn't make any sense.'"

(Below) An off-camera moment with the *ER* cast and crew during the taping of a live episode. As Eriq La Salle says of the show, "We accomplished the most amazing things, we did it as a team, we did it as a group."

The character of Carol Hathaway was originally killed off in the pilot of *ER*. But Julianna Margulies, shown here with George and Anthony (directing), happily recalls getting a message from George that said, "'We don't think Carol Hathaway is going to die.' That's an actor's favorite line to hear on the phone."

Quentin Tarantino directing an episode of *ER*. For ten of its fifteen years, *ER* was a top-ten-rated show.

The cast of *3rd Rock from the Sun*, from left to right, French Stewart (as Harry Solomon), John Lithgow (as Dr. Dick Solomon), Kristen Johnston (as Sally Solomon), and Joseph Gordon-Levitt (as Tommy Solomon). *"3rd Rock from the Sun*—that was crazy," says Karey Burke, former executive vice president of prime-time series, in remembering the "openness to everything" at NBC.

On taking the part of alien Dick Solomon, John Lithgow says, "There were two things that *completely* sold me. One was the fact that on a dime, the four actors could sing Cole Porter like Manhattan Transfer."

Will & Grace creators David Kohan and Max Mutchnick (back row) with Megan Mullally (as Karen Walker), Eric McCormack (as Will Truman), executive producer/director Jimmy Burrows, Debra Messing (as Grace Adler), and Sean Hayes (as Jack McFarland). As Kohan tells it, "NBC gave us the keys to the car, and they said, 'If you dent it, we'll take it away.'"

At the time, the creators of *Will & Grace* "didn't believe a network would put a show on with a gay lead." They couldn't have been more wrong.

(Above) Megan Mullally recalls that she was instantly taken with Sean Hayes: "I was like, 'Oh my God, who is that cute little elfin person?'"

(Right) Debra Messing says of the chemistry between Eric McCormack and her during the audition process, "Immediately there was just this click. You don't know why it happens, but it was just instant. We were like, 'All right, let's play.'"

"I remember the cast going over to Max's house to do the very first reading of the script, and we were crying we were laughing so hard," says Debra Messing, shown here with Eric McCormack and Megan Mullally at a table read-through.

"I remember being asked, more than once, 'What world do you live in to think America wants to watch this gay TV show?'" says David Nevins. It's hard to believe, looking at this photo of the cast (including Shelley Morrison as Rosario) celebrating the show's hundredth episode.

The *Seinfeld* cast takes a bow. In May 1998, the last episode of *Seinfeld* aired. It marked the beginning of the end of Must See TV.

At the end of 1998, after twenty years at NBC, Warren was fired. Perhaps Sean Hayes puts it best when he says, "There was this guy, this Warren Littlefield, who took us through this huge success at NBC, and then suddenly he was gone."

That's the good and the bad. Here's the ugly. More and more, I was the recognizable name and face of NBC Entertainment. One day at the height of our Must See success, the mail room received a suspicious package addressed to me. Security evacuated our Burbank offices and called in the bomb squad. A robot was used to dispose of what turned out to be an actual explosive device. The police told me it resembled the sort of bomb preferred by the Unabomber, Ted Kaczynski. Fortunately for us all, my specimen had been clumsily made and wouldn't have exploded. But even still, I was just running a TV network, and somebody wanted to kill me over that? I was tough but it was a sobering afternoon. I remember ducking into John Agoglia's office and all but breaking down.

So it wasn't all laughs at the network, but it was mostly laughs, thank God.

Marta Kauffman: We didn't experience the success of the show the way the cast did. We could walk through the airport, and we'd see pictures of them on the magazines, but that wasn't us.

Lisa Kudrow: When we were on *Oprah*, I think that first summer, she showed us all of these people in Internet cafés. People were online talking about the show, which was the first time that people were using the Internet to connect with each other, like the new watercooler. I thought, "Okay, this is something then. This is a big deal." That's when I got it. She was telling us this stuff, and we were watching their little film that they'd made, and she was like, "You all look like you don't know what I'm talking about. You have to know." And we just went, "No, but this is great news."

David Schwimmer: I had never been a part of the entertainment industry. I didn't know anyone famous. I'd never seen it. I had a girlfriend at the time, and I remember walking down the street with her holding her hand, when some girls came up, pushed her out of the way, and asked for my number. They were like, "Oh my God, can you come out with us right now?" As if my girlfriend just didn't exist. I found it *very* difficult to handle.

Matt LeBlanc: I remember I was living in an apartment in Beachwood Canyon, which, ironically, ended up being the apartment building that they used for the opening credits on *Joey*. I had to move *so* quickly. It was unbelievable. All of a sudden the people in the building were banging on my door. People knew I lived there.

I was like, "I've got to get a house. I need a house with a gate, because I need to be able to hide." It's funny, nowadays people that are famous get chased by the paparazzi. They have this fame, but they don't have the money to hide from it. We were really fortunate that we were compensated well enough to be able to turn the switch off, as much as one can. Kind of disappear. Barricade yourself in.

Lisa Kudrow: We did a photo shoot for *Entertainment Weekly*. When we walked out of it—our cars were all the way across the street—and there were tons of paparazzi, and it was nighttime, and we were blinded by all the flashing. It was scary, because we hadn't had that before. It was unnerving, because they yell at you. It's more of an assault than any kind of congratulations or "we love you." That's not ever how it feels. So that was jarring, and then I think all of us understood, "Oh, I get why people get so antagonistic with paparazzi."

David Schwimmer: For me, the fame is something I've wrestled with and struggled with since it happened. I don't think I responded very well to the sudden celebrity, the sudden fame, and the loss of privacy. There were several moments that were quite traumatic for me. I remember in the early days of just going to the airport and walking to my gate when I heard bloodcurdling screams, and I thought someone was being killed. Before I knew it, a group of girls was running at me and literally grabbing me and wouldn't let me go.

Lisa Kudrow: Fame doesn't cure whatever is going on inside of you, however you feel about yourself. The lucky thing was that the six of us had each other to go through it with. All we would talk about is, "What about people who have this and they don't have you and you, and they are just on their own dealing with this?"

Matt LeBlanc: I don't think America can relate to celebrity and wealth. You become an alien, basically. They're not going to have pity for you. They're not going to have compassion for you. You need to represent the common man, or they can't identify with it. They're like, "I really can't feel bad for you in your big mansion." Or, "Aw, your Ferrari had a flat."

David Schwimmer: As an actor, the training I received was that I walk through the world as an observer of life and of people. That's my training. My job is to actually be looking out all the time and watching people. But the effect of celebrity on me was that I suddenly found myself with a baseball cap, with my head down, hiding everywhere I went. And I realized that I was going to have to figure out a way to still be an actor filled with wonder at the world and curious about life and watching people. It's like those two couldn't coexist. It's been very difficult to navigate that.

Lisa Kudrow: I think before you are famous, you think, "Oh, if you're famous, you're loved and adored. And then maybe I can love and adore myself. If I'm good enough for the general public, then I might be good enough for myself." Then, when you really experience that attention and everyone cares what you're doing and wants pictures of you, it doesn't feel like a warm hug. It *really* feels like an assault. Then not long after you start to realize, "This has *almost* nothing to do with me, and I better do the work."

At first it was all thrilling. I remember going to the Golden Globes, and I was at a table with Kathy Bates. Then you learn soon enough that you're meeting these people, but you're not friends. It's just meeting people. That's all it is.

Matt LeBlanc: I never set out to be a role model. I set out to pay the rent.

Warren: For the first time in my memory at NBC, we had to worry about overexposure. We became gatekeepers for the *Friends* cast. Everybody wanted a piece of them—an electronic interview, a photo shoot, something. We realized the cast was so white-hot that we had to pull back, to help protect both them and their show.

To their credit, they all just kept their heads down and worked. Worked hard. The writers and actors on *Friends* were notoriously particular about what made it onto the air. A *Friends* shoot night could extend well into the small hours of the morning.

David Crane: Our hours were crazy. There were so many mornings when we were still finishing the rewrites. We'd get notes from the studio and the network.

Marta Kauffman: But it was *our* notes that killed us. We knew we had to listen to the audience. Their silence tells you a lot. Laughing in good and bad ways. Laughing at setups instead of jokes.

David Crane: We also felt everyone's opinion was valid. There was no hierarchy. It made everything better, but longer too. Sometimes we lost our energy because we took so much time trying to find a better joke when we should have just moved on.

Warren: Audiences on shoot night—and shoot night can run for many hours—are kept engaged by people like Mark Sweet, who has been warming up crowds for network shows since 1981.

Mark Sweet: The bleachers hold a couple of hundred people. You've got hours of time to fill, and doing stand-up doesn't translate well in that environment. I try to make the audience members feel that the taping is an event and they're valued. I did the whole run of *Coach*, the whole run of *Everybody Loves Raymond*. On hiatus from *Coach*, I'd go over and do *Cheers*.

One of the writers from *Coach* went over to *Friends*, and I went with him. That show used to go until one or two in the morning. They'd have to bring in a whole new audience, always had one in reserve.

David Crane: We'd walk out after every episode and say, "There's another one that didn't suck." And we meant it.

Marta Kauffman: We only had problems with standards. For a long time, we couldn't show a condom wrapper.

David Crane: The rules kept changing. For the first three years we could say "penis." Then we couldn't say "penis." Then we could say "penis" again.

Marta Kauffman: They're masturbating on *Seinfeld*, and we can't show a condom wrapper.

Warren: That made me crazy. I had a lot of battles with broadcast standards over that. What could be more socially responsible than these characters practicing safe sex?

David Crane: *Seinfeld* had different rules. Apparently, you can masturbate at nine but not at eight.

Lisa Kudrow: I think it was after our fifth or sixth year where it just got easier because we insisted. We had enough power at that point. "We only need *this* much time to get it done."

We insisted on starting in the afternoon. Marta said, "We won't find an audience at three." We told her, "People plan vacations around this show. Let's try." It worked, and then we weren't done at two in the morning. It was a lot easier.

Matt LeBlanc: It was sometimes hard to get through scenes because the crowd knew what you were going to say before you could say it. We would do it just for kicks sometimes. With a joke, you could get ten laughs out of it. They knew every arrow that was in each of our quivers.

David Crane: Then in season eight or nine we had Joey fall for Rachel, and that scared everybody. She was pregnant. The actors freaked out. Matt kept saying, "It's wrong. It's like I want to be with my sister." We said, "Yes, it's absolutely wrong. That's why we have to do it." You can't just keep spinning the same plates. You have to go places where you're not expected to go.

Matt LeBlanc: It felt wildly inappropriate. That's how close we all were to the character. I was like, "That's Rachel. She was supposed to be with Ross. Wait a minute." Everybody got super-defensive about the whole thing.

We went to David and Marta as a group and said, "We're really concerned about this. It doesn't feel right. We have a problem with it."

David said, "It's like playing with fire, and then you put it down, and you go, 'Remember when we played with that fire?' We're aware of everything. The feelings that you're feeling, we're feeling them too, and we like it."

David Crane: Once it actually started, it was heartbreaking because it couldn't go anywhere. It was always going to be Ross and Rachel.

Marta Kauffman: The Ross and Rachel thing was fascinating. My rabbi, when I dropped my daughter off for Hebrew school, would stop me and say, "When are you going to get them together?"

David Crane: From a technical standpoint, it was really challenging to keep them apart without pissing off the audience. In the pilot, Ross says to Rachel, "Can I ask you out sometime?" We go through an entire season, twenty-four episodes, and he never asks her out. Every time it's about to happen—we brought in the Italian guy, we threw a cat on his back—we kept asking ourselves, "Will they let us go one more?"

Then they got together and broke up.

Marta Kauffman: And got married and broke up. Their fights were some of my favorite moments.

David Crane: The episode where Ross and Rachel are on a break and Ross sleeps with the Xerox girl, and the whole episode is in the living room with the other four locked in the bedroom. It's really sad, and we kept going to the bedroom for funny. That's probably one of my favorite episodes.

For the two of us, the emotional stuff was what sustained us.

Marta Kauffman: We did not want to go out on the bottom. We wanted to feel more like it was time for your child to go to college, not die.

David Crane: We wrote three last seasons. It looked for a while like season eight was the last season. Then season nine. Warner Bros. told us this has to be the last season. Two days later, they come back and say, "Jeff Zucker stepped up, and it's not the last season." Amazing reversal.

Marta Kauffman: At that point, we said, "Season ten it is."

David Crane: You can't keep writing the last season. You have to know where you're going and go there.

Having seen the *Seinfeld* finale and knowing when you depart from who you are, it doesn't make the audience happy, let's deliver to the audience what they want and what they've earned.

Marta Kauffman: Everybody knew where we were going to end up. Ross and Rachel were going to be together somehow. We just had to make it entertaining.

David Crane: We talked about doing a qualified ending . . . they're not *together* together, but there's the hope they can be together. We said, "Fuck it. We've jerked these people off for ten years. Who are we kidding? We've just got to do it well."

Lisa Kudrow: I felt like we could have gone longer. David and Marta were saying, "It is getting harder for Rachel and Ross, coming up with reasons why they're not together." And then ultimately, it's a good thing that we were done, because sometimes you have to be pushed out of the nest.

Matt LeBlanc: That whole ending, that was a rough two weeks. We went away for Christmas for two weeks, and then we came back for two final weeks to shoot the one-hour finale. I had quit smoking for four years, and in that final two weeks I started smoking again because we were so aware that our time together was coming to an end. "Yes, I'll talk to you. Yes, I'll always know you, but I won't know you like this. I won't see you every day, all day. Eat lunch together every day. To have this awesome, *awesome* experience every week. It's coming to an end."

So in those final two weeks, we would steal away these little moments. "Hey, let's go hang out. Let's go sit in my room." It was really . . . a lot of Kleenex.

David Schwimmer: You just knew intuitively that that's how it had to end, with Ross and Rachel together. It was a romantic comedy, so it must end—as in great Shakespeare—with the lovers together. So the challenge is how the writers are able to create enough obstacles to sustain over ten years.

I really sympathize. I think it's incredibly difficult, because I don't think anyone expected it to go for ten years. So for David and Marta to rise to the challenge of making sure every moment, and every choice, and every decision made by this group of writers—in conjunction and collaboration with the actors—kept this tension going without upsetting the audience or driving them crazy.

Matt LeBlanc: There's only five people in the world who know exactly what being on *Friends* was like, other than me. There's five of them. David, Matthew, Lisa, Courteney, and Jen. That's it. Marta, David were close, but when they left the stage, no one knew what they did. We could never leave the stage, metaphorically speaking. Still can't. Still on that stage. That will follow us around forever.

Sean Hayes: I remember when I was a young person watching *Friends*, I thought, "This is how we talk." I don't see anything out there now that's like that.

David Hyde Pierce: I remember going over to the *Friends* set before it went on the air to watch Jimmy shoot. It was an episode where David Schwimmer got hit in the mouth with a hockey puck. It's great to have that memory of that as yet unborn megahit.

Matt LeBlanc: More important than anything else is the look on people's faces when you cross paths with them in the street, or in the store, or in the grocery line. You can always tell that you were—maybe still are, maybe always will be—a part of their family. Movies have this thing where it's an event. You get dressed up, you go to dinner, and you go to the movies. You're outside of your element. But with television, people are watching you in bed, at their kitchen table eating. You're in their house.

I did not want it to end.

10

County General

Warren: I was on the phone with Bob Wright one day, and he sounded even more despondent than usual, so I asked him what was wrong. "We lost Diane Sawyer," he told me. Diane Sawyer was a rising star at CBS News, and she was in play for her next contract. Bob had had several meetings with her and was very hopeful of landing her at NBC. But she went to ABC, where she remains today.

I told Bob I was sorry, that she was great but there would always be someone else. That's when Bob explained to me that his plan had been to give Diane a newsmagazine show stripped from Monday to Friday, every night at 10:00. If Bob had been successful at wooing Diane, there would never have been an *ER* on NBC.

The original *ER* script was what is commonly known as a trunk job. By the time it came into our hands at NBC—in 1993—it was already a good twenty years old.

John Wells: Tony Krantz, packaging agent at CAA, called and told me Tony Thomopoulos [president of Amblin Television] had been going through the vaults at Amblin looking for material that might work for television. He thought the Michael Crichton script was something that might work. I'd been working on *China Beach*, so I had some medical background. Tony wanted me to take a look at it and see if there was anything in it.

Michael had written it. Steven Spielberg had said he wanted to direct it. Steven had worked in an emergency room as a kid in Phoenix or Tucson. His parents had made him volunteer because they wanted him to be a doctor. He had signed on to direct it sometime in the early eighties. As is his practice, he takes ownership of anything he might want to direct, which is how his name ends up on all this stuff over time.

Noah Wyle: We heard Steven wanted Michael to write *Jurassic Park II* and Michael didn't want to do it, so he dug up the *ER* script and said, "Why don't we do this instead?"

Warren: The two Tonys (Tony Thomopoulos and Tony Krantz) set up a meeting at NBC, bringing in Michael Crichton, John Wells, and Steven Spielberg. They presented Michael's feature script based on his early years in a Boston ER. They believed it was a basis for a medical drama television series. They certainly had my attention.

David Nevins: My job was head of drama development the summer *ER* was developed. It was the summer *Jurassic Park* was the big movie. An agent hyped the Michael Crichton script to me. He was incredibly vague, and the script showed up on a Friday.

Warren: It was about 180 pages, and it was all over the place. It probably had over a hundred characters. I remember getting to a scene in the script where there was a basketball game on a TV in a hospital waiting room. Tommy Heinsohn was handling the ball for the Celtics. Holy shit, as a big basketball fan I knew he had stopped playing in 1965—this was an old script.

Biggest author, biggest director. They wanted a series commitment.

David Nevins: We didn't see how we could go wrong with a two-hour movie, but they turned it down. Nobody bit on their ask for thirteen episodes, and Warren stayed after them. Maybe two months went by, and Warren kept calling them.

Warren: The ask had gone down to six episodes.

David Nevins: Crichton decided to rewrite the script on two conditions. No network notes and Crichton would take one pass to update the medicine. He ended up doing a dozen passes of the script with John Wells. He just kept whittling it down.

John Wells: It was a big, old mimeographed script. What the series was was in there, but it was still left over. The nurses were called "nurse" on every page. The doctors were all white, and they were all male. I remember thinking there was a really good idea in the script.

Michael was a remarkably talented researcher. He was interested in a million things, but character development wasn't really his strong point. Michael and I got together for lunch, and we had a very frank conversation about what I thought were the shortcomings of the piece, and he was very receptive. We hit it off.

Warren: Like John Wells, we could see potential in Crichton's script. It was either a glass half-full or a glass half-empty, but it was certainly half. Sure, the material was a mess, but these doctors felt both real and heroic. Don Ohlmeyer took a different view. He insisted we were just star fucking. At the time, I didn't have a programming answer for Thursday night at 10:00. *L.A. Law* was clearly getting to the end of its run. As much as I respected a project that I developed with the feature film talent Barry Levinson, *Homicide: Life on the Street*, in the few times we tried it Thursdays at 10:00, it certainly wasn't a blockbuster. When I asked Don if he wanted *Policewoman Centerfold* or *ER*, I got a reluctant okay to pursue the latter.

I kept pounding away at Amblin, Warner Bros. (because of John

Wells), and CAA. I told them NBC was their best bet. CBS was doing a new medical drama with David Kelley. ABC really didn't have the 10:00 p.m. real estate available, and Fox didn't program at 10:00 p.m.

I was offering a two-hour pilot, and if they did it well, it would probably be on Thursday night. I tried to sweeten it by saying if we couldn't agree on casting, they would have the final word. I had no idea if I could back that up, but I said it. Just go, make your vision. How can you argue with that?

John Wells: Michael Crichton called me up once we had the offer from NBC. We'd become friendly. He apologized for taking up so much of my time, but he really didn't think it was worth his time, and he didn't want to do it.

Then I got another call from Michael a few months later, and he said if he didn't have to do much work and NBC wanted to do the show, then he'd be willing. I said I'd need a certain amount of leeway, because we hadn't worked on the script. I've got to start casting tomorrow. I've got to hire a director. You're just going to have to say, "Go do it," if you feel comfortable. Michael was kind of a control freak.

Warren: Because Crichton had been so slow to commit, everything had to happen fast from finishing the script, to casting, to shooting the pilot. I did ask them to change the location to anywhere but Boston. I didn't want to be compared to *St. Elsewhere*. The bar was just too high.

John Wells: We cast it up in a hurry. I knew Rod Holcomb [the director] from *China Beach*, and he came on, and we started casting like crazy. I was rewriting during that time, connecting the characters up, adding the love story between Hathaway and Ross. It was all in there, but it was a lot of Michael's impressions. Lots of anecdotes that didn't entirely connect up.

Warren: Out of necessity came innovation.

John Wells: We had to construct a way to do the show for the money, which had a lot to do with the style of the show. We had to shoot a lot and shoot fast. Rod said here are the two things I need: a four-walled set and a Steadicam.

Warren: We talked to Rod about the visceral quality of the script and the need to have the drama feel gritty and real, not melodramatic.

To add to the pressure, we'd learned that CBS's new medical series was aimed for Thursday nights at ten in the fall of 1994. It was David Kelley's *Chicago Hope* starring Mandy Patinkin and Adam Arkin.

John Wells: We had a conversation about how to distinguish the show, which came partly from knowing *Chicago Hope* had already been picked up. I got my hands on a *Chicago Hope* script. I read it and realized pretty quickly we needed to be completely different from that. We decided we wanted to take people into this world.

There was an artifice for drama that developed first at Universal but came into full fruition at MTM. It was very stylized but felt real. It's what Bochco was doing and what NBC was doing on *St. Elsewhere*. It felt real compared to what had come before. That had become the audience's expectation of what *real* was. We wanted to make *ER* feel like it was realer than what you could get someplace else.

I wasn't sure we were right, by any means. It ended up working out fine, but we were using real medical dialogue without explaining it at any length, or explaining it at all. The hope was the audience would feel like it got dropped in a real place. We depended on the audience's visual literacy. Then we could do a soap opera in the midst of all that.

At one point, Michael Crichton said to me, "What the hell is this series going to be? A soap opera?"

I told him, "Never say that out loud again."

Every long-running dramatic show is a soap opera. That's what people care about and get hooked on. That's what they come back for and watch for years and years.

David Nevins: We were wondering what we were going to promote, with so many stories. Your every instinct as a programmer is a big promotable story line. A lot of people believed we were going to get our asses kicked by *Chicago Hope*.

Warren: The casting sessions for *ER* were memorable. Anthony Edwards's Dr. Greene was the first part cast, and his remarkable performance set a very high standard for the actors who followed him. Maybe we had something here.

Julianna Margulies: We weren't known actors but for Anthony Edwards, and he was mostly known for *Top Gun*.

Harold Brook: On the Must See TV shows, I don't think we ever negotiated where we signed somebody and thought, "We'll have to kill ourselves." We had an Aaron Spelling soap opera called *Titans*. There was an actor up for the lead. He had no quotes, but we were told we had to get this guy. The guy wanted $40,000 an episode. No reason for it, but we signed him. A week later, I got a call saying we had to hire an acting coach for him. Bad deal.

Lori Openden: They brought in Anthony Edwards to read in my office, and it's still one of the best auditions I've ever seen. He walked in and nailed it, so we wanted everybody to be as good as Anthony Edwards.

John Wells: Tony Edwards came in, and he'd never considered doing television.

Anthony Edwards: I knew when I read the part that I could see who Dr. Greene was. It reminded me of the beginning of *The Right Stuff*. The voice from the cockpit. You want to hear the guy who loves flying. That was Dr. Greene. He loved medicine.

I couldn't imagine anybody else playing Dr. Greene. I didn't know who else was up for the role. I didn't ask. I'd been in and out of NBC a lot for TV and network movies. I'd been acting since I was sixteen, so I didn't have anxiety. I just knew it was right.

David Nevins: I remember crying at Anthony Edwards's reading, the first time I'd ever cried at a casting session.

Anthony Edwards: I had talked to Michael Crichton at a Christmas party, and I remember telling him that I was done with acting. There I was, thirty years old, and I considered myself finished. And then I had the best acting experience an actor could have on *ER*.

I never felt anxious about getting the role. It was meant to be. I fell in love with acting again because of *ER*.

John Wells: George Clooney begged me for a part. George was the first person to audition. He came after me for it. I knew him from around the lot. He was always smart about knowing all of the assistants on the lot, so he knew what the material was. He'd give them flowers and candy and come around and flirt with them. Our second day in the office, George showed up and wouldn't leave until I'd let him audition. He did the "he's just a little kid!" scene. He had it memorized, and he didn't have a reputation for being a particularly disciplined actor.

George got his hands on the material and was like a dog with a bone.

Noah Wyle: George knew television inside and out. He'd done about twenty failed pilots.

John Wells: I've learned you can tell a lot about whether your show has a chance of succeeding by the actors who come into the room responding to the script. If it gets into the actor community that this is a show you want to be in, people you don't expect to show up start showing up. People you normally have to chase. There's an instinct in the actor community about what they want to be in.

Lori Openden: George Clooney pops off the screen. We knew him from *Sisters*. He was great with Sela Ward. It was on *Sisters* that he became a leading man.

John Wells: His name was Falcon or something. He had really long hair and rode a motorcycle.

Noah Wyle: When I started out, I signed with a wonderful small agency called Leading Artists. I signed when I was seventeen, and I told my agent I was interested in theater and film exclusively. I played that out for a couple of years, and then I signed with a management company, and they sent over the script for *ER*. It was a feature-length script, and I thought it was for a movie.

I called them all excited to go in and audition, and that's when they told me it was a TV show. I figured it wouldn't last. All these quality dramas, like *Brooklyn Bridge*, were getting canceled right out of the gate.

Lori Openden: Noah Wyle had a wonderful audition. Every Thursday night he would go over to his mom's house and watch the show with her.

Noah Wyle: I auditioned for John Levey and then John Wells, and they brought me into the network. I was up against one other guy, an actor named Raphael Sbarge. I remember seeing Raphael in the corner doing Tai Chi, and I thought, "Oh, fuck. He's going to be all Zenned out, and he's going to get the job." I started to spin myself into little concentric circles of paranoia.

Michael Crichton walks in, and he looks at Raphael and he looks at me, and he sees I'm melting down, and he walks over and says, "It's interesting, Noah, I was just reading a book about a woman who lived in Tibet four hundred years ago, and she was a potter. Nobody knows if this was something indigenous to the clay in the region where she worked or something to do with her kiln process, but the pottery she made is virtually indestructible, and a lot of it is still in practical use today. Good luck." And he turned around and walked away.

I thought, "What the fuck?" But what a great gift. He walked into the room and saw one actor centered and one actor uncentered and said, "I'm going to take this kid so far out of his head, I'm going to take him to Tibet four hundred years ago."

I went in for the audition, and I knew I'd nailed it. I got the job later that afternoon. I was sitting in my favorite coffee shop, and my agent called the coffee shop, and they called me to the phone.

Lori Openden: Sherry Stringfield had spent a year on *NYPD Blue*, and she was really good in the early years of *ER*.

John Wells: Sherry Stringfield was on the first year of *NYPD Blue*, and she was unhappy. I sort of knew her. She called and said she wanted to come in and play Lewis. I had to call Steven Bochco and ask him if he was going to let her out of her contract or not. There was this long pause, and then he said, "I hope you know what you're getting into."

Lori Openden: Julianna Margulies had had a role on *Homicide*. She got hired for the pilot of *ER*, and she got killed off in the pilot. Once the show got picked up, we wanted her, and she had a choice between *ER* and *Homicide*. Good choice.

John Wells: On *ER*, her character was supposed to die.

Julianna Margulies: I died in the pilot, so there wasn't a lot written about my character, Carol Hathaway. It's an actor's job to find his own backstory. She came into the pilot basically OD'd from pills. The research I did was on nurses.

It turned out my father had a distant cousin who'd committed suicide, and she was a nurse. I came to understand that ER nurses have a tremendous amount of pain because they're dumped with it all. Either they're left with a dead patient or a live one. To stave off depression, they sometimes get addicted to pills. They have the keys to the medicine cabinets.

Staying on *ER* was a decision sort of made for me because I wanted to be a part of a brand-new show. And I had George Clooney calling my answering machine saying, "You'd be silly to pass up this opportunity." With *Homicide*, the show had been on for four years. I knew that I was coming with the idea to help someone else's character wake up. With Carol Hathaway, I'd get to create who she would be. I was twenty-six years old. My God, what an opportunity.

I had a message from George. He told me he'd been sitting with Warren and John Wells at the upfronts, and they said, "We don't think Carol Hathaway is going to die."

"Okay, maybe you're not dead." That's an actor's favorite line to hear on the phone.

Lori Openden: We still hadn't found Dr. Benton. The producers wanted Michael Beach, but we kept saying no. He ended up on *Third Watch*. I was watching a pilot we'd done a few years before, a soapy kind of thing, and Eriq La Salle was in the pilot. I just happened to see him.

Eriq La Salle: I was doing a Warner Bros. project in Portland. It was called *Beyond Suspicion*. It was a cop show. I was one of the detectives on the squad with maybe an average of ten lines per episode. My best friend is Michael Beach, and so Michael Beach called me and said, "Hey, man, I just read this amazing pilot. It's called *ER*, and there's a really good role for a brother in there . . . blah, blah, blah." I was like, "Oh, great. I'm up in Portland, and I've got nothing to do." I called my agent, and she sent it up to me.

So as I read the pilot, I thought Michael Crichton and John Wells did something interesting. I don't think Benton was ever described as an African American, and I tried not to think the role was *too good* for an African American to play.

Warren: At the network, we liked Michael Beach for the part of Dr. Benton, but we hadn't said yes to him yet. We hadn't said no to him either. We didn't know exactly who we were looking for, but we weren't ready to sign off on Michael Beach.

I was hoping they wouldn't play that "we have final say on casting" card.

Eriq La Salle: So I get to the end of the script, and I'm like, "Ah, that's a really good script." But I kept looking for the *smaller* roles, and fortunately the men were all written *very* strong: the Greene character, the Ross character, the Carter character. So as far as regulars went, all of them were strong. I thought, "This is a great script. That Benton character, that's the best character in the piece. He's the most dynamic."

So I called up my agent, and I said, "I'm sorry, which role is the 'black' role?" And she said, "The Benton role." And I was like, "Get out of here!" So now I'm going crazy. I said, "You've got to get me in on this thing." And she says, "Yeah, I've been working on it." So at this stage, the network had gone through a few different levels. The actors that I normally went in with on projects had all gone through. All of my friends had gone through. Michael Beach was John Wells's first choice, up until that point.

Lori Openden: Eriq La Salle is a little off-putting when you meet him. He has a cold exterior, but that was right for the part. It was just timing and chance.

Eriq La Salle: I had a couple of days to prepare. Maybe four or five years earlier, I did a ten o'clock medical show with Dick Wolf. It was called *The Human Factor* with John Mahoney for CBS. I still had the scrubs, so I came in wearing scrubs, and I said, "Look, I'm going for it." It was really no thought process. I was just doing it. And people started making a big deal of that, but right away I was just like, "I know this guy. I know who he is. I'm just going for it." So I came in, in scrubs, and actors were looking at me kind of weird, and when I walked in the room, I just remember people perking up.

Warren: I can remember that audition as if it were yesterday. Eriq took the room. There was just a collective "Yes!" We had seen strong actors do their interpretation of that role. And they were very good, very solid, but Eriq La Salle nailed it.

Eriq La Salle: Benton was never happy with just saying what a medical procedure was. Benton had to be able to say it in half the time that everyone else said it. He had to rattle this stuff off. So I knew when I was studying, I was like, "You're about to create *a lot* of work for yourself, for a long time. Because once you establish this, that's who he is. You can never go back."

Warren: Our thought in the room was "We're a cast now. Thank God we held out." It was a really triumphant feeling as the filmmakers went off to see if they could put this thing together and actually make it.

John Wells: We still had a 160-page script, and we only had seventeen or eighteen days to do it. We were going to be doing lots of 12- and 13-page days. The normal pace is much lower than that.

We found a hospital emergency room to dress. We pre-lit it and brought the Steadicam up and started shooting like crazy.

Anthony Edwards: I didn't understand the script when I first read it, but I knew it was real. We weren't going to explain medicine to people. We were just going to do it. In an emergency room, it's an emergency for everybody, whether you have a splinter in your finger or a heart attack.

I have no idea how we made that pilot. I never knew what door I was going in or out. Our job was to make it look easy. If it looked hard, you were doing it wrong.

Noah Wyle: On the pilot episode, George pulled us all into his trailer. He said, "Okay, guys, this is going to be different this time around. I've done a lot of shows, and what's killed all of them in one way or another is a lack of cohesion. This is the show that's going to do it differently. We're going to be nice to everybody. We're going to know our lines. We're going to be on time. We're not going to have any division between cast and crew. This is going to be a family." He just laid it all out there, and we were young enough and green enough to fall in lockstep behind him.

Eriq La Salle: We had to make people understand that there are no insignificant actors. It's a unit, and if you are caught not concentrating, you can compromise *everything*. We got everybody to buy into it. The principals anchored it, but one little cable could have made a huge difference. It was such synchronicity, just seeing how people were operating things, and cameras and dressing crew members up as doctors, just to make sure that we could just hide this thing. We could move this over here so that by the time the camera ended up on the actor, they were able to speak. It was an *ensemble* effort that you were proud to be a part of.

Noah Wyle: We were absolutely merciless on each other in terms of the quality of the performances we were giving when we screened the episodes just for us every Wednesday afternoon before they aired on Thursday. We would be brutally honest, and it galvanized us into a really tight ensemble.

Eriq La Salle: When you're doing a show of that magnitude, that pilot, that kind of pace, you don't have a lot of time. As a director, when I cast actors, I cast actors based on two simple principles: Do I believe in your talent? And will you screw me up at two o'clock on a Friday afternoon with a big debate? Will we have to talk about everything or can we just go, when the crew is tired and everyone is ready to go? I think Rod Holcomb [the director] had arrived at that point where "we've got to move, we got to get the best work we can and move on, and these six actors are the ones that are getting me there." We didn't hold up production. That pilot moved because everyone showed up knowing that we had *a lot* of stuff to do. *A lot.*

My first day of work, I was in every single scene, because they had already started shooting, and they kept pushing the Benton.

Noah Wyle: I assumed the attractive thing about my part was that everybody else started at such a high level of proficiency—they all had to be established, credible doctors—while my guy was the new guy. He was dropping trays of piss on himself, and he was going to botch up a stitch or two, so he was comic relief for the first few episodes.

Eriq La Salle: I think it was literally my second day of shooting when I had to show Noah around. It was a three-page scene where I am saying 80 percent of the dialogue. "In this room we have this, and here we have this machine . . ." I had to hit it hard because I'm testing to see how smart he is. I *want* him intimidated. I *want* to see if he's going to crack, and you can't do that by spoon-feeding him. But if I can overwhelm him, then I know what kind of guy I have. If I can't overwhelm him, then I know what kind of guy I have.

That commitment created extra work for me, because every single speech after that became "How fast can I say it and how clear can I say it?" With strong conviction and clarity. It was an extra hour or two of studying each night, but it was worth it.

Warren: Dr. Benton's precision and confidence were reassuring and utterly believable. I remember watching the dailies of the pilot with David Nevins. At one point, I turned to him and said, "I'd go to Dr. Benton. I know he'd take care of me."

Noah Wyle: I'm particularly proud of the relationship my character had with Eriq's character. I don't think there'd ever been a relationship like that on TV with that power dynamic. He was the authority figure. We managed to work through the drill instructor/private, teacher/student, and we ended up colleagues and friends.

John Wells: The camera caught the camaraderie and the sense that they were in the trenches together. There's a lot of kismet that happens in these things. The cast just jelled.

David Nevins: I had an epiphany. I remember watching the third day of dailies, and there was a scene with Sherry Stringfield and Miguel Ferrer, who is a guest actor. All of the dialogue on the page was Miguel Ferrer. The way it was shot, you realized the whole scene was about her being there as Ferrer was processing the fact that he was going to die. I remember thinking, "Oh, it's not about that guy. It's about this person." The camera told you where to look. It was a doctor show that wasn't about the patients. It was about the doctors.

Noah Wyle: We reinvented the sense of pace. Employing the Steadi-cam on those long walks and talks. The multi–story line—you'd start a story on its third beat instead of the first. This idea that the ER was just a transition place, people were coming through constantly, and you only got a glimpse of the stories as the show went along.

John Wells: We turned the pilot around in a hurry because we got started late. We showed it to Les Moonves. He said, "You know, I thought I'd hate this thing, but I actually really like it."

Anthony Edwards: I think Les said, "Not since *Charlie's Angels* . . ." We thought, "Really? *Charlie's Angels?*" We were better than that.

Warren: With the delivery of the finished pilot from Warner Bros., the trouble began at NBC. Don Ohlmeyer had strenuous objections to the style and content of the show. He thought there was too much blood and far too much technical dialogue. My leading memory of the screening at our NBC offices in Burbank is Don Ohlmeyer storming out of the screening room halfway through the show.

He came back in at the end but was still pissed off. Don asked in a loud and angry voice, "Why do we want to be in business with people who don't listen to us?" The room was very quiet until Lori Openden spoke up and said, "I loved it."

Noah Wyle: We followed all the talk about the pilot screening and Don Ohlmeyer's reaction. Too much blood, too fast, all that. I do remember the pilot script being highly technical.

Anthony Edwards: The mythology was that Ohlmeyer was saying, "Nobody will watch *ER*. There are too many characters, and it doesn't make any sense."

David Nevins: When the rough cut of the pilot came in, it wasn't well received. I remember Ohlmeyer said, "These feature people don't respect our medium." It had seemed like the greatest thing in the world to me. It was a medical show that felt like an action show.

John Miller: I remember the electricity in the screening room for the *ER* pilot. It had the same feeling to me as the screening for *L.A. Law.* The research came in overwhelmingly positive—even though people died in the show and were screwing around. It violated too many tenets to get a false positive.

John Wells: We waited a long time for Don's notes. Rod Holcomb got upset and left. Michael Crichton was pissed. We tried to make adjustments that wouldn't damage the piece, but we wanted to get on the air. We were pretty sure we were right, but you're never absolutely sure. We could well have been wrong. We didn't know. I didn't know.

Warren: For Don it became personal. I told him he couldn't attend the notes session. His presence would just be counterproductive.

Our notes, Don's included, were largely fear based. We were in uncharted waters with *ER* and knew it. I flashed back to my early days on *Hill Street Blues*. Lots of the same feelings, and that one turned out pretty well.

John Wells: Don told me later he was really pissed that nobody had addressed his notes.

David Nevins: Les Moonves called me at home, and he said, "You've got to get your ass down here and watch this test." They were testing the *ER* pilot on the Warner Bros. lot. The dials were stuck at the top of the screen. I'd been the supporter at NBC, so if I went in the next day and said the test looked really good, nobody would believe it. So I called the head of testing at NBC, Eric Cardinal, and asked him to come down.

I wondered if it was real or if the audience was Warner Bros. employees. You turn a knob to the right if you like it, to the left if you don't. Probably seventy-five people there, and I was afraid it was a stunt.

The dials were stuck at the top, dipped down during a break, and then back up to the top. Two days later we had our own testing to confirm it. The highest-testing pilot ever. Five characters who tested really high.

When testing is in the top 10 percent or the bottom 10 percent, that's when you pay attention.

Noah Wyle: A funny thing happened on the way to my film career. Six episodes in, and we're on the cover of *Newsweek*.

11

He's Just a Little Kid!

John Wells: There's an alchemy to TV, like anything else. NBC just pounded the hell out of *ER* all summer long. We got put in after *Seinfeld* when that show was at its most powerful. We were helped quite a bit by the critical community over the summer because they all said *Chicago Hope* would win the time slot. We were underdogs. That made it a story.

John Miller: CBS put *Chicago Hope* against it. Another hospital drama, set in Chicago in the same time period. I knew from the get-go that *ER* would take it. We pushed all summer for *ER*.

Preston Beckman: CBS announced that *Chicago Hope* would be on Thursday at 10:00 like they owned it.

David Nevins: *ER* was going head-to-head with *Chicago Hope*. Around August somebody got the current report for CBS, and the second episode of *Chicago Hope* featured the transfer of a baboon heart into a little baby. They're going to kick our ass, and what do we have? We have dozens and dozens of stories, no A-story, and they've got a baboon's heart in a little baby.

Noah Wyle: And your leading man shows up drunk in the first scene of the pilot.

Warren: The network put together a promo for *ER* that featured two iconic moments in the show. One was Eriq La Salle's display of triumph over the success of a difficult procedure, and the other was George Clooney confronting an abusive mother with the words "He's just a little kid!"

John Miller: That line made Clooney a hero and appeared in most spots. We knew we had something special with *ER*. In the final broadcast of *Hill Street Blues*, we put in a spot for *L.A. Law*, and in the final episode of *L.A. Law* we ran a sixty-second spot for *ER*. With *ER* we had a very strong show taking the mantle from *L.A. Law*.

Eriq La Salle: Rod Holcomb, the director, said, "Okay, when you come through the door, I want you to do a 'yeah' or 'yippee.'" And I just said, "Rod, that just doesn't feel organic to who this man is. This man is *so* grounded, and everything he does is really about being grounded, and I feel to physically jump off your feet, I think, literally and metaphorically, it feels wrong." Rod was trying to make his day, so he was like, "Well, whatever."

We didn't get into this philosophical debate, but fortunately, by this time, we had worked long enough for him to trust me, and for me to trust him. At that point, I felt that he trusted my *instincts*, so at some point you don't need a huge, philosophical debate. It's like, "You know what, just show me something."

So just remembering my martial arts, *that* just felt so appropriate. I didn't think about this, but it was just the opposite: instead of taking it up, he took it *down*. And again, I'd love to say I thought about it in such detail. I wanted a powerful moment, a powerful gesture, a powerful physicality that felt organic and true to Benton's celebration.

John Miller: Fine use of words, music, and great cutting in the promo. You play reach and frequency, and you play impact. The *ER* promo was about impact. We carved out the time for it, and that minute was worth probably $1 million to the network.

We were positioning ourselves for the fall. I don't think we knew what we had in *Friends* at that point, but we knew what we had in *ER*.

Warren: Networks commonly say each May, "This was our highest-testing pilot," but with the data that came in on *ER*, we really had hit levels that NBC had never seen before. You hope to have one character test in the range of a strong lead. It doesn't happen very often, but that's what you aspire to. *ER* had five characters in a strong lead character category. Test audiences thought of the show as an action hour. They loved it.

At the upfronts in New York in May 1994, we gave the affiliates (and the cast) a taste of the look and feel of *ER*.

Noah Wyle: The first frame of the show any of us had seen was when Warren brought us all to New York for the upfronts at Avery Fisher Hall. We were watching from the wings, peeking around the curtain. The voice-over said, "If you thought there were no heroes left in the world . . . from the creators of *Jaws*, *Close Encounters* . . . ," this whole list of credits. They ran a four-minute clip. It was followed by silence and then this thunderous applause.

Anthony Edwards: The moment we knew we were on something really special was at the upfronts. We saw the first twenty minutes of the pilot. It had the music and the logo, and I still get chills. It was like, "Oh, shit." We all knew the show was something special.

Warren: The upfronts make for a great show, particularly when you have a sensational program to introduce and showcase. They're always in New York. We usually held ours in Avery Fisher Hall at Lincoln Center. The business of the upfronts is to preview the fall schedule for advertisers, affiliates, and journalists, but we also managed to have an awful lot of fun with our presentations during the Must See TV years. One year, I even allowed myself to be played by Bob Balaban. Why the hell not? He'd played me everywhere else.

In the 1992–93 season, *Seinfeld* explored the story of Jerry being wooed at NBC with a deal to develop a show. Balaban played the character of Russell Dalrymple, network president of NBC. In the episode titled "The Pitch," NBC asks Jerry to come up with an idea for a series. George decides he can write it but comes up with nothing. Sitting on the couch in Russell's office with Jerry, George explains that there are no stories and nothing really happens. To which Dalrymple replies, "Well, why am I watching it?" George: "Because it's on TV." Russell: (threatening) "Not yet." Bob Balaban made a number of memorable appearances playing that character. I was both honored and entertained.

Then, when Bill Carter's book *The Late Shift* was developed for HBO, Bob Balaban was hired to play me once Peter Horton, of *Thirtysomething* fame, turned down the part. So it wasn't much of a reach for me to recruit Bob to appear at the upfronts one May during our Must See run. Preston Beckman, John Miller, and Mike Mandelker all warned me that Balaban's appearance would be too inside baseball to appeal to advertisers, affiliates, and the press. This was one of the rare times when I failed to take their advice.

Fred Silverman and Brandon Tartikoff had taught me that we weren't just in business; we were in show business. I was convinced that Balaban's appearance at the upfronts—playing me one more time—had a good chance of bringing the house down.

Conan's band, the Max Weinberg 7, got the crowd going before the announcer Don Pardo took to the mic and said, "Ladies and gentlemen, please welcome the president of NBC Entertainment, Warren Littlefield."

Out walked Bob Balaban in a new Armani suit I'd bought for him. The closer he got to the podium, the louder the laughter grew. Bob looked out over the audience, smiled, and proceeded to launch into a laundry list of NBC's achievements. More laughter. The crowd loved it.

Finally, I walked out and joined him. "Bob, what are you doing? You're a wonderful actor, but I'm Warren." It was a great, warm, funny moment onstage. The audience roared, and it served as a chance for me to truly enjoy who I was and what I had achieved with my team at NBC.

Noah Wyle: After the upfronts, NBC threw a party at Match, the SoHo restaurant. Warren, in his cups, got up on a table and said, "I'm so fucking excited." I thought, "I like this guy." That was also the first night I took two women back to my hotel room. Memorable.

Warren: After screening the two-hour pilot, advertisers thought we'd be about a 23 share—the same number they were estimating for *Chicago Hope*. Don was pissed off again. He asked us how could they not see that we were so much better? He suggested we not sell much of our ad inventory at that low estimate. Bold move, but we'd all seen *Chicago Hope* by that time, and we had audience "intent to view" research for *ER* that was looking really strong. We agreed with Don—let's not undersell the show.

We couldn't afford to run the two-hour pilot of *ER* on Thursday night. Preempt *Seinfeld*? Never. It would have been a massive loss to the bottom line. That airtime was just too valuable, so we premiered on Monday night, September 19, 1994. The football game on ABC was Detroit playing in Dallas against America's team, the Cowboys.

I'd seen *ER* so many times, and I had to keep flipping back and forth to check out what was happening on *Monday Night Football*. I didn't care who won; I just wanted it to be a crappy game. Naturally, it was an absolute nail-biter with Detroit winning in overtime. I was afraid everybody would be watching football. Sleepless night, but the overnight ratings were quite good. The nationals were great. Nearly twenty-four million people watched that night. Then, on Thursday, in the head-to-head matchup with *Chicago Hope*, we had twenty-three million, and *Chicago Hope* had under fifteen million (Nielsen Media Research). And it just kept getting better each week.

Anthony Edwards: The success of the show came in an abstract way. In overnights. I knew things were good when George got excited.

Noah Wyle: I remember Clooney calling me and saying, "We did a 42 last night." I said, "Is that good?" I just didn't know.

Warren: Ka-boom! Now the sales department could take the available commercial inventory and sell them at over a 40 share. While we didn't own the show, it was going to be a huge profit center for us.

Remarkably, Rod Holcomb only directed the two-hour pilot of *ER* (and the final two hours fifteen years later). While we all desperately wanted his vision on the series on a full-time basis, he had a conflict. Before series production was scheduled to begin, Rod's agent called to tell me that Rod had previously agreed to direct a cable-TV movie and he was going to honor his commitment. I believe I said, "This is Hollywood. Who does that?"

I called Steven Spielberg and asked if he'd direct an episode of the show. I figured there was no harm in asking. Steven told me, "I would if I thought there was something I could add, but no matter how many times I watch it, I don't know what else I'd do."

Eriq La Salle: I remember we were on the cover of *Newsweek*, and this was the whole Hillary Clinton time and the introduction of a lot of the same medical issues that we have now.

Noah Wyle: That *Newsweek* cover was very big. They'd sent me to

New York to school me in publicity. I think I did *Regis and Kathie Lee*, sort of the spring training of talk shows, and a guy came up with the *Newsweek* cover. I thought it was one of those things like you can get printed at Disneyland. I said, "I've got to get me one of those." He pointed at the newsstand. It didn't make any sense to me. I walked over to the kiosk and was staring at twenty images of the cast.

John Wells: *ER* took off in that weird Beatles way. The cast suddenly couldn't go to the supermarket anymore.

Julianna Margulies: *ER* ruined me for life. People say now, "You got really good ratings, a 13 share." I'm used to a 44 share. We got Super Bowl numbers. When they tell me now we're in the top ten with a 13 share, I'm shocked. I can't believe it.

John Wells: I remember talking to Julianna Margulies, who was going to New York for Christmas, and I came to understand she was flying coach.

I said, "You can't fly coach. You have to be in first class. You don't realize what will happen."

She said, "I don't want to be in first class. I don't want to waste the money."

I told her, "People will be angry at you for flying coach. They'll think it's not cool for you to be in coach. You'll have a miserable time. You're a star. People expect you to be a certain person and act a certain way."

She flew out coach. She flew back first class.

Anthony Edwards: Most of the time, people are really respectful. Dr. Greene was that guy mothers wanted their daughters to marry. The guy daughters thought they ought to end up with.

Fans relate to you depending on their interests. I'm a race fan, and when I go to races, it's all *Top Gun* fans. Actors make a choice about whether to be removed or not. You can play the role of a celebrity or not. It's a part too.

Noah Wyle: If I hadn't had George and Anthony and, to an extent, Eriq as well as guides through those uncharted waters, I don't know how I would have made it. I credit them with keeping my feet on the ground and giving me a sense of perspective.

John Wells: Sherry Stringfield couldn't handle the lack of anonymity. She was coming apart at the seams. I tried to tell her it was a momentary thing. The moment could last three or four years, but it can't be recaptured. You may regret having stepped away because it won't happen again. You only get to do it once, and you may not want to miss it.

The agents and the press agents and managers are the biggest problem. The desire to take this person and turn him into a commodity. Sometimes it works, but mostly it's a disaster. It's the same thing that happens with professional athletes.

Tony and George had seen this sort of fame and been around it, and they tried to counsel the cast. Eriq La Salle had a hard time with it. Noah Wyle had a hard time but came through it whole. Sherry couldn't. Julianna turned into a diva for a while, left the show and had a real-life experience, and is still a lovely person I like. She walked away from $26.2 million for two years for a movie career that didn't happen. That's the toughest part of these Zeitgeist shows.

Julianna Margulies: Because I've been lucky enough to have some success again, I understand now, and there's never a moment when I don't appreciate it. But for *ER*, I wouldn't know how to handle what I'm doing now.

Noah Wyle: We were on a seven-day shooting schedule, so the average workday was fourteen to seventeen hours. I remember thinking the analogy was Neil Armstrong, who said he always felt like he missed out on the moon landing because he was on the moon. I felt like I missed the initial splash of the show because we were always onstage filming the show.

Anthony Edwards: We never had any time. We'd go over to the *Friends* set, and they had all kinds of time. "What do you mean you come in at noon?"

Julianna Margulies: When actors walk on the set of *The Good Wife* and say, "I'm so tired," I think, "You have no idea." *ER* was the best lesson for being an actor—film or television.

John Wells: It's that whole watercooler thing that it's almost impossible to have happen anymore. On the show, we were the last to know. We were nose to the grindstone. I remember the movie-of-the-week guy here at Warner Bros. came over and said, "You guys are a big hit." It was after the second week, and I remember looking up at him oddly. We were just trying to make enough pages for the next day. Our heads were in the feed bag, just trying to get the damn thing done.

Anthony Edwards: It was always clear to me that the person who was telling the story was John Wells. Inspired by the experience of Michael Crichton, but it was obvious that John Wells was in control.

Because the material was so good, we had to keep our game up. All of us. The writers, the actors, the art department, all of us. I knew if I was going to get through this material, I had to be prepared. We were doing eight to ten pages a day. Forget one minute a page. We were probably at thirty seconds a page.

We kept the actors on the stage and the writers in the writers' room. We decided early on that if you had a problem, you had to deal with it early. We just didn't have the time.

Noah Wyle: I got spoiled on *ER*. I think all of us have gone on in our careers and walked onto sets and said, "This is grossly inefficient, or this is very unprofessional, or I can't believe nobody has the esprit de corps like we had on *ER*," but the world doesn't work that way.

From the top on down, the crews don't really hustle like they did on *ER*, the writers don't push the envelope, and they don't have the support from the executives and the network to take those risks and those chances anymore.

Anthony Edwards: It felt like John Wells was always pushing the writers, and we were always pushing ourselves as actors, and the camera people were always trying to push what they were doing. If *you're* interested, the audience is too.

The show needed the consistency of a backboard. That was my job as Dr. Greene. It wasn't flashy. It didn't win me any Emmys, but it was important to the show, and it was fun to play Dr. Greene. I was part of a good team.

Noah Wyle: I think I hold the record for most love interests on *ER*—Rebecca De Mornay, Mädchen Amick, Maura Tierney, Thandie Newton . . . I'll forget a bunch.

I was at a party four or five years ago, and somebody said, "Do you know Rebecca De Mornay?" I said, "No, but I love your work." She said, "Noah, asshole. I did six episodes. We had a sex scene."

John Wells: We had good fortune with the cast because the cast had a lot of fun with each other. We had great good fortune with George, who had been around for a long time. He understood that as he started to break out of the cast, it was incumbent upon him to make sure that he didn't break with the other cast members. He went to great lengths to remain humble with them, include them in everything, and kind of talk himself down. That worked for about three years. He didn't stop doing it, but they stopped believing him.

Noah Wyle: George is an amazing individual. He's one of the few men I know who can engender goodwill among men without it being competitive or jealousy based. He's the only guy I've ever met who every woman wants to go home with and every man wants to buy him a beer.

Eriq La Salle: In the first year, when we started doing interviews, one of the moments that I was very proud of was when George one time said, "I think Eriq La Salle has the hardest job on this show because we all know him, we know who he is, but each week he comes in and he plays this character to the hilt who is not always the most likable or whatever, but it's the commitment of being an actor."

I'll make my own mistakes, but I'll also be that much farther ahead of the game and have more victories because of what I learned by having a front seat in one of the biggest shows in history, and one of the *best* TV shows ever. Damn, we did get a lot of shit right.

Noah Wyle: There was one mandate: don't stop. If you take a private moment, it has to be earned by the content of the episode. If any of us tried to take a little acting moment, you knew you were going to be in the crosshairs on Wednesday.

When Alan Alda came and did a turn on the show, he said that's what they'd done on *M*A*S*H*. They'd call it a gut-check session. He said if somebody took an inappropriate moment or milked a line, they were merciless with each other.

Anthony Edwards: We decided if you had a moment, walk away from it. We didn't linger, because real doctors never stay for a moment. It was *who could get out of the scene faster*, and the directors trusted us on it. It became the style of the show. The audience had the moment, not the actors.

That was the trouble with *Chicago Hope*. They lingered. "God, it's hard being a doctor." That sort of thing.

Warren: It really wasn't much of a contest in the end. *Chicago Hope* spent half a season in the 10:00 slot on Thursday night, opposite *ER*, before CBS shifted the show to Monday. *ER* dominated the competition at 10:00 and regularly delivered over a 40 share.

Preston Beckman: CBS always used New Year's Day to launch shows. I said, "Why don't we repeat the *ER* pilot on that day." Mandy Patinkin came up to see Ohlmeyer, he was so pissed about it.

Dan Harrison: It would take a hundred ad spots on the USA Network to reach the number of discrete eyeballs you could get with one spot on *ER*.

Warren: We were paying about $3 million per episode for that 40 share. We were charging a fortune for the advertising spots and making hundreds of millions of dollars on the show. *ER* never lost money. We'd already made a billion dollars before the renegotiation began. For ten years in a row it was television's highest-rated drama in the coveted adults eighteen to forty-nine. I didn't want to be a dick, but just once I did say to Bob Wright, "I bet you don't miss Diane Sawyer anymore."

John Agoglia: I was expecting a bloodbath with the renegotiation for *ER*. I think we were paying $3.5 to $4 million per episode. I put in $8 million for the negotiation. People told me I was crazy. I think it ended up at $12 million per episode. Bob Wright went nuts.

Harold Brook: For the *ER* negotiations, we went in at a high number. They were stunned, but we'd decided not to nickel-and-dime them. We came in at $8.5 million and closed at $10 million. It took about four days to strike the deal. Warner Bros. had a deficit on this show—$50 mil—and they wanted it back in one check.

Warren: We didn't own *ER*. We just rented it. After the first four years, we rented it for a lot more.

Harold Brook: In two weeks after we closed the deal, Warner's announced that they'd sold the repeats to Turner, and they were going to run it on Thursday nights. Not at 10:00, but on Thursday night. That was the angriest I'd ever seen Don Ohlmeyer. We hired outside counsel and sent an ugly litigation letter. Don said, "We're not buying anything from Warner Bros. anymore." That lasted two weeks.

John Landgraf: After the renegotiation Don Ohlmeyer said to me, "I'm paying $13 million an episode for *ER*. They're going to take all of my notes, and you've got to make it happen." And I'm thinking, "Right. I'm going to tell John Wells he's got to take Don's notes. He's got a show with a 40 share."

Noah Wyle: Every time a contract renegotiation would come up, I'd look around and say, "I don't think there's any better writing or directing around," so I'd sign back up.

Anthony Edwards: We had to pay strict attention to the details. We couldn't afford to get sloppy about the technical stuff. We had all these doctors and nurses on the set, and everywhere we went, people said they liked the show because it was real. The tone had to be real too.

If we weren't going to stop, the camera couldn't stop. I actually directed an episode with a twenty-two-minute scene. One shot.

Noah Wyle: I suddenly flashed on the "Love's Labor Lost" episode. It was one of the most amazing hours of television I'd ever seen. I think it was the only Emmy we ever received for writing. I was doing a play in Hollywood at the same time, and I got mononucleosis. We were shooting the show that night, and I had a fever of 104 degrees, and I was hallucinating. I didn't think I was going to make it.

I turned to Dr. Joe Sachs, our medical tech, and I said, "Joe, I don't think I'm going to make it." Joe said, "I don't have anything for you." He looked around the set and said, "I guess I could take one of these IVs and give it to you." There were IVs all over the set. He squeezes a bag of saline into me. When we were shooting, I'd put it in my pocket. I remember thinking that wasn't odd. It was something we'd all consider doing.

I was twenty-two or twenty-three and working eighteen hours a day. Going home seemed like it wasn't on the table.

Eriq La Salle: There was a time when Noah's character was dealing with an addiction—this might have been season six or so—and so I say, "I'm going to put you into rehab," and there's a point where he hits me. The way we approached the work—this was symbolic of how we approached all the work—was "How do I help you sell your punch?" You're getting ready to punch me, and this isn't about me being cool. That was our attitude: How do we make each other look good?

Noah Wyle: I remember John Wells calling me and telling me I would be stabbed by a psychotic patient. It would be a near-fatal injury, and I'd be left with debilitating pain and have to self-medicate in order to regulate. He said he wanted to show that the face of addiction was every face, any face. "If it can be you," he told me, "it can be anybody."

I don't think I'd ever seen a slight, peripheral character move closer to the core as a series went on.

Anthony Edwards: George and I came up with the idea of doing the live episode. It came out of doing oners, long shots. It was like acting in a play. If you screwed up at the end of a oner, you really caught it. George is a big TV history buff, and we talked about doing the show as a play, as a live show.

I don't know if the execution was as good as the idea. I don't know that the show looked that different from what it normally did.

We had five days to rehearse. We all had theater backgrounds. I have a picture I love, taken about four minutes before we went live. We were on the couch in the doctors' lounge, and we were laughing. Thinking, "All we'd have to do is walk out that door, and what would they do?" Such power.

Warren: Don thought we were nuts. "You better not destroy this series." Once again I put my faith in John Wells but with Don's words ringing in my ears I was also right there in the director's booth for both live shows.

Eriq La Salle: It was such an ensemble thing. It was such a team effort. Just like the theater. You're running around backstage, and then you come off nice and easy and say your last line, and then you bolt over here. "Hey, man, yeah, been there, done that, and loved it and still love it." But again, it was that unit, that team, relying on each other. I knew where Noah was; I knew where George was. I knew we could do the no-look passes. They knew if they needed me over there, I'd be there, and they could do the alley-oop.

Anthony Edwards: Very little went wrong. I think we dropped a tray or something, but that happened all the time anyway.

Noah Wyle: The only advantage network television still has is the ability to command a very large audience on a given night at a given time. That was never lost on us. For forty-eight minutes a week we had the opportunity to tell half the country anything we wanted. We could give them soap opera, or we could give them an episode like "Love's Labor Lost." It caused pregnant women all over America to call their ob-gyns the next morning to ask, "What is preeclampsia and do I have it?" We enriched, we informed, and we entertained at the same time. You just don't see that anymore.

Eriq La Salle: We accomplished the most amazing things, we did it as a team, we did it as a group. We are a part of a proud history, and to be included in that group is obviously one of the greatest achievements of my professional life and personal life. We're a part of history.

Anthony Edwards: It was a phenomenal time. And the show stays. Nothing goes away now, good and bad. Everything just lives on. People loved the experience they had on Thursday night. My wife wouldn't let me near her between ten and eleven.

Noah Wyle: I walked on the show at twenty-two, and after the final episode I walked off at thirty-seven. It was very much like stepping off a fast-moving freight train and saying, "Where am I now?" I got on a train fifteen years ago, and now I'm stepping off a different person in a different land.

Anthony Edwards: The number of angry, older women in my neighborhood who have told me, "How dare you leave the show!"

"But I wanted to be with my kids."

"We don't care about your kids. We want our Thursday night at ten o'clock, and we want you on it."

Noah Wyle: Two weeks ago I had an audition at Warner Bros. for a Clint Eastwood movie. I'm looking at my directions, and it says, "Gate 3." It was a parking structure. I go up and park at the top, come down, and go through the metal detector, and the guard won't let me in without my photo ID. I've left my wallet in my car. I tell her, "I used to work here on a show called *ER*." She says, "I'll call my supervisor." I finally get in. I go by stage 11, and the doors are open. It's empty. You'd never know we were there.

12

It Rhymes

Warren: I would like to be able to say that the phrase "Must See TV" was the product of hard work and assiduous calculation. Not remotely the case.

The "Night of Bests" began in the eighties on Thursday with *Cosby* at 8:00, *Cheers* at 9:00, and *Hill Street Blues* at 10:00. We felt we had the potential to get that Thursday magic back.

John Miller: We had a few pieces. This was the end of the *L.A. Law* time. *ER* had not yet come on. *Seinfeld* was birthed by *Cheers* but was struggling. We had *Mad About You* sitting over between Thursday and Saturday. *Wings* was still on the network, had been sort of the offshoot of *Cheers*. We had little pockets of strength.

Don Ohlmeyer said he wanted to label our night of appointment television on Thursday. "You guys figure out what you want to call it." That first lineup was *Mad About You*, *Wings*, *Seinfeld*, and *Madman of the People*, *L.A. Law* at 10:00. That was the fall of 1993.

We wanted to come up with a name for this night because we wanted to package it. There was a guy who worked for us then named Dan Holm. He suggested, "How about Must See TV. It rhymes."

We said, "Okay. Let's go with Must See TV."

You'd think it was focus grouped or researched. Nope. Must See TV. That was it.

John Agoglia: Must See TV was an era of incredible teamwork and understanding. Of course, we were insufferable at the affiliate meetings because we're paying the affiliates to carry product that made them money.

Bob Wright would take someone to dinner and puff them up and say how much money we were making from their show, which was like a stake in my heart. I could feel it.

Warren: My philosophy as president of entertainment at NBC was simple. I knew I didn't have all the answers, so I kept my office door open, and my colleagues were always welcome with their suggestions and their ideas. In the end, it probably helped that Don Ohlmeyer drove us together with his explosive personality, but as a longtime exec at the network I'd grown to appreciate the value of opinions other than my own.

Karey Burke: Warren never created an air of "no, this won't work" or "I know better." There was openness to everything. An openness to every kind of idea. Conventional wisdom was out the door. It was energizing and very attractive to creators. *3rd Rock from the Sun*—that was crazy, and *ER* was daring.

Harold Brook: In business affairs, we're negotiators. Everything from options and scripts, acquisition of literary material, pilots of movies. Focusing on the network, our biggest liaison was with the studios. They had to coordinate with us. Warren and his group would make decisions of what they wanted to do. Then we'd get the deal memo and negotiate the deal. Paper it.

It wasn't straightforward negotiation for me. That was the easy part. You met in the middle, and the parameters were pretty well set. In the nineties, the personalities made it different for me. I was in the yard with a lot of kids, and everybody wanted something. I had to figure out how to do that. We had a great group of people, except for a couple of odd ones.

We had contact with every department in the entertainment division. Financial, creative, promotion—we did deals for series, movies, late night—we really covered the group. We were very into making deals, not figuring out roadblocks. And it's a thankless job.

I could go to Warren and say, "This is going to be ugly. Trust us. We'll make the deal." When we had that, it was always smooth.

Karey Burke: The culture of the place attracted people. People knew we'd back their shot. It may not work, but we'd back it. That wasn't alchemy. It was leadership.

Steve McPherson: The Must See TV era was a special time. I think collectively we all felt NBC was a collegial, passionate place. People worked together and partied together. We felt like we were on the cutting edge of TV. It was a work hard/play hard environment, and it was really fun.

Warren: And *really* profitable. Looking at ad sales figures, I could see in black and white the vast differential between what was charged for a spot on Thursday versus what we would get on Saturday. At the height of Must See madness, a thirty-second spot on *Seinfeld* sold for $800,000 while *ER* commanded $550,000 for thirty seconds.

My question was simple: Why not create more advertising time on Thursday? Why did a Thursday comedy have to be the same running time as a Saturday one? Why not adjust and follow the dollars?

By the time *Seinfeld* went off the air in 1998, the episodes were at least a minute shorter than they'd been early in the run of the series (remember, $800,000 for each thirty-second spot). I could rarely have a conversation with Jerry Seinfeld or Larry David in those final few years without them telling me, "Stop making the show shorter!"

Mike Mandelker: We had properties on Thursday night. It became like folklore that you couldn't release a movie successfully unless you had an ad on *Cheers* or, later, *Seinfeld*. It probably wasn't true, but I didn't want a movie to open successfully unless it had been advertised on our Thursday night.

We started off selling four minutes per thirty-minute show. By the time we were done, we had five minutes. Everybody was lined up. We had twenty-two to twenty-four original episodes of these shows, and that's why NBC was the first network to hit $2 billion in the upfronts.

Bob Wright: Thursday night during Must See TV basically carried the entire network. That night was driving as much income as each of the other networks was making together. It allowed the network to develop sports and do other things we would have been constrained on at the time. We got back into football thanks to Thursday night.

We did close to $3 billion one year during upfronts, and the next guy was $1.8 billion. When you get on a roll like that, the advertisers are right with you. They don't want to be left out.

Warren: With the tremendous profits flowing from Must See TV into the network and into NBC's owned and operated stations, Bob Wright was able to solidify his vision for the future of NBC. Bob aggressively pursued the acquisition of cable channels with their dual-revenue streams (ad sales and subscription fees), a move that would keep NBC in profits even as the struggling entertainment division slid all the way from the top spot to fourth place after the Must See TV years.

Mike Mandelker: If we'd had three nights of Thursday programming, I'm not sure we'd have gotten three times the revenue. Maybe twice the revenue. We got our pricing because of supply and demand. Change the supply, you change the demand.

Warren: I like to think the freewheeling atmosphere contributed to our success in the nineties. I do know that our openness to shows like *Seinfeld* and *Mad About You* did serve to make NBC a beacon for everyone who wanted to work in TV comedy. When Thursday night took off, the creative community watched our shows along with everybody else. Even when agents would tell their clients, "They have a full stable at NBC. They don't need you over there," they'd hear back, "Yeah, but they *get* us."

The quality of our Must See shows became our greatest sales tool to the creative community. Better still, we'd begun to promote our shows in a way no other network had attempted at the time. We produced the network rather than just the shows.

John Miller: Producing the network was a year in the making, and then we had a year on the air by ourselves doing this. We took the credits—and we had a unit make what we called promotainment. Not pure promos, but talking about our shows, the stars, where they'd come from. It was to keep people engaged.

Warren: We invited over one hundred artists to create their versions of the NBC peacock. A lot of credit for reimagining what NBC looked like on air should go to Jeff Rowe, a guy who never went to college, had a background in radio, and whom I hired because he just impressed me. He bounced around a number of different departments, and then fortunately John Miller said, "I'll take him." That's where Jeff started to flourish. Under John Miller and Vince Manze's guidance, Jeff helped hatch a new vision of what we'd look like on air.

John Miller: We said, "You have to end with the correct peacock. How you get there, we don't care." I was the peacock police. My idea was let the journey be the magic and end with the logo.

Then I had to go to the guilds and tell them their credits wouldn't be full frame but off to the side. Not crawling over action, off to the side so the show could continue. Research indicated that we would cut down on our audience loss—from 25 percent to 5 percent.

We could usually keep audience through the first minute because of how we flowed the shows. Some shows that shouldn't have made it probably did because of the way we produced the network. If a network has a persona throughout the day, it has a brand equity, and advertisers know what they're getting.

Warren: Producing the network cost us $1 million because we had to reshoot all of the credits, but everybody at NBC understood that the changes would make us *the* network rather than *a* network. Nobody was more tuned in to what we were up to than the creative community, which gave us the best shot at the best shows.

With Thursday night performing like a weekly rocket ship, I had good reason to exhale and enjoy what we had accomplished. Despite the many predictions that I couldn't fill Brandon's shoes, under my guidance NBC had surged to dominance in the coveted adults eighteen-to-forty-nine category in the 1995–96 season. On Thursday night we were beating the combined competition (ABC, CBS, and Fox) by 36 percent and had improved the night 58 percent from our 1992–93 collapse (Nielsen Media Research). Better still, our programs held particular appeal for upscale urban households with college educations. Our advertisers were proud to watch our shows and patronize them. These weren't just popular programs. They were Emmy Award–winning, and our advertising spots were going at premium prices.

As luck would have it, my contract was expiring just as we were hitting our stride. Clinton and Gore had delivered on their promises, and the economic recovery looked as if it would last. Jack Welch and

Bob Wright had every incentive to make me happy and keep the team together. They left the details to Don Ohlmeyer, who invited me to dinner to discuss my new deal.

We met at the Morton's in West Hollywood, an industry power spot. I approached the dinner as a negotiation of sorts. After all, Don would be my advocate with management in New York, and I wanted him to urge them to stretch to make it work for me. I'd composed a list of creative goals and financial benchmarks I felt I'd been responsible for achieving.

The dinner didn't go well. Don had a few vodkas. He listened to what I had to say, but it was clear he thought he was a far larger part of our success than I did. I believed I was the quarterback of a team that was currently kicking ass and he was the coach on the sidelines. Since my contract was expiring, I felt I needed to state my case, not just cheerlead for the team.

The next morning Don's assistant asked him how the dinner went, and Don said, "The young man certainly has a high opinion of himself." With that, the negotiations were handed off to Bob Wright and NBC's longtime head of human resources, Ed Scanlon. My attorney, Skip Brittenham, took my side.

Unlike with the earlier "take it or leave it" offers, we were finally in a position to negotiate. We proposed three streams of compensation: an annual salary, performance-based bonuses, and GE stock. Ed Scanlon agreed, so the real question would be the amounts. It was NBC's and GE's belief that the best compensation they could pay would take the form of GE stock and options. It built company loyalty and wasn't an instant drain of cash. We agreed to a base annual salary, bonuses for ratings achievements in the November, February, and May sweeps along with the full-season ratings standings in prime time and late night, and finally a package of stock and stock options.

In all of the discussions, the length of the deal was always three years. But on a visit to Burbank, Bob Wright asked to see me and said, "I understand we have a done deal, but I need to change it to five years. That's what Jack and the board want." I thought about that for a moment. Freedom or a guarantee? I took the five years.

I couldn't have predicted the windfall I'd enjoy, thanks to NBC's continued ratings triumphs, and the ballooning value of GE stock in the nineties made that component more valuable than all the others. Thank you, Jack Welch!

Not bad for a kid who put himself through college driving a truck for J. Rosenblum & Sons, purveyors of fine foods in Paterson, New Jersey.

With our success everybody wanted his or her show to air on Thursday night, a problem usually tended to by our scheduling genius, Preston Beckman.

Preston Beckman: Kauffman, Bright, and Crane created *Friends*. Then *Jesse* and *Veronica's Closet*. Two *real* gems. They heard, erroneously, that we were moving their shows out of protected time periods. They called me and asked if I would come up and see them. I go.

Marta says, "We hear you're moving our shows. That troubles us."

I said, "When I come to work, I only have two goals. I have to put food on my table and the tables of everybody at NBC, and I have to make sure we can all send our kids to college. That's all I care about. I have a feeling you can send your kids to college, your grandchildren to college, your great-grandchildren to college, and the whole state of Idaho to college. I don't care about you." And I walked out.

I have virtually no friends in the business.

Dan Harrison: Preston said to me on my first day at NBC, "I want you to go in the bathroom, look in the mirror, and say one hundred times, 'Get the fuck out of my office.' If you smile when you say it, you need to start again."

Mike Mandelker: Preston always looked at the schedule in the aggregate way rather than as component parts. He was a genius at making his ideas mine.

Dan Harrison: Preston was a real strategist. It's very easy for the creative executives to believe so much in the show they're working on that they don't see the bigger picture of how the network is going to do. Preston was always the honest broker.

Preston Beckman: I gave Warren and Don jigsaw puzzles one Christmas and told them, once you've put 999 pieces together, call me, and I'll tell you how to move a few. That's what scheduling was like.

Warren: The big difference for us was that in the nineties, we had the opportunity to develop and produce shows people actually wanted to watch. In that era, NBC comedies that would have led in the ratings at one of the other networks were down the bench for us. We were that stacked with talent.

Two such shows that spring to mind immediately are *3rd Rock from the Sun*, with John Lithgow, and *Just Shoot Me!*, created by Steve Levitan, whose current show, *Modern Family*, is a runaway hit for ABC.

Karey Burke: *3rd Rock* was an ABC pilot that Jimmy Burrows had directed. It was from Bonnie and Terry Turner, who'd run *SNL* for years [and produced by Marcy Carsey and Tom Werner]. It was a broad idea about aliens in Ohio. It wasn't seen as an NBC show— bigger, broader, set in Ohio, physical comedy. ABC failed to put *3rd Rock* on the fall schedule, and the Turners called us, and we screened the pilot.

Marcy Carsey: I had been very clear to ABC. I spoke very slowly, and I told the absolute truth. I said, "I know how you guys feel about this show. Maybe it won't work, but we have more faith in it than you do. I'd like to take it somewhere else, so if you could release it to us, we'll bring you something better mid-season." How much clearer could I be?

Warren: The fix was in. I told Marcy I'd buy *3rd Rock* if she could get ABC to pass.

Marcy Carsey: They decided they'd release it the day after NBC announced its schedule. They thought they were accomplishing everything. Then NBC picked it up at mid-season. ABC was furious. "NBC is picking this up!? What!?"

I said, "I told you I wanted to sell it somewhere else," and they said, "But we didn't think you could."

Warren: I picked it up officially an hour after they passed.

John Lithgow: I had hosted *Saturday Night Live* three times in the eighties. The second and third of those three times, Bonnie and Terry were on the writing staff, and we became *really* good friends. I saw that they did *The Brady Bunch*, *Tommy Boy*, and *Wayne's World*. They had a booming movie career after seven years on *SNL*, but I talked to them not at all during those years.

My agent called, and he said that Bonnie and Terry wanted to have lunch with me. I thought this was just a social engagement, and they didn't know how to reach me, so I said, "Sure! I would love to see Bonnie and Terry. I love those two!" So we made a date, and I went to the Four Seasons thinking I was just having lunch with Bonnie and Terry to catch up—that's how stupid I am. I was shown to the table, and there was Bonnie and Terry and Caryn Mandabach, Tom Werner and Marcy Carsey, and David Tochterman—all of them. And I thought, "This is not a fun lunch with my old friends. This is a pitch, goddamn it!"

It was Terry's job to pitch the show to me. He had given a tremendous amount of thought to his first sentence, and he said, "Well, it's about a family of four aliens." In my mind, there was this neon light that went off. "Noooooooo!" I thought, "How am I going to say no quickly, politely, and get this meal over with?"

Warren: As unlikely as it might have seemed at that moment, John Lithgow was soon won over to the idea of playing the alien Dick Solomon on a network sitcom.

John Lithgow: There were two things that *completely* sold me. One was the fact that on a dime, the four actors could sing Cole Porter like Manhattan Transfer. If required, they could sing. They also pitched the episode of the professor that everyone loathes who dies of a heart attack, and Dick finds himself in the position of having to deliver a eulogy. Bonnie recited, by heart, the eulogy that she had written for this occasion.

John Mahoney played the character. Dick Solomon is at such a loss because he doesn't know what he is going to say, because everybody hated this man; Dick even hated him. But he gives this speech in which he says, "There comes a time, there comes a moment when all things pass from matter into light." And it was so beautiful. Bonnie just spoke it off the top of her head, verbatim. That was the speech that I spoke two years later, when we finally shot that episode.

Those two things—that and the fact that I looked around the table and thought, "These are the best people I've ever met in this business." I *loved* Tom and Marcy; it was the first time I'd ever met them. I thought, "Jesus, what am I waiting for here?" I don't know whether it was their calculation, but my most recent jobs had been *Raising Cain*, *Cliffhanger*, *Ricochet*. I was slowly turning into this kind of John Malkovich, this strange movie heavy. This was beginning to bother me.

I almost got the role of Hannibal Lecter, and when I didn't, I rattled off all these penny-dreadful villains. I was beginning to feel, "This is what I'm known for, and it's not entirely what I want to be known for. People have now forgotten about *Terms of Endearment* and *Garp*."

So I got up from the table that day, and I said, "If I do end up doing this, I just have to tell you, you will have gotten me at *exactly* the right moment." Because it was true; it was the perfect thing for me to do right then.

Karey Burke: We stole *3rd Rock*, and then it was uh-oh. We weren't sure it was an NBC show.

Marcy Carsey: We had to shoot that pilot twice. We screwed it up, and we added Jane Curtin.

John Lithgow: I *loved* the process of putting together the cast and plotting the series. It was so much fun. Those historic moments when Kristen Johnston came in, and French Stewart came in, and Joseph Gordon-Levitt came in. In the case of Joey and French, *that* was when those characters came to life. In the case of Kristen, we already knew what the character was; we just couldn't find the person for it. Then bam! There she was. It was uncanny and great.

What people loved was the scene on the rooftop at the end of the episode. We only did that about a third of the time, but everyone thought we did it every time. It was so emblematic—where we simply talk wistfully. I remember Bonnie so wanted to have James Taylor's music—whatever the song was, about outer space and stars; I'm a pop music illiterate. But James was an acquaintance of mine, and they deputized me to find him and get his permission. I did, and we got it as the closing music of the first episode. I hope he's glad that he said yes.

Preston Beckman: It was a strange show. I thought it was an A or an F, and I didn't know which.

John Lithgow: Taking the role of Dick Solomon was like being handed a magic wand. It was just extraordinary. So much fun. I honestly think

I'll live ten years longer than I would have, just from the pure rocket fuel of laughter. It's such a fun thing to do. I hadn't realized how, when it's right, there's nothing like a sitcom.

Warren: *Just Shoot Me!* was a show I was always in like with but never truly loved, no secret from its creator, Steve Levitan.

Steve Levitan: The show wasn't beloved at all. We'd shot six episodes, and we heard from the network, "We think three or four of them are airable."

We were the little show that could. The show was a breech birth, and at every turn the show had to fight for everything it got. We were only the third or fourth most important comedy at NBC. The bench was so deep that we were the utility player.

I think we were in thirteen or fourteen spots in seven years.

Warren: We were looking at a competitive matchup where ABC had put a comedy starring Arsenio Hall on Wednesday night at 9:30. I didn't know if Steve had created a hit show, but I knew it was better than Arsenio Hall. We had a chance to succeed.

Steve Levitan: A week or so away from *Just Shoot Me!*'s premiere, and you couldn't go anywhere without seeing Arsenio. Every billboard. On buses. Everywhere. Nothing for us.

Then the show debuted, and we beat *Arsenio.* No advertising, nothing, and we beat him. Warren called. "Steve! Steve!" They smelled blood in the water and were going full bore.

Warren: We suddenly knew we had a sophisticated, adult hit. Preston and I patted ourselves on the back. "How smart are we?" Jack Welch called and said all the young GE execs loved it. *Just Shoot Me!* premiered in 1997 and died an inglorious death at the hands of Jeff Zucker in 2003.

Steve Levitan: Jeff Zucker killed us in the end. I think he cost us two years. We were scheduled on Wednesdays at 8:30 for the new season, and a week and a half out they put us in a different spot. It was listed in *TV Guide*, everywhere, and nobody knew when it was on. You couldn't TiVo it. Nothing. We got the numbers, and they were really down. Of course. Zucker's response was, "I guess *Just Shoot Me!* isn't as strong as we thought it was."

I defended the show to the press. How could you expect the show to do better under these circumstances? Jeff lashed out at me. Never one to miss a good fight, I lashed out at him. The crowning indignity was the series finale. They burned it off in the summer.

My wife once asked my daughter, "What are some bad words in our house?" She said, "Jeff Zucker."

13

*Batting for
the Other Team*

Warren: Out of all the shows of the Must See era, I probably feel the warmest connection to *Will & Grace* because it featured a relationship I had often seen in life but never on TV. I had floated the idea for a similar show with Brandon Tartikoff in the eighties, when I was vice president of comedy—gay guy, straight girl, best friends. As I recall, he said, "Get the fuck out of here." But in all fairness to Brandon, attitudes had changed by the time the writers Max Mutchnick and David Kohan came into my office to pitch a large ensemble comedy with a straight couple as the primary focus and a *Will & Grace* couple off on the periphery.

David Nevins: *My Best Friend's Wedding* was doing very well along about then, and we were more interested in the Will and Grace characters than the rest of them. *Mad About You* was six years old, so we already had that show.

Jim Burrows: Warren is responsible for *Will & Grace*. The boys had written a script with three couples in it, and Warren picked out the Will and Grace couple. He wanted a show about them.

David Nevins: Max and David resisted us. They didn't believe a network would put a show on with a gay lead. Eventually, they said,

"Okay, but we don't believe you. We'll write a great script, but you'll never put it on the air."

Max Mutchnick: I felt as a viewer as much as a writer I understood what Thursday night on NBC was all about.

David Kohan: We were working on *The Single Guy*, and we felt like we got the sensibility of that show, and we'd write our drafts based on that. Glenn Padnick, the president of Castle Rock at the time, took notice of us because of those drafts.

A comic named Anthony Clark had made a splash at one of the festivals—at Montreal or Aspen. Anthony and Max were friends from college, and Anthony came to us and said he'd be signing a deal sometime soon, and he asked if we would write him a script. Max and I wrote a script and put it in a drawer, and then Glenn Padnick called us in. He said he'd signed Anthony Clark, and he said he understood we'd written a script for him.

He read it, and he said, "I don't like it. I don't like the idea. But I like the way you've written him."

Max Mutchnick: Glenn said he was having success with writers who had relationships with the leads of shows, meaning *Seinfeld*.

David Kohan: We were still officially *pisseurs* at this point. We'd not crossed the *pisseur* Rubicon yet. We ended up doing a completely different idea about a guy who brought his sister to college and fell in love with a grad student there. Glenn liked it and brought it to NBC as *Boston Common*. We were eager to do it, but NBC said we were too green to run the show.

Max Mutchnick: That was our first pitch at NBC, and we were told we were too young to be doing this. And my whole issue in the elevator going down was "David, you've got to wear a good white shirt!" Look at him. It's still a problem.

David Kohan: The people who ran the show were just figureheads. They were doing it as a favor to NBC and a favor to us. NBC gave us the keys to the car, and they said, "If you dent it, we'll take it away." They took a chance on us, and you'd never see that today. Never.

Max Mutchnick: I remember Warren showing up on the set, and I was too young to understand what he was trying to say. He wanted more from our show, but I was too young to know what he meant.

Anthony's character wasn't supposed to be on Thursday night. He wasn't part of that rainbow.

David Kohan: On Thursday at NBC, if you had something good, it would take off. If you had something bad, it would reveal itself.

NBC had a legacy of taking chances on writers and producers who had a vision for what they wanted to do. We had a sense that we were being nurtured and given the latitude to do something we felt was interesting.

Jim Burrows: "This is my *Wings*" has become an expression in the business for start-out shows. *Boston Common* was Max and David's *Wings*.

Warren: So in the spring of 1997, I canceled *Boston Common*, but I told Max and David and their fearless agent Scott Schwartz, who discovered them, "Don't leave. Come join the club." I wanted them to create and produce not just shows that we would put on NBC but product that we would also own. As thrilled as we were with the success of *Friends* and *ER*, we knew we had helped to nourish hits for Warner Bros. We didn't own them. We had to take more shots with people whose shows we owned.

Max Mutchnick: We were set up in an overall deal at NBC and had offices in a bungalow where Charlton Heston was attacked by David Kohan.

David Kohan: I had one question for him: "Do you think fewer guns would mean fewer murders in the U.S.?" And he totally ducked me.

Max Mutchnick: I don't feel like we were in that deal for very long before we had a pitch with Warren. We pitched a show that took place in San Francisco, and Will and Grace were the neighbors. Jack and Will were the same guy in the first draft, and we split them off. We wanted to get all of that color in there.

Warren: Hearing that first pitch from Max and David was a flashback moment for me. I'd had a similar experience with Susan Harris about *The Golden Girls* more than a decade earlier. On a Saturday night in August, I put on a tux and watched Selma Diamond and Doris Roberts onstage together in 1984 at a network promotional taping, and they'd been hilarious. They confused *Miami Vice* with a fictitious new sitcom, *Miami Nice*. Their chemistry had inspired me and the others in attendance to think of the possibility of a comedy starring actresses over fifty. The pool of available talent was extraordinary.

Through Paul Witt and Tony Thomas, I reached out to their partner Susan Harris—the creator and writer of my favorite comedy, *Soap*—and told her what I was thinking. I'll never forget what she said: "I love the idea, but will you put it on the air?" I assured her, "If you write it, it'll be wonderful, and we'll have to."

I found myself saying much the same thing to Max and David. They were deeply skeptical that we would find a spot on our schedule for a show about *the gays*. JoAnn Alfano was the talented creative executive working with them at the studio; I knew they'd get the support they needed. I told the boys, in essence, if you write a good script, we'll have to make room for it.

David Kohan: It was right as *Ellen* came out, and that show got a really big hit. I remember pitching romances for Ellen to the show runners, and they kept saying, "No, I don't think we're going that way." We wondered, why not? Then Ellen came out. Needless to say, we didn't get the job.

Max Mutchnick: We turned in the *Will & Grace* draft, and it was largely left alone. But it didn't start with Will and Grace doing their thing. Warren made us write the cold open—them on the phone talking about how they were both attracted to George Clooney. And people still didn't know the guy was gay.

Warren: When NBC put together the selling package, Will wasn't identified as gay.

The promotion department certainly liked the pilot, but they feared alienating advertisers and audiences. Despite Ellen's trailblazing, we were still in territory that was quite new to network television.

David Kohan: "They're not a couple; they're a couple of friends." That was the promo line.

Max Mutchnick: That's how we were supposed to know Will was a homo. Ohlmeyer called it *Grace & Gay*. So warm.

Warren: Don had been fighting me on the idea from the beginning. He didn't think the country was ready for this relationship on broadcast TV in 1998, because he wasn't ready for it. Instead of having yet another confrontation with Don, I decided to string him along. "It's just an idea. Nothing usually comes of them." That was followed by "It's just a pilot script. Most of them don't go anywhere." But then it became "Hey, you know that Mutchnick and Kohan script? Jimmy Burrows wants to direct it." Don loved and respected Jimmy Burrows. There wasn't much he could say after that.

Max Mutchnick: Warren was crossing the street, and as we passed each other, he said, "Jimmy Burrows read the script and wants to meet with you guys."

Warren: Writers who don't know Jimmy can be intimidated by his credentials. My approach with Max and David was exactly the same as it had been with Reinhold Weege, the creator of *Night Court* in 1983. "Just sit down and meet Jimmy, and I'll pay for the meal."

Max Mutchnick: I said, "I don't know that we want to do that. I'd rather we star in the show than Jimmy Burrows."

Warren called a couple of hours later and said, "You're meeting Jimmy tomorrow afternoon at Nate 'n Al's in Beverly Hills."

David Kohan: I remember us deciding to say, "Thanks, but no thanks, Jimmy. We have a good idea of what we want here, and we don't necessarily need the corrosive influence of a remarkably successful director."

We found Doris Day parking, right in front of Nate 'n Al's. We sat down with Jimmy. He said, "I think I want to do it." And we said, "Okay."

Jim Burrows: I had a great meeting with Max and David. They *were* Will and Grace. They thought they were auditioning me. Writers always do. I tell writers what I think the script needs, and if they're defensive about it—"No, it's funny"—then I don't want to work with them. If they can defend their material and tell me what's going through their heads, then I can work with them.

Max Mutchnick: He had a change on the script too, what we came to call the Jimmy Burrows double/double. Jimmy likes for things to fall apart in the second act, and then everything fixes itself.

Jim Burrows: The boys wrote a really good script. In the second act, it lacked fire. They wrote a scene where Will goes down to the courthouse to talk Grace out of marrying Danny. I told them I'd seen that scene before. I suggested a scene where Will admits that he doesn't like Danny. Grace gets furious and then comes in the next day and says, "You broke up my marriage." She screams at him. He goes to his office, and she comes in to apologize. So at least you'd have some heat there.

I also said they needed a kiss at the end of the show. I thought it was really important to make America think Will was going to take the magic pills and become straight.

I'd never done a political show, and I never intended this show to be political, but it changed—in a small way—the perception of gays. I would drive carpool every Thursday, and the thirteen-year-olds would want to know what was happening with *Will & Grace*. They were comfortable with it.

Max Mutchnick: I remember Warren asking us what we thought about casting. It was a conversation. Don came to the audition for Eric McCormack. He said Eric reminded him of Paul Reiser, and then he got up and left.

Eric McCormack: In 1993, I was doing a pilot outside of Dallas, and Constance Marie was in it. I remember dragging her to my hotel room to watch *Seinfeld* and *Mad About You*. By the time I got to L.A. in 1996, I was dreaming of a Thursday night sitcom that Jim Burrows directed.

I got *The Jenny McCarthy Show*. I had a very funny character. We had thirteen shows guaranteed. I was playing a Charlie Sheen type, a spoiled TV star. We shot the pilot, and then I got the call from Warren that the character was being cut entirely. It was seven months later that I went in to read for Max and David for *Will & Grace*.

The part was basically mine, and I was told I had to meet with Jim Burrows. It was *happening*!

Jim Burrows: When I got on *Will & Grace*, they had Eric McCormack and Marin Hinkle. I told them I thought they had a Will but not a Grace. I'd known about Debra Messing from *Ned and Stacey* and *Prey*.

Warren: I was a big fan of Debra's from *Ned and Stacey*. She's beautiful and funny. I wondered how she'd gotten away from us at NBC. She should be over here. Now we had a show for her.

Debra Messing: I was working on the spectacular, futuristic drama *Prey* on ABC at the time, where I played a bio-anthropologist, and we were supposed to be counterprogramming for *Friends*. It was my first drama, and I was the protagonist, and so I was working sixteen to eighteen hours a day.

I was completely, completely exhausted. I would come home and fall asleep on the couch, and five hours later my husband would wake me up and say, "You have to go back to work."

The show got canceled. It ended on a Saturday, and I e-mailed my agent and said, "Don't wake me for four months. I'm going to sleep, and I'll see you in a while." Then Bob Gersh, my agent, called on Monday and said, "We have a special script. You have to read it." And I was like, "No, no, no. I'm exhausted. I cannot move. I'm in bed." And he said, "We'll send it over. Don't leave bed. Just read it in bed."

I read it, and I thought, "Uh-oh." It was a very ambivalent feeling, because it was like, "You know what, he's right. There is something really special on the page. The characters are already specific. It has such a unique comic voice that jumps off the page. This doesn't happen in a pilot script." And I thought, "Yeah, that is kind of special, but I'm too tired. So I'm just gonna go to bed." And Bob told me, "Okay, look. Sleep for a couple of days, and then why don't you just go in and talk with the writers?"

Max Mutchnick: Debra Messing was sick of earning $35,000 a week since she was eighteen. She was exhausted.

David Kohan: The first meeting was at her apartment. We walked in with a big bottle of vodka and said, "Let's sit down and talk." We all got along well. It was like we'd gone to camp together.

Max Mutchnick: A big moment in our career was the drive to Debra Messing's house when we were casting *Will & Grace*. We were on the phone with Warren for thirty-five minutes, and he told us how to get the actress. It was incredible.

Warren: My advice was essentially this: You're romancing her. Take baby steps. Try to get her to say, "Yes, I will go on this date with you."

Debra Messing: It was pouring outside, one of the rare times it rains in Los Angeles. It was 6:30 at night, and it was really dark. I opened the door, and they were drowned rats holding a liter of vodka and a lime. I said, "Hi." And I thought, "Oh, boy."

We popped the vodka and cut up some lime and sat in the living room, and we talked for three hours. So much of it was my fear that the end product wouldn't end up being what everyone wanted it to be. I was fearful of having this gay character as the center of the show and this woman, and then this gay supporting character. I thought, "Now, it's about time. This is really exciting, but is Middle America going to be okay with this? Will the network ultimately be okay with this? Will GE be okay with it?"

Warren: All fair questions. I got a call from Debra following her "meeting" with Max and David.

Debra Messing: I was blasted.

Warren: And she said, "I may be a little drunk, but I feel really good about this." My heart started to race.

Debra Messing: After that night with the vodka, I was in with them. But then I was scared about signing on to a contract for six-plus years and not being happy. So then came the weekend and the audition at Jimmy's mansion. Seeing the art on the wall and seeing the framed pictures from *Cheers* on the piano and the twenty-five Emmy Awards all over his office.

Max Mutchnick: I don't know why the audition was set up on Saturday at Jimmy's house.

Debra Messing: Bob Gersh kept calling, and he was like, "Okay, you know what, why don't you just go over to Jimmy Burrows's house, on the weekend, and meet Eric? You know, Eric has been cast. And you can just do some reading. No pressure. No one else will be there. It's not an audition per se, but if you read it and you love it and you want to do it, then you'll do it."

David Kohan: There were two other women auditioning just in case Debra Messing said no. Nicollette Sheridan auditioned in ridiculously tight leather pants.

Max Mutchnick: The other one was Rebecca Kleenex commercial. She was in the hottest commercial at the time.

David Kohan: The actresses were each told by the casting director that they were the only one auditioning, so we staggered the times and informed the town car company that none of the actresses could see each other as they were coming and going.

Debra Messing: I thought, "Oh my God. I get to go to Jimmy Burrows's house in Bel Air!" That had a lot to do with it. I thought, "What does a home in Bel Air owned by Jimmy Burrows—this icon of television history—what does that look like?"

So a car showed up at my apartment, and I was like, "A car!" It was the first time that a car had been sent for me, and I thought, "Oh my gosh. This is very different from Fox." Because I had been on *Ned and Stacey*, and that was my first experience.

Jim Burrows: We set up this incredible ruse at my house on Bellagio. We invited the studio and the network and the three girls, but the girls all came in separate limos because they each thought they were the only one reading.

Eric McCormack: Three actresses, and it had to happen on the weekend at Jim Burrows's house. I was shooting a movie with William Shatner, and my mother had had a heart attack the day before. I'd shot until 4:00 in the morning, and then I had to come to Jimmy Burrows's house to be Will. I was a mess.

Jim Burrows: The first girl read. Rebecca Boyd. She wasn't any good. Nicollette Sheridan read, and she was okay.

Eric McCormack: Nicollette Sheridan said, "Any notes? Anything?" Jimmy told her, "Wear tighter pants."

Debra Messing: I only found out after the fact that two other actresses came over on Saturday to audition. Bob called me beforehand, and he said, "I have been assured there is no one else coming to audition. It is only you. This is not a screen test. This is not a test day. It's only you." Then I find out that Nicollette Sheridan had been there, and I was like, "What! They lied to me!"

Everywhere I looked, it was television history, and Jimmy was at the center of it. I was so nervous. I remember walking in and seeing Eric. He had scruff, and he had just flown in from Canada. And immediately there was just this click. You don't know why it happens, but it was just instant. We were like, "All right, let's play."

David Kohan: Debra and Eric were amazing together. It was as if they had been great friends for a really long time, and it was right there on Jimmy's couch. It was thrilling, but then . . . was she going to do it?

Warren: It was so wonderful to see the two of them together. Chemistry like Paul and Helen, Ted and Shelley. I loved it. I knew we had to get Debra to commit. I also knew it wouldn't be easy.

Jim Burrows: When Messing read with Eric, it was magic. Messing had been flaky, wouldn't commit to a lot of projects. I walked her out, and I said to her, "I don't know you, but you were genius down there. This is a great show. Don't fuck this up."

Debra Messing: I looked in his eyes, and I just saw the gravity. He was telling me, "You know. You gotta do it." And I said, "Okay. I'll go home, and I'll think about it." And I got into that car, and I remember the whole ride back to my little apartment I was thinking, "Jimmy Burrows is telling me I should do this show. *Jimmy Burrows.*"

Harold Brook: The reason you make deals before the actor reads is because if somebody loves him in the room, you don't want that actor coming out and saying, "They love me. Now let's go hold up the network."

We had that problem with Debra Messing. She read with Jim Burrows on a weekend. We didn't have a deal closed, and he expressed his love for her. She "agonized" until she got one point on the back end.

Warren: It wouldn't have worked any other way. Debra was in demand.

I knew she'd have lots of choices. When Harold made his final offer, I called Bob Gersh and said, "You've stretched the rubber band as far as it will stretch. There is no more money. We love her, we want her, and if she does this, it will be a hit." Bob closed the deal.

David Nevins: The idea for Jack came along in order to make Will a little more butch. Sort of a Frasier/Niles thing. Sean Hayes had done *Billy's Hollywood Screen Kiss.* That was the only year I went to Sundance, and Lori Openden and I saw the movie. He had this incredible winning sweetness to him, and I had no idea he had the comedy chops he had.

Sean Hayes: I was sitting in the screening of *Billy's Hollywood Screen Kiss,* and the projector broke. The lights came back up, and somebody tapped me on the shoulder. It turned out to be a guy who worked for Lori Openden. He introduced himself and said they were casting a new show called *Will & Grace* and they were looking for their Will. I said, "Watch the movie. Maybe you've found him."

The script came to my hotel room the next day. I read it. It was very well written, but a lot of scripts are. I didn't have money to fly home to audition, and I wanted to bask in my first big role at Sundance.

By the time I got home, I was told Will was already cast, and I was asked to come in and read for the other guy. I couldn't pay my rent, so I said sure. It upped my confidence that I was coming from something—*Billy's Hollywood Screen Kiss.* I went to see Max and David, and as I was leaving the room, I told them, "Stop staring at my ass," and went out and slammed the door.

Max Mutchnick: Sean Hayes came in to read for the part of Jack, and it was like there was a star standing in our office. We had him read twice because it was such fun to watch him, but we thought it would be a difficult deal to make.

We knew we had him when his manager called and said, "I don't know if I'm going to do this network deal, but let me ask you a question. Is he going up against fifty or sixty other guys?"

Then I knew we had him. He was represented by Murray's Talent Loft in Tarzana. No experience there at all.

Eric McCormack: When the role of Will was mine to have, I got scared. I backed off. I think it went through Christmas and New Year's. I phoned Max and David and said, "I think I have to back away from this." Max said, "You're making the biggest fucking mistake of your life!"

Right after New Year's, like a scene from a movie, I sat up in bed. I said to my wife, "I made a terrible mistake, didn't I?" She said, "Yeah, I think you did." I got on the phone with my agent and said, "See if they've cast this. Let's get it back."

I found out after the fact that all four of us—the actors—had crises committing one way or the other.

Sean Hayes: They called me back to test for Jimmy Burrows. It was just for Jimmy, and then I tested again at NBC, and the job was between me and Robert Arquette, who is now a woman. I'd never done any TV shows, guest starred on a TV show, nothing.

I used to think, "Wouldn't it be great to be on a show like *Cheers*." You just come in and do your job and you go home. You're not that famous. The *show* is. And then there I was, and I couldn't believe that I was part of this legendary NBC.

Megan Mullally: I first auditioned for the role of Grace. I thought the script was fresh and more modern feeling. I went in and read, and it was just flatline. They couldn't have been any less impressed with me. So that was that, and I forgot all about it. Then a couple weeks later, I get a call from one of my agents.

She said, "Oh, we have an audition for you for a pilot, *Will & Grace.*"

I said, "I already went down there."

She said, "No, it's for a different role."

And I said, "What other role?"

She said, "A secretary."

And I was like, "Oh, all right. Well, send it to me again."

Mind you, I was stone-cold broke. It's not like I was rolling in dough and could pick and choose. I was mysteriously being sort of particular. It got to the point where it was the day of the test, say the test was at 1:30, at NBC, in Burbank. At 11:30, my agent called me and said, "Are you going to the test?"

I'm in my pajamas eating a plate of scrambled eggs, and I was like, "I don't know. I don't know what I can really do in that role. I'm not really sure if that's what I want to be doing, but okay, I'm just going to go." So I went. That's how close a thing it was.

I guess because I wasn't feeling like I *had* to get it, it made it better. When I did get it and the deal was closed, I had $200 to my name. Two hundred dollars. I don't know what I was thinking.

Sean Hayes: We did a table read. I met Megan, all dressed in black, and I thought, "Who does this girl think she is?"

Megan Mullally: When I first saw Sean, he pulled up in his car, and he had that incredible smile. I was like, "Oh my God, who is that cute little elfin person?" I was very taken with him right away.

Debra Messing: I remember the cast going over to Max's house to do the very first reading of the script, and we were crying we were laughing so hard. I remember just looking around the table, looking at this Sean Hayes. It was like, "Who is this Sean Hayes guy? He is a genius."

To this day, I think Sean might be the most talented person I have ever worked with in my entire career. He is really touched with magic. And then Megan. She literally can't say anything without making me laugh. Then the warmth between Eric and me. It felt like this best friendship had been in place for years. We didn't have to put any effort into it.

Warren: Even still, airing *Will & Grace* came with no little risk for the network. There had been no sitcom like it before. Would we embrace our fears or run from them?

David Nevins: I remember being asked, more than once, "What world do you live in to think America wants to watch this gay TV show?"

14

Story Camp

Eric McCormack: *Will & Grace* was what Must See TV had to do next.

I had more a fear of success than of failure at the beginning. I had the fear of getting the wrong thing. The fear of getting *Full House*. To see John Stamos only now overcoming that role. I recognized that if I got the part, Will Truman could be my Sam Malone. You add gay to that, and you might have something that will brand you.

Around that time, there was a gay character on *Melrose Place*, and the actor didn't want to talk about it in interviews. I remember thinking, if I do this, I'm going to have to really do it. I needed to take on that side of me and wear it proudly. I didn't have to go off and play a football player during hiatus just to prove my manhood.

Debra Messing: My first experience on TV, I felt like a dancing monkey, in fact so much so that I named my production company Dancing Monkey. It was *Ned and Stacey*. We had some really amazing fans, and a lot of the experience was really special. I had never been on a TV show in my life. I had just come from doing plays and being in graduate school, where it's collaborative. My contribution was not valued. It just felt like, "We're going to decide what the scene is. We're going to decide the way it should go, and it's your job to execute it."

That *is* my job as an actor, but after a while if you feel like you're just a shell and you're not actually contributing something, it drains you of the creative lifeblood that made you want to act to begin with.

To be able to come on the show and to be allowed to be physically comedic, that was life changing. That was such a huge gift. And there wasn't a lot of precedent for it at the time. *Suddenly Susan* was on, *Caroline in the City* was on. *Friends* was on, and *Seinfeld* was ending. At that time, there were a lot of leading ladies who were the stars of sitcoms, and it was the men who did the pratfalls. I said, "I want to be one of the men."

Megan Mullally: Because *Will & Grace* is farce, I wanted to bring a different element to the character. My natural speaking voice is very low, and I didn't feel like that was right for the character. I wanted to bring something to it that would create more energy. I tend to be a sort of voice and hair and wardrobe actress. Once that all comes together, I can really nail the character better.

I knew that if I did that voice in the pilot, they would fire me. So I didn't want to. I worked it in pretty slowly. I would say by maybe the tenth episode, it's fully in there. But I really didn't come out of the gate with that, because I thought, "They'll replace me. This is too weird. Too bizarre."

Sean Hayes: I was so sick during the shooting of the pilot because I was riddled with nerves. And I remember the first time I saw the monitor, and I said to myself, "Oh my God, I'm on TV."

David Kohan: The main thing we learned from Jimmy Burrows initially was that the story is king. It didn't matter how funny you were if the audience wasn't invested in the characters. We didn't necessarily get the idea that the story was paramount.

Max Mutchnick: We also learned to listen and not watch. With *Bos-*

ton Common we were always glued to a monitor. Jim ran a show where there were no monitors on the stage, so you couldn't see what the cameras were doing.

David Kohan: He'd say you assume the director is going to get the shots.

Max Mutchnick: All you had to do was hear that the music was in key, and you knew cameras would cover it.

Eric McCormack: Jimmy has supreme confidence. It's what makes him Jimmy. With that confidence, there was also the ability to be surprised. He'd prefer not to direct. He'd rather actors come in and be brilliant. When that doesn't happen, he's got his work cut out for him. When Sean Hayes would come in and do some outrageous piece of physical business, nobody was happier than Jimmy.

We worked three hours a day. Jimmy didn't believe in belaboring it, and that was so my style.

There were no marks on the floor. You didn't have to hit marks. Jimmy trusted his crew to find us, and they found us. We all felt we were in great hands. That left Max and David to forget everything else, just go and just write a great show.

David Kohan: Working with Jimmy was an education and story camp in a lot of ways.

Sean Hayes: We only worked three hours a day because the writing was there. We were actors and a director, so what were we going to fix? Sometimes Jimmy would send us home. "It's not ready yet. Go home."

David Kohan: In the pilot, there was a law partner in the show named Andy Fellner. He was a straight single guy who'd get all his romantic advice from Will. Will would explain what a woman would want in every situation. But the character felt extraneous, and he was making the show a little long.

Then a directive came down from the NAACP or something that there wasn't enough color on Thursday night.

Max Mutchnick: So Warren said to us, "No matter what, this guy's going to be black."

David Kohan: Cress Williams as Andy Fellner. Suddenly it didn't work. He wasn't a nebbish. He was something else.

Max Mutchnick: We had run-throughs every day, and everything worked until you'd get to Will and this black guy. It just didn't work, and that was the gift of Jimmy Burrows.

David Kohan: He said, "We've got to cut it."

Max Mutchnick: And once that character was gone, the script sang. Jim knew that the show was peaking too early. We released everybody and gave them two days off in the middle of the pilot—unheard of. It was a brilliant move because it made for an incredible filming.

Sean Hayes: All you ever heard was "the great Jimmy Burrows" like "the great Oz." He knows how to read a script and give great notes on a faulty story line, and he knows how to read and balance actors.

Warren: I remember a moment on *Caroline in the City*. It was a rehearsal, a run-through, and on the counter there was a vase, and Lea Thompson was supposed to slide the vase away. As she did it, Jimmy said, "Other hand." Then she did it again. Though I have no idea why, it went from a movement that meant nothing to a burst of comedy.

He knew for her, in that moment, that's how it would work. I couldn't figure it out. Jimmy just instinctively knew.

Megan Mullally: I'd met Jimmy at a couple of auditions, and I thought he was *so* intimidating. Of course, if you know him for more than two hours, you realize that he's the biggest softy in the world. The thing that I love about Jimmy is his incredible talent and facility for comedy, particularly physical comedy.

You always know where you stand with Jimmy. He does not blow smoke. He's no bullshit. That was the best thing because I knew I could trust him. If I had any questions about the character or the direction it was going in, I could just ask Jimmy, and he would settle it in one short sentence. But in a nice way. He's a man of few words. He's very blunt, but he's kind. I'm sure you know ours is the only series that he directed every single episode of.

Sean Hayes: I don't think the show would have lasted without Jimmy. Max and David used to just write in jokes and didn't seem to care about the characters until Jimmy came along. Max used to call it *The Jimmy Burrows Show*, and I said, "You *should* call it *The Jimmy Burrows Show*, and you should thank him for it."

Eric McCormack: I was intimidated by Jimmy at first. During the pilot, I was doing something, and I was trying to be funny. Jimmy said, "Let me tell you something I told Teddy." I thought, "Teddy? Oh my God, Ted Danson. Now I'm his Ted!"

Sean Hayes: I remember my first fitting, before we shot the pilot. I said to Lori Eskowitz, who's doing wardrobe on the show, "We don't know if this is any good, do we?"

She said, "Are you kidding me? It's an NBC Studios show with Jimmy Burrows. It's going to go."

I said, "How do you know?"

She said, "I just do."

Debra Messing: We were shooting the pilot, and we were all looking like scrappy New York theater actors in our sweatpants and ripped T-shirts and no makeup, and we were sitting outside the stage at a picnic table. I was smoking at the time. The four of us were there, and I had this old matchbook from a restaurant that was all ripped up and it had two matches left. I lit one, and the wind blew it out. And then all four of us came together to try and help me with my last chance to light this cigarette.

Megan Mullally: Don Ohlmeyer comes walking by, and all we knew is that he was some big chief, but we really didn't know what he was.

Debra Messing: I'm sucking on the cigarette trying to get it to stay lit. It's going out, and all of a sudden this hand comes in with this glittering yellow-gold Dunhill lighter.

It was Don Ohlmeyer, and he said, "May I?"

Megan Mullally: He's a fancy guy. He was like, "Well, hello."

We were like, "Oh, hey. Hi." I don't even think we knew what his name was, and we certainly didn't know exactly what his job description was. I still don't. But Eric and Debra were a little more business savvy than Sean and me. Sean and I were just idiots.

Debra Messing: We did not understand who this man was. We knew he was powerful, but we had no idea exactly what he did. He was in his sweatpants, and he was walking by. It was the sweatpants era for Ohlmeyer. And he said, "Well, hello, everybody, how's it going?" Then we realized who it was, and we were like, "Oh, it's going great."

He handed me the gold lighter and said, "Here, you need to have this. You can't be using those matches any longer." My mouth dropped, my eyes bugged out of my head, and all of us were silent. I was like, "Ohhh, okay. Thank you."

Megan Mullally: She went to hand it back to him, and he said, "No, no. Keep it."

Then he walked away a minute later, and we were like, "Oh my God! Our show is gonna get picked up! We're in!"

Debra Messing: A couple of months later, I find myself in bed watching David Letterman, and Adam Sandler is on promoting one of his huge comedies. Letterman says, "When did you know that you were on the road and you were going to make it?" And Adam said, "I was on *SNL*, and Don Ohlmeyer gave me this lighter. It was a gold Dunhill lighter. He just took it out of his pocket and he said, 'Here, you need this.' I'm this kid at *SNL*, and I remember feeling like, 'Okay, I'm in.'"

And I'm thinking, "I've got a lighter too!" It was like I had been knighted, but instead of with a sword it was with a gold Dunhill lighter. I still have it, so every time I look at it, I think about the pilot. I'm very sentimental that way.

Sean Hayes: Don gave gold lighters to Eric, Debra, and Megan. I didn't get one. I still have issues about it.

Eric McCormack: We shot the pilot, and Debra and I were sitting on the couch on the set, and I looked at her and said, "Are you thinking what I'm thinking?" She said, "Yeah. I think we're going to be here for a while."

Debra Messing: We were sitting next to each other, and we held each other's hands. We looked at each other, and it was almost like we were saying, "Okay. We're jumping off a cliff together, because this is going to fly. This is going to be really exciting. This is uncharted territory."

Eric McCormack: Then Warren came out, took my hand, and said, "Aren't you glad I fired you from *The Jenny McCarthy Show*?"

Warren: The greatest feeling in the world is standing on a stage and watching 250 strangers in the audience laughing, clapping, and cheering for characters they've never seen before. You've made a connection with them, and that night with this pilot it was as if we brought the Beatles back together for that audience.

Debra Messing: I will never forget the thing that shocked me most about the opening scene in the pilot. Grace and Will were talking about *ER*, watching *ER* and watching the gorgeous George Clooney. I think after the pilot was shot—I don't know if there was testing or something—but there was a huge percentage of people who, after that scene, did not get the fact that Will was gay.

And I thought, "What?" He said, "I'm batting for the other team." I thought, "Wow. This is going to be an interesting journey."

Sean Hayes: I kept waiting to get fired. I got an apartment that cost $1,250 a month. I got it after we shot the pilot, and the landlord wasn't going to let me rent it. I told him the show had been picked up for thirteen. It hadn't yet. He rented me the apartment.

Megan Mullally: I bought a Range Rover. It was a ridiculous thing to do, but I just knew the show was going to get picked up. I bought it with my pilot money.

Jim Burrows: The pilot was great even without a great Megan character because she didn't find that voice until about six shows in. The audience will laugh at places you don't expect. They'll be quiet, the worst thing possible if you're doing a comedy. Television is usually one or two people watching the show. The goal is to get the feeling of the studio audience into the living room. We want the viewer to feel like they're part of the audience. The audience responds, and then the actors respond to the audience. It was never canned laughter on *Will & Grace*. All real laughs.

Warren: Developing this particular idea with writers we're paying a lot of money to and then going out on a limb and making the pilot raised the stakes considerably on *Will & Grace*.

A crucial moment for me at NBC was the first week of May 1998, when we ran the pilot of *Will & Grace* during screening week for a roomful of NBC executives, including Bob Wright. It was the usual mix, development and current executives from the West Coast, the promo department, sales executives from New York and Burbank, and the research department. They were laughing in the right places. I thought it was going well, but I knew I was too close to this one. When the episode finished and the lights came up, Bob Wright turned to me and in a voice that the whole room could hear said, "That's the best thing we've ever had our name on." Then people started clapping.

Game over. If Don Ohlmeyer had any thoughts of raising further objections and continuing the fight, Bob Wright's reaction put an end to them.

Preston and I debated many times where we should first schedule the show. I loved it and believed it was the essence of the Must See brand. But Preston helped me to see the long-term picture.

We started *Will & Grace* on Monday night. We didn't want to invite controversy, and on Monday we didn't ask the advertisers for a mountain of cash—as we did on Thursday. We didn't start on Broadway. We opened in Boston.

Jim Burrows: I begged NBC not to start the show on Thursday night. It had to be in a spot where it could sneak into town. It had gay people in it. They're bad. They can hurt your television. They put it on Jimmy Burrows night. Monday. There were four comedies, and I'd directed all the pilots. It ran after *Caroline in the City*.

Twenty percent of the country would never watch the show, because it had gay people in it. I thought if you could make people think Will and Grace might get together, then a lot more people would watch the show. If you could get them to watch, they wouldn't care after they saw how funny it was. That was the funniest show I've ever done. Ever. I called it a fairy tale, figuratively and literally.

Megan Mullally: That's why that show was able to happen with the groundbreaking aspect of two of the four regular roles being gay. It was never politicized in any way. It was just about four people, four friends who were in relationships with each other in one way or another.

Had it been politicized at all, it never would have worked. That's what happened with *Ellen*. It was amazing and fantastic and historic. It was very cleverly done, the way she came out in that episode. But from then on, everything was about her being gay and the problems that that would cause.

Jim Burrows: At the beginning of the second year, Max wanted the guys to look better. Eric always looked great, but we do the first scene, and Sean comes out in Prada pants, pointy Prada shoes, and a suit jacket.

I say, "Cut, cut. I've got a technical problem." I went over to Max and said, "No." This was a man who claimed to have fucked most of the men in New York, and the best thing we could do was keep him in Jack Purcells and a sweater vest. That made him innocent, so he could talk about all that stuff. His costume never changed after that.

Debra Messing: The first time we had a moment of "you can't do this," it had nothing to do with homosexuality, with sexual politics. It was Megan's character yelling at her maid, played by Shelley Morrison, and using a derogatory word that the censors were concerned the Latin American community would find offensive.

I remember that day. It was so vivid to me. Them coming down and telling Megan they're really concerned about this. And the character had been established that she is just offensive to everybody. This is what she does. She is just offensive to everybody who walks the earth.

We really struggled with "Why do we have to edit this? Because if we edit this now, aren't we opening a door to editing everything in the future?" And again, when you talk about strategy, I remember the discussion being "This is our first season. We might have to make more compromises and be a little more careful our first season. And as we go, we are going to be able to be bolder and bolder." It was really interesting that the one and only thing that was tagged was that. It never happened again.

Eric McCormack: The show was very much a living entity. It had a lot to do with how Jimmy rehearses and shoots. It had a lot to do with how good that writing staff was. We got to a point where the reigning thought was "We just shot it. Why would you shoot it again?" Put in fifteen new jokes. Replace the ones that don't work, and replace the ones that do work.

Very often what ended up on television in any given scene were two or three or four jokes that were brand-new. Had never been rehearsed. Never heard by the crew, not heard by the audience. That's the reason the laughs were so big. The jokes were fresh—Laura Kightlinger or somebody had just thrown them off the top of her head—and we thought they were funny. All four of us had the ability to do it off the cuff. These characters were alive for the audience. They were seeing us create. Shoot night was alive. It was a rock concert, and there was nothing better.

Sean Hayes: One time I said, "Jimmy, is it funnier if I go straight for the refrigerator or should I stop at the couch?" He said, "I don't care, honey. I've got to pick up my daughter in an hour." There was a compliment buried in there. He was so comfortable with the marriage of the actors and the material that he trusted our instincts. Before Jimmy, I didn't know it was up to me.

The laugh is everything. When you're taping a show, if an actor was about to step on his own laugh, Jimmy would stop and go back. Jimmy was a theater guy, and sitcoms are theater.

Debra Messing: I thought that it was so ingenious how Max and Dave found a way to navigate around the censors in terms of the language and metaphors that they were constantly using for sex acts, for body parts. The craziest words and the craziest things put together, which made it okay to be put on prime-time television, and younger kids had no idea what they were referencing, but the adults could feel smart.

Megan Mullally: It's key that all four of us had a theater background. Every one of us had done plays or musicals or both. That made a huge difference, because, like I said, it was farce. Everybody had a great sense of pace. And of course, Jimmy.

Debra Messing: The rewriting was so constant that there were times when we would get a word and "Oh, we couldn't say that. It's too on-the-nose naughty." Then because we had Jimmy, and he had such authority, he'd be like, "Just shoot it anyway. We'll make them see it, and we'll make them cut it after they see it." No one can overestimate the importance of having Jimmy direct every episode for eight years. It was unlike any experience I'd ever had. It was just pure joy.

I always tell people, if you can, go to a taping of his and just watch him direct. It's like he's a conductor. He often doesn't even watch the action. He walks back and forth along the line of the stage, and he listens to the musicality of the comedy. As soon as he hears us veering off rhythmically, he'll say, "Stop, go back!" He will not let us finish the sentence, because he doesn't want to blow the punch line. But he already knows that it's not going to land as well as it could, so, "Let's go back. Let's start that section again." He'll walk up to one of the cameras with his toe in the middle of the scene. He'll push it, roll it so that the angle is just a quarter of an inch different. It's this intuitive thing that he has. You feel so safe with him, and you always feel when you're around him his love for actors, for stage-trained actors.

Sean Hayes: At the beginning, the scripts were all jokes, and Jimmy would come in and say, "There's no story." That was his go-to line that we'd all imitate later: "Honey, there's no story."

We used to sit down at a table while we were rehearsing and talk about what was working and what wasn't. Jimmy always said it was about the writing: if it ain't on the page, it ain't on the stage.

Eric McCormack: People think anybody can do this. You always run into those guys who say, "Yeah, I was going to be an actor." They think, "How hard can it be? You're just up there being you." So when you get a chance to not be you . . . it's a good thing. It was complicated. It had its moments, but eighteen or nineteen million people a week were buying it.

Debra Messing: The NBC comedies were so sophisticated and so smart there was an assumption that if anybody can take a stab at this and succeed, it would be NBC. Then the letters started coming when we would show up in the morning to do our rehearsal. The letter from a fourteen-year-old gay boy from Arizona whose best friend disowned him and wouldn't talk to him anymore because he said that he was gay, and he has been watching with his mother—who was devastated when he told her—but now they laugh together. And, "Thank you because you have bridged this huge thing between my mother and me, and hopefully one day my best friend will talk to me again."

It was so shocking because of the crazy hilarity and goofiness that was going on on that stage and then to have these letters of real impact. At the end of the day, it's the greatest gift to all of us involved in *Will*

& Grace to be a part of something that made people feel like "for the first time in my life, I am represented on television."

Eric McCormack: You get spoiled by the words you get to say. You get spoiled knowing Jimmy Burrows will be there every week. You get spoiled by a big audience share. And the money they had to spend on my suits! If Grace is always out of money and always borrowing from me, why does she have so many fantastic clothes? It's TV. You don't ask.

Max Mutchnick: Jimmy came to us after the thirteenth episode and said there was room on his mantel for another Emmy and it was time for us to make him an executive producer.

Jim Burrows: I told Max and David the only reason I wanted to be a producer on *Will & Grace* was so I could get an Emmy if they did. I haven't gotten a directing Emmy in years.

David Kohan: We decided, once again, we were going to say, "Thanks, but no thanks, Jimmy."

Warren: Max called me and said, "They're going to jam Jimmy Burrows down our throats. We don't know what to do." NBC had just dumped me, but that didn't keep me from having strong feelings for one of my "children." We had dinner at Spago. I said to Max and David, "This is the greatest thing that can happen. Embrace it. Embrace Jimmy. This means a hundred episodes are in your sights." I also knew if I couldn't be close to offer guidance and protection for their vision, having Jimmy locked in would mean no one would fuck with it.

David Kohan: That night, Joan Collins and Nancy Reagan were at Spago. Barbara Davis was there too, and then in came Marvin Davis's chair. A couple of big guys came in carrying Marvin Davis's chair and put it at the table with Joan Collins and Nancy Reagan.

Max Mutchnick: It was huge. It was like a Barcalounger. It was the weirdest thing, and it went with him wherever he went.

David Kohan: We loved the whole procession of it, and we wondered if he was going to come or if he was just sending his chair.

Max Mutchnick: At the Beverly Hills Hotel, Barbara Davis came over to our table and said she was sick of her Bentley. She said she always had a chase car, a duplicate Bentley to follow her because hers always breaks down. I've lived on that story. A chase Bentley.

Megan Mullally: I remember there was a moment, just a regular episode in the first season, and I opened the door to make my first entrance, and the audience started screaming. Then we had to start again, and Jimmy had to ask them not to scream. That's when I first realized that people were responding to the character. We aired that first season, and they reran it over the summer, and over the summer it really kicked in.

Warren: Sound familiar? Patience and risk rewarded once again.

Eric McCormack: Near the end of the first season, I ran into Jimmy on the lot. He'd usually be off playing golf or something. I said, "Jimmy, what are you still doing here?" He said, "I was just talking to the boys about what we're going to do with your character next year." I said, "Next year? I like the sound of that." Jimmy said, "Jesus Christ, McCormack. Buy a house."

I went home that night and told my wife, "God said we can buy a house."

Debra Messing: None of us saw what ultimately happened coming. We didn't see any of it coming. We had no idea that the show was going to become something that was socially and politically important outside of just being a piece of entertainment and that it would be important to so many people.

Eric McCormack: Initially, it was gay men and women who loved the show. Then, second season, straight guys would say, "My girlfriend likes the show." Then by season four it was "Sometimes I watch it with my wife." Then it became "I make my wife watch your show."

Megan Mullally: The role of Karen is a perfect example of an incredible writing staff that was extremely intuitive. Any little thing that I would bring in that was new and different that they liked, then they would write to that. Then they would write something that I hadn't expected, and I would play to that and build on that. It was all very collaborative and symbiotic, in the sense that we took the best of what each other was doing and then tried to add to it.

Debra and Eric wanted to spend a lot more time hashing out story. Sean and I had the luxury of not having to do that because we didn't have the A-story, so we didn't have to really worry about overarching themes or season arcs. We were just over in the corner, flashing our tits and falling down. We didn't have to worry about the real stuff.

Sean Hayes: It was very exciting to be famous. I'd be lying if I said it wasn't, but I learned the only thing you need fame for is to get a table. That's it.

Eric McCormack: With the exception of Sean, we were all in our thirties. We had been around, most of us. There was growth from the first year to the second year, so there was time to get used to the idea of our success. It was *Friends, Frasier,* and us—we were the big shows on NBC for a few years.

I so wanted to embrace my good fortune, and I think I did. I was involved with AIDS charities and gay charities, and it could have been that gay America wouldn't have accepted it and straight America wouldn't have accepted it. But that didn't happen. I just relaxed into it.

Debra Messing: When Megan and Sean were let out of their cages, so to speak, all bets were off. There was literally nothing that was too big or outrageous that couldn't be done on our show. Because you always knew you had Jimmy, Max, and Dave to figure out ways of grounding it. Make it real, make it grounded. Having that balance so that the extreme vaudeville that we ended up falling in love with with Jack and Karen could soar. Then you could ground it with whatever was happening with Will and Grace.

Megan Mullally: We would have fun talking about different ways where we wouldn't see Stan, my husband on the show, but we would see parts of him, like his dental records or an X-ray. One time, I'm in the bathtub—we found the person on the set with the biggest feet, who was one of our PAs and like six five—and you just see his giant, hairy foot next to my head.

Once I feel like I've become familiar with a role, that character becomes very real to me, as if it was actually its own real person. It was no problem for me to have this husband that we never see, because in my mind Karen loves him and that's all that matters.

Jim Burrows: The *Will & Grace* writers' room was the funniest room in the world.

Megan Mullally: Our worst episode was great. Off the charts. We were so spoiled by that. Our writers were not only great, but there was great chemistry in the writing room too, just as we had a chemistry on the stage, with the actors and Jimmy. I'm trying to think of a sports analogy, but of course I don't know anything about sports.

Jim Burrows: Everybody wanted to be on *Will & Grace*. Lots of guest stars. It almost ruined *Friends*. Julia Roberts et cetera. What it tends to say is "our cast sucks." It was different with *Will & Grace*. The guest stars just made our actors better.

Debra Messing: Every time someone came on—Madonna—we'd be like, "Really? Really? Us? Okay." We'd feel a little nervous at first, and then we'd be like, "Wait. This is our playground. This is our home. This has been our home for years. We're not the nervous ones."

Jim Burrows: The only note I ever got from a high-placed executive on *Will & Grace* was "too many gay jokes."

Debra Messing: Maybe after the sixth season was the first time that the cast got together and said, "How are we feeling? Is it time for us to stop?" And we would have the conversation "No, there's more. We have more that we can do."

The thing that drove those conversations was that this was something that was so precious to us, that we were so proud of, we just wanted to protect it. We had seen *3rd Rock from the Sun* go from being this trailblazing, Emmy-winning, creative, original, fantastic show to a time when people are like, "Oh, is that still on?"

It really is impossible to have perspective when you're in it. Because when you love something, you're too close to it. We consciously said, "We have to err on the side of leaving before we're comfortable."

Megan Mullally: We all had a lot of fun together. We never had any huge drama. We were lucky in that too, because there are successful shows that have drama behind the scenes, but we really didn't have that. Everyone got along.

For an actor, just having a job for eight years straight, it's almost unheard of. The same job. You're lucky if you have a job for eight days in a row.

Debra Messing: Until we die, the four of us are going to be like siblings. It doesn't matter how much time goes by, when we see each other, it's family. You can't even hope for something like that to happen. Certainly, when you go to acting school, you don't say, "I'm becoming an actor because I want to play one role for eight years." Usually, it's the antithesis. It's "I want to play all kinds of roles, in different genres." But playing one role for years has its own glory in its own way.

Eric McCormack: I made a pilgrimage to come to L.A. with just Canadian stuff on my résumé because being here mattered. I got to walk on the lot every day where *Seinfeld* was filmed.

Debra Messing: We laughed every day at work. You don't really have to say more than that. To be able to go to work every day and to laugh is such a blessing.

Jim Burrows: America got tired of the show after eight years. I don't know why. It never lost its edge.

Debra Messing: When we were done, everyone was talking about what they wanted to take from the set as a memento. I said, "I want the door to my office. Just the door that says 'Grace Adler,' and I want to put it in my office at home as a piece of sculpture against the wall." I get it, and I'm so moved by it. Then, two weeks later, I get a call. NBC wants $225 for the door to pay for the wood.

I said, "Are you kidding me?" They were like, "Well, no. They could use the door on another pilot." I said, "Tell them to sue me." So much for being part of the family.

Eric McCormack: I was inside something that was hard to share with other people. And it was hard to believe it would ever end. Must See TV felt indestructible.

15

Thank You and Good Night

Warren: In 1996, Larry David left *Seinfeld*. Being a show runner is grinding work under the best of circumstances, and Larry had also taken upon himself the job of rewriting every script for every episode of the show.

Jason Alexander: Larry was always saying, "It can't be done again." Next week's show was impossible, and we'd done seven years. He was done after every week.

Glenn Padnick: Larry told me once that leaving the show was the biggest mistake he ever made. He loved the show, and he hated the thought of it going on without him.

Jerry Seinfeld: Larry and I created the show together. We were absolutely bonded. It was a very tough thing when Larry left.

Larry had to go. He wanted to do what he's doing now, though he may not have known it at the time. Out of everything he did for me, I'm most grateful that he left me and caused me to swim on my own. I know I can run a ship now.

Glenn Padnick: Jerry had something to prove to himself and the world. After the show became a hit, the media said the secret of *Seinfeld* was Larry David. There was some truth to that, but in my view the secret of *Seinfeld* was—guess what?—Jerry Seinfeld. Jerry softened Larry's dark edges. There were so many things Larry might have done . . . but he put them in his notebook and used them on *Curb Your Enthusiasm*.

Jerry Seinfeld: When Larry left, I knew I wasn't ready to stop, and the audience wasn't ready.

Jason Alexander: The show was originally written about some pretty complex people, and that ship was being steered by a guy who was pretty complex and kind of dark. Larry had a real gallows humor. Now you've got the same characters, but the writing staff is all in their twenties, and they're being led by a guy who's not dark.

It felt like it shifted from a show where George was the most compelling character to a show where Kramer was the most compelling character. He had a youthfulness, an innocence, that that writing staff knew how to write. And Michael was so easy to write for. "Kramer comes in." You're done.

Jerry Seinfeld: Then I did two years without Larry. The half-life of an executive producer on a sitcom is a short one. It's a grueling, exhausting life. I was starring in the thing. I was in pretty much every scene. I'd rehearse from 9:00 to 3:00 and then write from 3:00 to 7:00. I loved that the show was working.

Warren: Any day at any time, if I needed to find Jerry, he was over at the show. Onstage, writing, or in editing, always fully committed to the show.

Bob Wright: Those last two years, after Larry left, Jerry was really concerned that the show be as funny as it was in the preceding years.

Jerry was his own worst critic. It was almost like Jerry was concerned that he was too close to the product.

Jerry Seinfeld: If you look at the last season, when we did "The Betrayal"—the entire show in reverse—or "The Bizarro," when we met our opposites, those were signals to me that we had broken enough china in the china shop. There wasn't much left to break down, and I didn't want to twist a dry sponge.

We had to keep pushing, but at a certain point we just got to the end of the path.

I never was out in the world, and that's where you get stuff from. I started to feel isolated from the world, and as a comedian that's a horrible feeling. I remember going into a deli on the Upper West Side and seeing phone cards. I said, "What's that? I don't even know what that is."

Warren: It had become a tradition with me and Jerry that around Halloween I would go by Jerry's office on the Radford lot to tell him formally, "We want you back next year. The audience wants you back." I would always cite some of the amazing performance stats of the new season for the show. Jerry and I would talk about how he was feeling and how the show was going, and he would eventually say, "Okay. Let's try and work it out."

My next call was to John Agoglia to say, "Jerry's up for it; let's make a new deal." We weren't the only ones in Burbank who thought creatively. As head of business affairs, John came up with a complex equation of rewards for our most important star.

As an additional reward for their great success, I told Jerry to take the GE jet and the writing staff to New York for an all-expenses-paid "research" trip. It became an annual event. In one contract negotiation, I had the art department take an eight-by-ten photo of the jet and write "AIR JERRY" on the tail. It was the final bit of icing on Jerry's financial cake that year.

Then there was the NBC-Nike connection. It was a close second in perks to the GE jet. Nike Inc., in the form of the West Coast rep Tracy Hardy-Gray, was enormously generous to the NBC talent. The actors on our Must See schedule got loads of swag from Nike's Marina del Rey warehouse, and they didn't even have to wear it on the air. Though I was assured it would be perfectly all right if they did.

I have a copy of a well-known *Seinfeld* poster hanging in my house. It shows the legs of the *Seinfeld* cast from the knees down. Jerry just happens to be wearing a pair of sneakers. Guess which brand? This sort of thing drove the sales force nuts. "Nike should be paying us for that!" But Tracy was helping us keep the talent happy, and you couldn't really put a price on happy talent.

I'd usually get a call from Jerry just before Christmas, often on the afternoon of December 23. "We're coming back for another season," he'd tell me, and that was that. It was a reliable, professional, honorable relationship. No drama. No tantrums. The honeymoon never ended. There was always the sense between the network and Jerry that he'd brilliantly done his job and we'd done ours.

When I visited Jerry in late October 1997, things went a little differently than they had in years before. We chatted for a while, and then I told him, like usual, "We want you back next year, Jerry. The audience wants you back." For his part, Jerry went off script. "Warren," he said, "I need you to know that I don't have a life yet. I'm not in a relationship. This show is my life, and at some point I have to have a real life." There was no "Let's try and work it out," and for the first time I left a meeting doubtful that Jerry would sign on for another year.

Jack Welch, Bob Wright, and Don Ohlmeyer all believed that if we made a rich enough offer to Jerry, he'd have to continue with the show. My feeling was that we usually had Jerry emotionally on the five-yard line and just had to come up with a few enticements to shove him into the end zone. The Jerry I'd met with on this particular Halloween was well back down the field. A meeting was set in New York.

Howard West: We were the number one show, and we got a call from Bob Wright, president of the network. Welch would like to have brunch with Jerry, George, and myself.

George Shapiro: In Bob Wright's apartment on the thirty-eighth floor of Trump Tower.

Howard West: For two weeks we negotiate what Jerry would like to eat. Oatmeal. French toast. Whatever. They were very nervous, catering to Jerry. It was a far cry from where we'd started.

Bob Wright was at the head of the table. To his left was Welch. I'm to the left of Welch. Across the table was Jerry and George. There were three waiters for five people.

We're eating. I'm discussing everything with Jack Welch but *Seinfeld*.

George Shapiro: Howard was like a kid meeting his baseball hero.

Howard West: They bring in research on *Seinfeld*. Charts. They're making a presentation to us. We turn from beggars to the network begging. Welch tells us *Seinfeld* hasn't yet reached its peak. It was a very warm moment. It felt so good.

Jack Welch: We pitched Jerry in Bob Wright's apartment and thought for sure we had the sale. We made the pitch to Jerry that if he quit, he would be quitting with increasing ratings.

Howard West: A magnificent presentation, but inside I'm laughing my ass off. Jack Welch said, "You know, Jerry, I go all over the world. People only want to know about one thing—Jerry Seinfeld and his show."

Bob Wright: We gave Jerry all kinds of reasons to believe the show was still as popular as it always was, but that wasn't enough for him.

Jerry Seinfeld: I almost wished it was a regular show, like a grocery store. You don't close it. You leave it open. "We're making money here!" But the show had its own rules, so I felt like I had to play by them.

Howard West: Jerry sent signals that it might be time for him to get off the stage. Jack Welch said, "Jerry, come here."

They go off to the side, and Jack Welch writes on a piece of paper and gives it to Jerry. He writes $5 million a show. That's for twenty-two shows. A hundred and ten million dollars. Firm offer. We didn't negotiate. That's the offer. That's the beginning.

Jerry Seinfeld: It was the most backward meeting ever in show business. Where the people are telling you you're worth more, and I was saying, "I don't want it." Normally, you tell them you're worth more, and they say, "We don't have it." They can't give you any more, and you won't work for any less. This was backward. We want to give you more. I won't take it.

I felt the giant wheel slowing. A big part of that was the writing staff, the engine that supports the show. The writers had all set up deals all over town for their own shows and their own production companies—not a one of them panned out—and they weren't giving me the support I needed. I probably should have fired them all and brought in fifteen new kids who were excited.

But my own wheel was slowing also. My only interest was, "What would make this most exciting for the audience?" I thought of the Beatles. They did nine years and then were gone.

Howard West: The meeting ends, and George and Jerry and I go for a walk. All around Central Park, and Jerry sits us down on a bench.

George Shapiro: Eighty-first and Central Park West.

Howard West: Jerry says, "Guys, when I was twenty-one, I sat on this same bench."

George Shapiro: The same bench he sat on when he told his father he was going into stand-up comedy.

Jerry Seinfeld: We went to the park bench where my dad and I had sat before I moved into my first apartment. I told him I was going to be a comedian, and he thought it was great. He said he wished he could have done it. And he could have. He was very talented, a very funny guy.

Imagine sitting there trying to figure out if this was the time to leave the show.

Howard West: Now we're walking to lunch, and Jerry said, "What do you think?" We'd been well paid as an extension of Jerry. Me, I'd have loved to have done one more season.

George Shapiro: I thought it would be great to quit while Jerry was on top.

Howard West: I told him he was the guy working seven days a week to turn the show out.

George Shapiro: Jerry said he didn't want to stay too long. He was getting a standing ovation, and he wanted to leave while he was still getting that ovation.

Jerry Seinfeld: I really didn't think about the money at all. I thought about the audience. How are they feeling? Where are they? I was trying to perceive it like a comedian on the stage. When you've been onstage for a pretty long time—and nine years is a healthy run—and they're still screaming, if you can get off, they'll scream even louder. They'll never forget you.

Jason Alexander: It was the right artistic thing to do. Every comic wants that. "Good night, everybody." No, do ten more minutes!

Jerry Seinfeld: There's something about a thing that's in your life for a brief period of time—a little bit less than you really want it—that makes it special. I thought, "If I go now, the level of excitement the audience feels will last." There's a peak of energy that everything has. I thought if we ended the show when we did, we'd leave a buzz in the room.

Howard West: Jerry said he would have gone back if the writers had come to him and said, "Jerry, one more. Let's do it together." But those writers were spoiled, indulged, and overpaid. We started with three and ended up with eleven or twelve. No one ever created a show and had it on before or after.

George Shapiro: They won Emmys and got credit for the scripts, but Larry and Jerry rewrote every word. They acted out every word. Performed every word.

Jerry Seinfeld: My only regret is that we never found out where that deal would have come out. Nobody knows.

Howard West: I was deballed! I didn't even get to make a counteroffer.

Warren: On December 23, 1997, I got the fateful call from Jerry. "Warren," he told me, "this isn't going to be like those other phone calls." The tone of our conversation was like everything else that passed between NBC and *Seinfeld*. It was straightforward and good-humored. Jerry told me the show was over, that he was ready to go out and live.

Seinfeld was one of those shows where there were never any problems, and this wasn't a problem either. Jerry had had enough, so *Seinfeld* was finished. Jerry would go out on top. *Seinfeld* would end the 1997–98 season as the year's most watched series, averaging thirty-four million people a week (Nielsen Media Research). I called Bob.

Bob Wright: At the meeting at my apartment, I thought we had convinced Jerry to stay on with the show. But I got a call later that day or maybe the next day. It was George Shapiro telling me Jerry didn't want to keep doing the show.

Jack Welch: When I think of Jerry calling me on Christmas Eve to tell me he wasn't going to do the show anymore, I couldn't believe somebody could turn down $110 million.

Jason Alexander: I don't miss doing the show. I miss the people, and I miss having a reason to hang out with those people. We did not become friends outside of the show, so we knew we were splitting up that family. My feeling was we couldn't surprise the audience anymore. We could make them laugh, but we couldn't take characters down a road where you couldn't anticipate what they might do. I think that's the dictionary definition of jump the shark. It felt like a good time to go.

I think I'm the only guy on the planet who liked the finale. It was what we never were, which was sentimental. It found an organic reason to bring back all the people who had been meaningful to us and to the success of that show. The experience, for me, out-colored what it was for everybody else, which I guess was underwhelming.

Mike Mandelker: For the finale of *Seinfeld*, we went out asking $2 million for thirty seconds. We ended up getting $1.8 million. We'd gotten less for the Super Bowl the year before.

George Shapiro: When the show went off, Jerry's picture was on every magazine. He said he was sick of himself. The last telecast was May 14th of 1998, and that was the day Frank Sinatra died.

Jerry Seinfeld: In around 1997, somebody interviewed Steve Case of AOL, and they asked him, "Who is your competition?" He said, "My only competition is Jerry Seinfeld. When that show comes on Thursday night, our connections go in the toilet. I'm only scared of Jerry Seinfeld." Then I left, but it didn't save him.

Warren: The end of *Seinfeld* occasioned another programming conversation with Jack Welch. It played out a little better than our *Wall Street* chat. Preston Beckman and I were in New York, and Jack summoned us to his office at 30 Rock to discuss what we had in mind for replacing *Seinfeld,* not that anything could replace *Seinfeld.*

We walked into Jack's office and found him beaming like a little kid. "I think we're into one of the most exciting businesses we've ever played in," Jack told us, and with that he opened an envelope and spilled diamonds all over his desktop. Some of them skidded off the blotter onto the floor. "They're synthetic!" Jack said.

He told us how, instead of needing a thousand years to make a diamond, they could now do it in a couple of weeks. Preston and I were on our hands and knees gathering up the synthetic spillage off the carpet and looking at each other. Synthetic diamonds? Jack was beside himself, downright giddy.

He got to the topic of television only eventually. Jack just wanted a heads-up on the *Seinfeld* replacement—what would go on Thursday at 9:00—whenever we made our decision. "I'd like to know about it before I read about it," he told me.

That was as close as Jack Welch ever came to "interfering" with programming. We left him with his synthetic diamonds scattered all over his desktop.

Jason Alexander: There was not a day we were together on that set when we weren't laughing. Every day. It was pretty miraculous. If they said today, "Come back and do *Seinfeld*," it might be a stupid career move, but somebody's going to pay me to laugh?

Warren: In 2009, the invitation to "come back and do *Seinfeld*" was extended by Larry David for his HBO show, *Curb Your Enthusiasm*.

Jerry Seinfeld: The reunion on *Curb Your Enthusiasm* was perfect for us—perfectly wrong.

Jason Alexander: I had tons of hesitation about going on *Curb Your Enthusiasm*. I'll be brutal. It was far too valuable for HBO. A *Seinfeld* movie? We could have made gazillions. There was only going to be one. That was it, and we were just giving it away.

The other hesitations were really practical. We hadn't worked together in ten years. Could we do it, and without a script? I was forty when we shut down the show. Now I'm fifty. George was a lot to handle at forty, now maybe I hate this character. Between us not knowing if we could work together and whether or not these characters had aged well, I was concerned. But we were in Larry's hands, and he knows what he's doing.

Jerry Seinfeld: Look how easily the shows collided. People loved the scenes with me and Larry in the office. People said, "It looks like that's what it was really like." That's what it was really like.

Jason Alexander: It was so *Seinfeld*ian. When we walked into that stage and there were those sets again. There were people at that table read who would have been at that table ten years ago. It was a pretty remarkable thing.

Jerry Seinfeld: The syndication story of the show is, to me, more interesting. The show flourished in syndication, found a new audience, and kept going.

Howard West: We've been on, in one form or another—network to syndication—for twenty years.

Jason Alexander: Our audience grew at least fourfold in syndication. It's beyond a TV show or an acting job at this point. *Seinfeld* has a resonance and a power that nobody could have imagined.

George Shapiro: With Turner, we're set for a deal through 2016. There's a whole new generation discovering the show. Funny is funny. The kids are loving the show.

Jason Alexander: The thing that has shocked me since we've gone off the air are the places where I have to assume I'm a face in the crowd, and I'm not. I thought there was no way in the marketplace in Budapest in the middle of the World Cup that anybody is going to know I'm alive. Nope.

Walking into Ramallah as an American Jew and having Palestinians running out of their homes and their shops yelling, "George, George!" There's no explanation for it.

Jerry Seinfeld: Somebody just asked me about the show yesterday, asked me how many viewers we had. I told them seventy-five million, and they couldn't believe it. Outside of the Super Bowl, you can't come near that today.

There's never a control group for any of these experiments. We did what we did, and it's pretty cool for me to think that I got one of the last big rides on the television rocket where you could literally control the dialogue of the country.

16

"You're Fired!"

Sean Hayes: There was this guy, this Warren Littlefield, who took us through this huge success at NBC, and then suddenly he was gone, and I had to ask, "Why did Dad just leave? Where did he go?"

Warren: A few months before my firing, I had an ugly run-in with Don Ohlmeyer. Don held a daily strategy meeting in his office, a kind of huddle focused mostly on advertising and promotion. It always started at 2:30. One day my colleague Karey Burke and I were on the panel at the Hollywood Radio and Television Society luncheon in Beverly Hills, and I called Don's assistant, Sandi, to remind her where we were and tell her we probably couldn't make it back in time for the start of the meeting. She said, "Fine. I'll tell Don." She called back a few minutes later with this message: "Don says if you're not here, the door will be locked and you can't come in."

I asked her, "What the hell does that mean?" She couldn't say. I told her to tell Don we'd be there when we got there, and if the meeting was still going on, we'd join it.

A few minutes passed. Another call from Sandi. "Don says if you don't make this meeting, don't bother coming back." This was how my wars with Don usually started. Every conversation would escalate until we got to the "don't bother coming back" part.

Of course, Karey and I came back, well after 2:30. The meeting was still going, and we joined it. Once it had broken up, I asked Karey to stay behind, and I cornered Don and said, "You big fucking bully. What the fuck is your problem? How dare you! We didn't go for a round of golf. We didn't go to the video arcade. We were representing this company. Karey Burke was asked to sit up onstage along with me as a senior development executive and a spokesperson for NBC. We should celebrate that. What the fuck is your problem?"

Don didn't say anything. "Apologize," I told him. Don mumbled something. "Just say you're sorry."

"I didn't mean to . . . ," Don said. That was about as much of an apology as anyone could ever expect from Don.

"Okay, fine," I told him. "Good-bye," and Karey and I were out the door. Yes, it was childish and petty and just the sort of thing that was growing all too frequent between us.

Jack Welch: Somebody had to leave, and we weren't going to fire Ohlmeyer. The thinking was that Warren was a dry hole. Ohlmeyer's personality and charisma made us a bigger force in Hollywood, in our view, so we weren't going to get rid of him and be left with Warren. Then we still wouldn't be getting hits and wouldn't have any presence.

Warren: I have to think Don convinced Jack and Bob it was time for me to go. The success Don and I had enjoyed at NBC had made our relationship more contentious rather than less so. I'd come to feel I no longer had to listen to everything Don had to say, and Don seemed to believe he was more responsible for NBC's turnaround than I was. It was a clash of egos and measuring dicks.

Our last big battle was over the show that would become *The West Wing.* Following *ER*'s phenomenal success, CAA approached me with a proposition to make a multi-series commitment to John Wells. John had distinguished himself on *ER* as a remarkable show runner and all-purpose talent, and it seemed perfectly sensible for us to secure his services on any and all future projects. John was a hot commodity, and I knew if we didn't lock him in, our competition would steal him away.

One of the first projects John Wells brought to us was in partnership with Aaron Sorkin and was based on Aaron's experiences as a White House intern in the press corps. Aaron knew the ins and outs of the West Wing of the White House intimately, and his pitch was compelling. I was well aware that network television's track record for political drama was deplorable, but Sorkin's pitch hooked me, and John Wells was supervising, so I said, "Yes!"

The script they delivered was every bit as electrifying as the pitch. Though I struggled with the decision, given the history of such shows, I eventually told Don I thought we should make the pilot. I believed John Wells more than deserved the benefit of the doubt and that the Sorkin script was damn good. This was very much in keeping with my philosophy of trusting the talent. John Wells, in particular, had more than earned that trust.

John Wells: Don thought *West Wing* was elitist or something. This is the same Don who'd once told me he thought *ER* was great but it wouldn't last. I don't know if he actually believed it or just said it. When I kind of took the paramedics off *ER* and wrote *Third Watch*, I remember Don telling me, "This is the kind of show you want, kid."

Warren: Harold had the deal closed, everything was ready but Don was adamantly against moving forward, and this time he dug in his heels. Despite all my efforts, there was no budging him. Don and I had always fought, but somehow business had gotten done, shows had been made. This was different. This was a stalemate.

I think our mutual success had exhausted us a little, and Don—as I would soon learn—had come to believe our relationship was too contentious to continue to be productive. To Don's way of thinking, it was time for me to go. So the Ohlmeyer/Littlefield thing ended, fittingly enough, with a battle and a snarl.

Bob Wright: It seemed like the play was ending. Don was a handful, no question. We all enjoyed a lot of success during that period, and it was like the band was breaking up.

Warren: I called Don at home one night in October 1998 and said I was hearing rumblings—what was going on? He said, "Maybe there should be a statute of limitations on these jobs. I think you should talk to Bob."

Wow. That's what you get after twenty years at a company? After delivering billions in profits? Statute of limitations?

Bob Wright called from New York the next morning to fire me over the phone. I left my position as president of entertainment and my twenty-year career with NBC within weeks of the airing of the final *Seinfeld* summer repeats. I had been announced as entertainment president the same month the first episode of *Seinfeld* aired. There are worse bookends.

When I was running NBC Entertainment, the shows that made our schedule were my choices, and I didn't ask approval of anyone. I brought many voices into the process. I listened, but then I made the call. Maybe Don allowed me that because it was my ass on the line, and he's a pretty shrewd guy. Maybe he believed that we had a pretty good track record, and I had earned the right to do what I believed was best for the schedule.

For a long time, that's how we functioned. There wasn't chaos. There wasn't resentment. There weren't decisions that were made in the moment. Rather, our motto was "this is our long-term strategy, this is what we believe in," and patience was rewarded. The audience was sending us really positive signals. We believed they deserved something in return.

At the height of the Must See era, NBC was generating over $1 billion in annual profit for GE. During my last three seasons NBC sold an industry record $6.5 billion in prime-time advertising, $2 billion more than our closest competitor. On Thursday night in the 1997–98 season we beat our combined competition by margins of 60 percent (Nielsen Media Research). This was the essence of being at the top of the Rock. We had climbed a mountain and delivered award-winning high-quality entertainment that America embraced and our competition coveted. A generation of television watchers were weaned on Must See TV, including my two most passionate fans, my kids.

The network was valued in the recent Comcast deal at $0 and was estimated to run at a $600 million annual loss. The reversal has been remarkable. In the nineties we produced little short of a financial geyser at NBC, and many of our Must See shows have gone on to realize staggering revenues.

Friends, owned by Warner Bros. Television, has generated over $5 billion in revenue worldwide and for all ten years of its run was a top-ten-rated series. *Seinfeld*, distributed by Sony and owned by Warner Bros. Television, has worldwide revenues that exceed $4 billion, and the show still generates over $40 million a year in domestic syndication advertising sales. Three billion dollars in revenues for *ER*, and for ten of its fifteen years it was a top-ten-rated series. Two billion dollars for *Frasier*. About $1 billion apiece for NBC's *Will & Grace* and Sony's *Mad About You*.

Our prime-time success drove large audiences into our owned and operated local stations' late-night news and right into *The Tonight Show* with Jay Leno. Again, decisions and actions that were ultimately worth billions. While not part of the Must See brand, let's not forget over nine hundred hours of the *Law & Order* franchise and still counting.

Not bad for a dry hole. NBC was the most watched broadcast network for the 1995–96 season and would hold on to that crown for eight of the next nine years. After running out of quality product in 2004, the network dropped to fourth place and has stayed there since.

My replacement as president of entertainment, Scott Sassa, soon replaced Don and then brought in Garth Ancier in my old job. Garth lasted a little over a year, and then Jeff Zucker took over.

Sean Hayes: Warren Littlefield. Garth Ancier. Scott Sassa. Jeff Zucker. Kevin Reilly. What bigger red flag do you need to know something isn't being managed correctly. Our show ran eight years, and we had five different presidents at NBC.

Jack Welch: NBC was a great asset for GE. Employees loved it, were proud of it. They felt like it was part of the family. It's been a tough run for NBC. You look in that top ten every week, and you never see a show.

Warren: A few months after my transition, Bob Wright invited me to breakfast at the Peninsula hotel in Beverly Hills. He said he had something for me. I had begun the healing process, and Bob helped that along when he handed over several bonus checks based on year-end performance by NBC. They were still number one.

I asked Bob who was going to be making the key creative decisions at the network? Bob told me there was a system in place that would suffice. That was the moment it dawned on me that I must have done a shitty job of managing up. Every day, using NBC's money, I had made dozens of financial and creative decisions that impacted the quality of the product we aired and our performance as a network. As smart as he was, Bob didn't have a clue about what I really did.

Bob Wright: It's clear in hindsight that we weren't able to recover the way we had before. To this date, we've not seen the level of performance at NBC that we enjoyed.

Warren: Only after I was gone did they start to realize what we had achieved in the Must See era.

Dan Harrison: Today the average home has two hundred channels. You're never going to aggregate up an audience like there was in the Must See TV era. It was as much of a cultural milestone and touchstone in size and scope as Frank Sinatra or Elvis or the Beatles were in the music business.

The highest-rated entertainment program in history was the *M*A*S*H* finale. Seventy-seven percent of American households watching television on February 28, 1983, were watching the finale of *M*A*S*H*. Then you get to *Cosby* at 50 percent shares and thirty-plus ratings. Now you're down to *American Idol*, where a 20 share is massive. The shows that are hits today would have been canceled after a week in the nineties.

Steve McPherson: I do think I was lucky to be along for the ride. It was intimate and close at NBC, and people knew each other very well. Everything meshed together. It wasn't as if the workday ever ended. Agents for drinks. Out to dinner with the studio. Notes for producers. It never stopped.

It makes me sad to see what's happened at NBC. It's a shame. There's been a complete abandonment of what made NBC great. It was *the* brand, and now it's just been thrown into the Comcast deal. It's really sad, but I'm sure Jeff Zucker will get promoted over it.

Dan Harrison: Working at NBC in the Must See era was like playing for the 1927 Yankees.

Dick Wolf: Getting a commitment on NBC in the glory days was better than your birthday party when you were six, because you knew you had a shot.

I recently said to Jeff Gaspin [former president of entertainment, NBCUniversal], "I honestly don't think you want your legacy to be two hours of fat people." He said, "Fat people who cry."

Harold Brook: One of the biggest things that went on during the nineties was Warren. We had this amazing confluence of people. Warren threw a Christmas party a few years ago, and he invited everybody who'd worked for him. I looked around this room, and it was amazing. People who'd gone on to bigger jobs, and it had such a good feeling about it. I went to CBS after NBC. I only lasted eighteen months. It was dreadful.

We all worked so well together. It was like kicking the tires at a hundred miles per hour, but it didn't feel like it at the time.

Bob Broder: The allegiance, the belief in talent, kept people like Jimmy Burrows hanging around to work with them. Today at NBC, they have no belief in talent, no relationship with the creative community, and they have too many people doing the job.

John Wells: The hubris that came after Warren leaving and the way NBC is run still exists to this day. I was at the Olympics, and I got stuck in a car with Bob and Suzanne Wright. Suzanne was a big fan of *ER*, and I saw a moment from Bob. He steeled up—like he ran the network and knew how it should work. I remember thinking, "He has no idea how this works, but I think he thinks he does."

Max Mutchnick: We were the last Must See show because we were part of a generation that got the last bit of a company and a president of a network who cared about writing. No one loved writing and actors after Warren.

David Kohan: We were at a meeting recently for a show we were doing with the brass of a network. By far the most dominant voice was the sales guy, who I've never met and probably will never see again. And he was giving us notes about what would work and what wouldn't. And this company shall remain CBS. Les Moonves [president and CEO of

CBS] wasn't even talking. And I remember walking out of that meeting saying, "Why are we listening to *that* guy?"

Lisa Kudrow: I have been trying to produce shows and ran away from the network because it wasn't possible to do something different. Because if it's different, it has to stay on the air so people learn what it is. *Seinfeld. Friends.* It was a little easier to get what it was, and Warren also gave the shows the best chance possible. It's really hard to do something different that's going to last a long time, something that's based on those little moments of character.

Paul Reiser: If you hire people you like and trust your instincts—I like this talent, this package, these people; go do it—then you're much more likely to have a success.

Steve Levitan: After Warren left, I don't think the people in charge were interested in having quite as much fun. Everything seemed so grand at that time. We talked about that NBC brand all the time. That brand represented smart, sophisticated, urban comedy. It stood for quality. NBC was my first stop with a pitch, my first choice going in.

Jason Alexander: What's fascinating to me is it feels like the lesson of *Seinfeld* wasn't learned. On my subsequent shows, the network and studio executives micromanaged those projects, micromanaged them into failure. With Jerry and Larry, people looked at this singular take on life and knew there was no negotiating with them. You either decided to trust them or decided you couldn't. That lesson doesn't seem to have been learned.

Warren: TV historians may find other events to mark the death of Must See TV, but it was a January morning in 2004 when I called Preston Beckman at Fox, my former consigliere and scheduling guru, and said, "It's over." NBC had just announced that Donald Trump's *Apprentice* would be their new Thursday night program at 9:00. Must See TV didn't end with a whimper. It ended with The Donald barking, "You're FIRED!"

Bob Broder: Thursday night, the best night of television on television, and you put *The Apprentice* on? You just piss it away? There's no question that the world has changed, that media has changed, that digital is making everybody insecure as we try to figure it out. But some of the basic principles of programming and scheduling don't evaporate or dissipate because of those changes. You almost have to work harder to make sure you have content in a place where the audience is going to come to see it. After twenty years of being number one on Thursday, that legacy ended with the conclusion of the '03–'04 season.

Tom Werner: There are all sorts of ways to bring people to the television. You can do it with exploitive programs or good programs. NBC proved you could do it by producing excellent programs. Now we've gone from Must See TV to *The Apprentice* and *The Biggest Loser.*

John Landgraf: NBC lost sight of its perch. It owned quality television.

Warren: Bob Wright was correct in predicting that the broadcast business would change. He bet that the cable business model with dual-revenue streams (advertising and subscription fees) would be a hedge against an eventual weakening broadcast schedule. So Bob continued to invest in cable and diversify the NBC portfolio.

Dan Harrison: The broadcast networks were slow to move into cable generally, and most of the broadcast/cable networks that exist today were built by acquisition. ABC bought ESPN, and Disney bought ABC primarily because of the value of ESPN. What NBC did early and smart was launching CNBC. And then there was America's Talking, run by Roger Ailes, and that's what became MSNBC in a partnership with Microsoft.

CNBC and MSNBC had direct revenue streams from subscribers. In the nineties, you had all sorts of new people becoming cable subscribers, and that added more money to the network's bottom line. That was really the beginning of NBC's cable bet.

Warren: Meanwhile, cable television, after living primarily off of network reruns (like *Law & Order* on TNT) and theatrical films (HBO's primary thrust in the early years), made the strategic decision to invest their profits in original series programs. As the cost of failure continued to rise in network television, the response by the large corporations that ran the networks was to tighten the creative reins, add more layers of supervision, and manage the process more aggressively.

Program development became "systemized" with more controls in place than ever before. Story area documents and story outlines were written again and again. Once they'd been okayed to go to script, writers discovered there was no time in the process to experiment or detour from the approved documents.

Teams of well-intentioned, industrious studio and network executives all put their imprint on the material. But breakthrough success in television has never been about control. It's about nurturing and guiding and allowing creative people to flourish. It's about taking risks. I encouraged an environment where mistakes could be made, where boundaries could be pushed and even broken. Cable television has embraced this philosophy and is proving an extremely seductive alternative to the networks.

Cable TV offers freedom in language and far fewer restrictions on violence and nudity. After HBO broke through with *The Sopranos* and *Sex and the City*, the world of television changed.

Eric McCormack: Nowadays, it's all a crapshoot. There is no brass ring. There's no obvious place to aim for, and everything is second place.

Max Mutchnick: There's no bedside manner left anymore. None. And it shows itself in very strange ways. You used to go up to Warren Littlefield's office, and the big move was you go behind the glass doors. That's a big move for a writer, and then you're waiting in the small anteroom before you get into the big office.

Now you'll sit at the guard gate for forty-five minutes, and then maybe you'll be brought to the third floor for another thirty minutes, and then you'll be brought in. There are all of these little slights that make you feel like shit.

When you're interacting with the guy making the decisions at the network, you feel invested, you feel better about your work, and you work toward making it better.

David Kohan: We're not that adaptable. We write what we think is good, and the networks say no. We go in now and ask the networks what they want.

Jason Alexander: When I go in and pitch shows, and they're laughing and they get the characters, and the guy says to me, "What happens in season four?" I say, "I renegotiate for more money, because apparently we're in season four." That's a great problem to have. Why not figure it out when you get there?

I can't tell you how many times people have told me, "This is so good. It's not for us."

Warren: I couldn't sell *Friends* or *Mad About You* today to a network. No hook.

Sean Hayes: I remember a phone call to Jeff Zucker. It was toward the end of *Will & Grace*, and the ratings weren't that great, and I called Jeff. He said, "Yeah, Sean. What's up?"

He talked fast to let me know he didn't have much time.

"What can we do for marketing?" I asked him.

He said, "It's over, Sean. Nobody cares about the show anymore. It's over." I couldn't believe he was telling me that.

I hung up on him.

Steve Levitan: It's been very depressing to watch NBC sink. Zucker's tenure at NBC, that really got to me. From the first minute I met Zucker, I knew he was a guy who didn't love TV. He didn't love entertainment. Didn't love Hollywood.

David Kohan: The upfronts in the nineties were fun to go to. It was a party, a kind of celebration. Now there's a pervasive sense of "I hope we made the right choices. I hope we didn't screw this up."

John Wells: When Zucker started making noises about canceling *Southland* in 2009, I called him up and said, "Jeff, don't do it. You're not in a position to cancel shows that ABC and TNT both want. They're going to put it on the air, and it'll be terrible for you. Just the PR of it is terrible in the creative community. You're already the fourth or fifth place people pitch anything. Even if *Southland* doesn't work, at least it looks like an interesting television show." He just doesn't get it.

He had no idea when he took over, and he had too much ego to admit that he didn't know.

Steve Levitan: If you're a network president, you'd better believe in what you're doing. You'd better believe broadcast television is relevant and can be what it was. If you don't believe in the network, nobody else will either. If you don't bet big, you become a niche.

Jeff just wanted to go back to New York from day one. You knew it. He didn't want to be here. You could feel it. Why am I at the kids' table? He wanted to be in New York with Jack Welch and Bob Wright.

David Kohan: The president of Warner Bros. [Peter Roth] loves television, and he loves to make the sort of TV he enjoys. There's something nice about that.

Steve Levitan: Look at the Emmys this year. Jimmy Fallon came out and said, "I love television. I love this stuff." You have to believe it.

Max Mutchnick: They're not happy unless it's horny guys trying to score with a slut. Be a nerd who wants to fuck a blonde, and you might get on the schedule. There's no quality or level to the people you get to write.

David Kohan: We recently wrote a show about a strong woman. They said it's too alienating, and we don't want an older woman at the center of the show. It was an Auntie Mame story. I asked the executive, "Did *you* like it?" He said, "Yeah." I asked, "Well, what makes you think nobody else will?"

Max Mutchnick: It's comical now to go to a network and watch all of the lower-level execs. They wouldn't dream of saying what they thought. At one network, you're not allowed to laugh. At another, you look at the shade of red of the head of the network's face.

Bob Broder: Jeff Zucker's NBC has been going down a long ski jump, and they fell off the end. Like the thrill of victory and the agony of defeat. From 1982 until two years ago when *Scrubs* came off NBC, I or my agency has represented a successful half hour or more on NBC every year.

Steve Levitan: Jeff Zucker is the worst thing that ever happened to network television.

Max Mutchnick: The script we're about to do notes on we call *Chipped Beef in a Cone*. I call it that because I saw a PBS documentary about scientists in London who were trying to devise a food that the most people would respond to—in terms of texture and taste. It was a croissant-like cone filled with a creamy whipped beef. What we've just written is chipped beef in a cone.

Jason Alexander: When we went off the air, Fox was really starting to come alive. So it was the networks, HBO, and Showtime. There wasn't much entertainment on the Internet. *Now* if you have four million viewers, *Woooo!*

Dick Wolf: It's still the same-size pie. Total viewers haven't gone up. The slices are just getting thinner and thinner.

Tom Werner: In the days of *Cosby*, because there were so few channels, it was possible for America to sit down and watch something all together. *American Idol* gets a third of the *Cosby* audience, even though it's the number one show on TV.

Dick Wolf: *Monk* did a 6.8 for the finale. You put on a public execution, the last episode of *Monk*, or Tiger's home movies, then you'll get a number. But that's not programming.

Tom Werner: Rick Rosen told me a story recently. He talked to fifty people about some show they all watched, and he asked how many had watched it live, during its regular time slot. Two people raised their hands.

Warren: To complete the circle, remember Paul Klein? He of the "big-event" philosophy at NBC and LOP? Least objectionable programming?

Dan Harrison: Paul Klein's theory was that the network that had the best second choice was the one that was going to win. You had a very passionate first choice that would lock in a specific audience, but if you had the most popular second choice, people would gravitate toward that in large numbers. Today that would never work. It's a larger passionate base, but people are never looking for their second choice. If you love shows about cooking with margarine, there's a show about cooking with margarine. If you love shows about Hitler's bunker, there's a show about Hitler's bunker.

Now you can zero in. There is no second choice anymore. This is my passion at this moment, and I'm going to find a show to satisfy that. If I change my mind and tomorrow I'm passionate about something else, there's another channel that will serve me that. That's how the viewer watches television now, and that's a big change from the Must See era.

Steve Levitan: During the darkest of the years, at least for me—Bush in the White House and Zucker in the NBC chair—I wondered if the magic era was gone. Too many choices, a fractured audience. Can we ever get back to the days when something means as much as those shows did? I think people are rediscovering some of the quality work that's out there. I'm hoping we can recapture that Must See TV feeling.

Warren: Ultimately, it is the programmer's creative instincts that determine what shows get the love and the promotional support at the network. There are easy calls when the research document screams hit show—like *Cosby* and *The Golden Girls*—but most are harder, murkier, gray instead of black or white.

In deciding what got on our air and what didn't, I went back to the guiding principles of Grant Tinker. Respect the audience, he told us, and they will come. Grant taught us to get into business with the best-quality writers and producers the industry has to offer and let them do what they do best—create and execute. "First be best, then be first" was his mantra. And rather than fear change, as I did with the loss of *Cheers,* I learned to embrace it. It meant opportunity. These were lessons that served us well during my tenure running NBC in the nineties.

I wasn't born with a silver spoon in my mouth but I was always curious about how the world tasted. I've been a teamster truck driver, shoveled coal in a plastics factory, and poured cement with a crew of French Canadian ex-cons. Those were hard jobs, but not nearly as hard as television and not nearly as much fun.

The Zuckerization of the network in recent years has been marked by the belief that viewers exist to be manipulated rather than nourished. In the Zucker worldview, the audience doesn't count. Only the dollars do. This philosophy in practice resulted in Jay Leno at 10:00 five nights a week, and we all know how well that went.

In January 2011, Comcast took over controlling interest of NBCUniversal, and their senior management group did not include Jeff Zucker. They reached out instead to Bob Greenblatt—producer of *Six Feet Under* and past president of Showtime—and the creative community breathed a collective sigh of relief. I breathed one myself.

Here's hoping the peacock struts again and NBC does indeed recapture that Must See TV feeling. Cheers!

Acknowledgments

It began with my mother. She first figured out that despite the fact I loved sports, I didn't have the talent to be a professional athlete. Thankfully, she encouraged me to join the junior wing of the Montclair Dramatic Club during my high school years. That program was run by Charlie Mortimer, who, after many years in advertising in New York, launched his own production company, Westfall Productions. My first job in the industry was working at Westfall as a gofer on a television pilot, *The New Little Rascals*. It was during that production that I realized I didn't want to go to graduate school in psychology because I'd have a lot more fun in the wonderful world of entertainment. I never looked back. Jonathan Bernstein was the line producer who mentored me and taught me the art of TV and film production.

My father was a humble and loyal man who taught me many of the values I try to continue to embrace.

Through the years my wife, Theresa, and our children, Emily and Graham, have hopefully understood by my words and actions that they come first. I acknowledge that my career is a close second. Without their flexibility, support, love, and understanding I never could have accomplished what I did.

My sister, Pam, has never worked in television, but she loves to watch it and with my mom has always been one of my biggest fans.

In addition to being my valued and trusted assistant through my NBC years and ever since, Patty Mann gave the creation and execution of this book her laser focus and commitment.

Brian Pike, my friend and agent, suggested I write this book and then put me in the skilled hands of the literary agent David Black. David knew how daunting a blank page could be for a nonwriter and had the wisdom to introduce me to the writer T. R. Pearson. Writing partnerships are like marriages; some work, and others end up in court. With Tom the honeymoon is still going on.

To bring this book to life, Tom and I conducted over fifty interviews with actors, writers, producers, agents, and executives. To those who participated, thank you for your time and unedited truthfulness. The Must See story is as much yours as mine.

Michael Zinberg hired me as manager of comedy development at NBC in December 1979. Why, I'll never know.

Brandon Tartikoff was a tough boss but brilliant broadcaster whose infectious love of the medium was a gift.

Fred Silverman was an inspiration as a legendary television executive and prolific producer.

Grant Tinker was our compass at a time when NBC had none.

Bob Wright introduced a discipline of strategic thinking to an industry that mostly chased after hit shows.

Don Ohlmeyer chose not to fire me when he walked into NBC, and I'm grateful. It wasn't an easy ride with Don, but it was historic and as memorable as these pages reveal.

Preston Beckman and Dan Harrison remain valued friends and invaluable resources of knowledge of the history of the television medium. Their contributions were significant.

Without Jimmy Burrows there could not have been Must See TV. His talent runs through much of the Must See content, and his passion for his work is unequaled.

Chris Connor, Jimmy Burrows's indispensable assistant, expertly aided us in getting "must have" interviews.

Sari DeCesare was always a highly valued resource from the research department at NBC in New York, particularly on the long days and nights in preparing the upfronts. She's still there (senior vice president of TV network audience research) and was invaluable once again in clarifying what the TV world looked like and what we accomplished.

Barbara Tranchito, a senior NBC publicist during the Must See years, brought her wit and wisdom to helping us gain access to key talent.

Many entertainment executives embraced my quest to tell this story, and while they were not formally interviewed, their knowledge was readily supplied. Special thanks to Steve Mosko, president of Sony Pictures Television; Bruce Rosenblum, president of Warner Bros. Television Group; Joel Berman, former president of Paramount Worldwide Television Distribution and founder of Wavelength Media; and Jerry Petry, former executive vice president of NBCUniversal Television.

The guys I grew up with in New Jersey and remain close to today have always reminded me that I have no skills whatsoever. Any success I may have enjoyed in my career is pure luck. They are wise men.

Mark Streid came into my life when I became president of NBC Entertainment. He is a good friend and taught me that a strong body was needed to survive the job and would help build a strong mind.

Jill Young brings an energy and creative spark to my company's development and brought that same attitude to helping me accomplish this.

Rebecca Marks, executive vice president, NBC Entertainment Publicity, embraced our historical journey. Also at NBC, Jennifer Hozer and Julie Gollins were critical in retrieving from the NBC photo archives the wonderful shots that capture the Must See era.

Tom and I wish to thank Bill Thomas, our editor at Doubleday, who enthusiastically embraced our pitch like a good network executive and helped steer us into print. Working closely with Bill have been Todd Doughty and Cory Hunter, who both gave countless hours and unbridled support. And finally, many thanks to Elizabeth Bohlke for her tireless work transcribing interviews.